Office of the Provost   GREAT PAST. BRIGHT FUTURE.

With Our Compliments

Dear David,
Best wishes
from GRCC!
Laurie Chesley

In Memoriam

Richard W. Calkins
June 3, 1939–November 29, 2013

Open Door: Grand Rapids Junior/Community College 1914-2014

by Walter Lockwood

Research, photographic curating, timelines, and sidebars by Mike Klawitter

Layout and design by Jan Ensing

 Grand Rapids Community College
Grand Rapids, MI

Grand Rapids Community College
143 Bostwick Avenue NE
Grand Rapids, MI 49503-3295

Published by Grand Rapids Community College
Printed by Custom Printers in Grand Rapids, MI, United States of America

ISBN 978-0-692-22933-0 (cloth)

Acknowledgments

I have many people to thank for their parts in this 100-year history: Mike Klawitter, GRCC Archivist, for keeping a multitude of historical materials at my fingertips, for his work on researching and compiling the book's photographs, timelines, and sidebar stories, for reading and commentary; to Klaas Kwant, for ongoing editing advice and for filming and editing many hours of video interviews; to Jan Ensing for creative layout and design and her patient perseverance in readying the book for print; to Dr. Robert Riekse, for his doctoral dissertation on GRJC's first fifty years, for his broad understanding of the college and his valuable reading and editing; to librarian Nan Schichtel, so helpful with the early years of the college story and with fine-tuning the text; to Anita Cook, Archivist for the Faculty Association for Association and contract records; to Gary Eberle of Aquinas College for his initial encouragement and advice; to Bob Partridge and Donna Kragt for insightful interviews and editing assistance; to Dr. Karin Orr for her seventy-fifth anniversary GRJC history; to historian Z. Z. Lydens for his history of Grand Rapids; to the advisors, editors, writers and photographers of *The Collegiate* for providing an invaluable institutional history; to Marilyn Smidt, unofficial archivist of the Health Programs for historical materials; to Andrew Schmidt for assisting with digital photo editing; to Matt Coullard, Amanada Kossack, Michelle Rose, and Laurie Schaut of GRCC Graphic Services for layout and design proofing; to Rachel Bower of GRCCePrint for working as print liaison; to Melissa Polance-Nuñez, Liz Timmer, Jan Benham, Jerry Benham, Misty McClure-Anderson, Arthur Johnson, and Deb DeWent for helping compile the 100-year employees' list; to the Grand Rapids History and Special Collections Department of the Grand Rapids Public Library for research materials and photographs; to David Hendrickson and Custom Printers for the finished product; and to my wife and family for patience and support.

Special thanks to former interim presidents, Dr. Patricia Pulliam for her detailed interview and ongoing advice, and to Dr. Anne Mulder for her interview, her history of the GRJC Music Department, and her vivid institutional memory; to the late President Emeritus Richard Calkins, for invaluable video and telephone interviews; to President Dr. Juan Olivarez, for his detailed story of the college in video and telephone interviews; to Faculty Association President Fred van Hartesveldt for his ongoing input, reading, and advice; to present President Dr. Steven Ender, for his ready availability to provide the college's most recent history and for his reading and editing advice.

I am indebted to others who provided video, telephone, or unrecorded interviews and/or written historical material, reading or advice: John Dersch, Janice Balyeat, Dr. Cornelius Eringaarde, Fred Sebulske, Tom Hofmann, Jonathon Russell, Bob Garlough, Jack VanAartsen, Jim Schafer, Shelly Richter, Dr. Don Boyer, Bruce and Tina Lockwood, Dr. Scott McNabb, Joy McNabb, Deb DeWent, Dr. Gilda Gely, Patti Trepkowski, Ken Bultman, Duane Davis, Kevin Dobreff, the late Barbara Eggerding (for material on her father, John Bos), Keith Longberg, Chuck Chamberlain, Phil Jung, Richard Andre, David Cope, Elias Lumpkins, Richard Bezile, Bill Foster, Lisa Freiburger, Dr. Till Peters, Lloyd Soper, C. J. Shroll, Julie Johnson, Maryann Lesert, Sharon Wynkoop, Richard Austin, Joan Berends, Gordon Hunsberger, John Regenmorter, Dr. Joe Hesse, Nick Antonakis, Dr. Robert Long, Dr. Gary Burbridge, Gary Schenk, Bert Bleke, Erin Cisler of the GRCC Foundation, Joyce Hofman, Richard Reid, Betty Robbins, Dorothy Terhune, Phyllis Fratzke, Janet Paasche, Jennifer Ackerman-Haywood, Chris Arnold, Dr. Matthew Douglas, Tom Worthington, Dr. Kathy Mullins, Vicki Janowiak, and Tina Hoxie.

100-Year Anniversary Steering Committee

GЯCC

Steve Abid
Raul Alvarez
Dr. Lilly Anderson
Margo Anderson
Elly Bainbridge
Dr. Andrew Bowne
Erin Cisler
Deb DeWent
Sara Dorer
Karen Ender
Laurie Foster
Dr. Gilda Gely
Dan Gendler
Nanci Guigue
Vicki Janowiak
Mike Klawitter
Klaas Kwant
Pamela Laureto
Donald MacKenzie
Jan Maginni
Eric Mullen
Dr. Kathryn Mullins
Leah Nixon
Julie Otte
Malinda Powers
Nan Schichtel
Liz Timmer
Michelle Urbane
George Waite

Foreword

Grand Rapids Community College is 100 years old and has the distinction of being the first junior college in Michigan and among the seven oldest community colleges in the United States. Through the pages of *Open Door,* retired English professor Walter Lockwood presents an amazing chronicle of this wonderful institution. The research is rigorous, and yet the story-telling is engaging enough to allow the reader to sit back and enjoy the fascinating history of GRJC/GRCC.

Professor Lockwood traces our history through the leadership eras of the nine individuals who served in the role of president, examining the historical events and local dynamics that affected students, faculty, staff and administrators. Time and time again through our first one hundred years, the college has experienced periods of explosive growth and significant enrollment decline, usually triggered by external events including political dynamics, the World Wars, the Great Depression and economic recessions in Michigan and across the country. Throughout it all, the college has never wavered from its goal of providing quality higher education at an affordable price for citizens in our service district and beyond.

This story is told through the people of the college—the faculty leaders and key administrators who weathered every storm and seized on every opportunity to continue the legacy of GRCC's greatness. Their dedication, contributions, and commitment are recognized and honored throughout this history.

GRCC's founding President, Jesse Buttrick Davis, has been described as "remarkable, visionary and a mentor to students, teachers and administrators alike." President Davis set the expectations for all faculty and staff who would come after him. Through their dedicated service, the college has never failed to reach the high bar that was set 100 years ago.

Steven C. Ender, Ed.D.
President

Table of Contents

East Building, 1964. (GRCC Archives)

Introduction

Fifty years ago, at midpoint of the 1964-65 school year, I began my teaching career as part of the Language Arts faculty at Grand Rapids Junior College. The college consisted of the Main and East Buildings, neither built for the purpose of housing a college. The East Building, constructed in 1891, had once been Central High School and later Strong Junior High. A gymnasium had been added in 1922. In 1925, the building became home of the Junior College. The Main Building, vintage 1923, was the former Davis Technical High School. In 1944, it became half of a two-building college campus.

In 1964-65 the student body numbered 3,500. There was an administrative staff of seven and 105 full-time faculty, most of whom I came to know. My starting yearly salary was $5,500, which seemed a fortune to someone 23 and just out of graduate school. I wore a suit and tie to classes. The Main Building had an elevator for staff only, with a female operator charged with keeping out students. In spite of my suit, she told me I would have to take the stairs. Elva VanHaitsma, a dear lady and colleague in English, vouched for me; the operator grudgingly allowed me aboard.

I had no parking space for my car. A scrubby vacant lot occupied the place where the east end of the Ford Fieldhouse stands today. Faculty paid for narrow, dusty slots there; they parked two deep and traded keys. I was granted tenure long before I was granted my own parking spot.

I shared an office-classroom with Dr. Marinus Swets in the basement of the Main Building. Through our ground-level window we could see feet and lower legs pass by. The journalism staff (Dr. Swets was the advisor), met in our room. Soon I would convene the literary magazine staff there as well. I quickly learned that teaching was hard work, and reading papers even harder. But the job never felt like a job. Language Arts Division folk and other staff members soon became friends, many of them life-long. The hand-me-down facility we worked in was not as important as the energy and creativity of the staff. The atmosphere was egalitarian. We all gave ourselves to teaching. We did not compete for rank or notoriety—there was no publish or perish policy. We were an experiment in democracy, a college with doors open to all.

Faculty for the most part enjoyed friendly relations with administration, even after collective bargaining began driving a wedge between us. Together, we watched the student body grow at a dizzying pace, scrambled to expand to accommodate it, and did our best to ride a tidal wave of social and technological change. We were blessed with visionary leaders, most of whom knew that a college must exist in a perpetual state of becoming.

For that and other reasons revealed in the pages to follow, Grand Rapids Junior (now Community) College, the first junior college established in Michigan, and third or fifth or seventh in the nation (depending on your sources), has managed to remain consistently—for 100 years—among the very best of its kind. Many who have come through that open door have been guided to other doors into new and larger worlds.

First GRJC football team, 1919. (GRCC Archives)

Beginnings
1914-20

Jesse Buttrick Davis

The story of Grand Rapids Junior College begins with one man—Jesse Buttrick Davis—the founder and first president of the college (**Figure 1**). What sort of man was our founder? Remarkable is the first word that comes to mind; visionary is another. Jesse Davis spent a lifetime innovating at all levels and areas of education. He gave himself to community service. He was a mentor to students, teachers, and administrators alike. He was a caring husband and father of three, a writer, a musician, a university professor. Describing him as a Renaissance man would not be far from the mark.

Raised by loving and supportive parents, a blueblood mother from the East and a Baptist minister stepfather, both of whom guided his life in positive and productive ways, Davis was also strongly influenced by an imposing great aunt whom he called Aunt Sally. She taught him to read before he began school and inspired in him a love of history.

As a student at Colgate University, he was shepherded by a Professor Charles Thurber toward discovering the profession he was best suited to pursue. Davis was considering the ministry and possibly law. By prompting him to examine the foundations he had already laid in his education and life experience, Thurber opened to him the possibility of becoming a teacher.[1] Once

Davis saw the light—that teaching was indeed his truest gift—he became a passionate advocate of the kind of vocational guidance he had received from Professor Thurber. Davis would eventually provide the energy for introducing vocational guidance counseling into the public schools. In 1912, Davis helped found the National Vocational Guidance Association.

Jesse Davis was a progressive educator with a head full of ideas for improving American education. Soon after graduating from Colgate, he was hired to teach at Detroit Central High School, which he did with distinction from 1895 to 1907, serving as head of the department of history and principal of the eleventh grade (during that time earning his M.A. degree from the University of Michigan [U of M]). Though concerned about administrative responsibilities pulling him away from the teaching he loved, when William A. Greeson, Superintendent of Grand Rapids Public Schools (**Figure 2**), offered him a job as principal of Grand Rapids Central High School, Davis said yes—with enthusiasm. Central had a statewide reputation for excellence. Superintendent Greeson's welcoming

(**top, Figure 1**) Jesse Buttrick Davis, founder and first president of Grand Rapids Junior College. (GRCC Archives)

(**left, Figure 2**) William A. Greeson, 1928, Superintendent of Grand Rapids Public Schools. (Grand Rapids History and Special Collections, Archives, Grand Rapids Public Library, Grand Rapids, MI 54-27-42)

1914

Jesse Buttrick Davis founded Grand Rapids Junior College and served as its first president. Initially dedicated to providing a transfer curriculum to the University of Michigan, he was also sensitive to the needs of the community and steered the college into terminal, occupational programs. During his tenure the college grew from 49 to 401 students.

Grand Rapids Junior College opened on September 21, 1914, and operated out of Central High School until 1925.

1914 Course of Study *Bulletin of the Grand Rapids Junior College*, August 1914. (GRCC Archives)

THE COURSE OF STUDY.

The subjects offered in the Junior College will be those of the regular literary department of the University of Michigan. The teachers of these subjects will follow the outlines of each course in co-operation with the professors at the University. For the first semester the work will be given as outlined below:

RHETORIC AND COMPOSITION. Three hours. Mrs. Hulst.
    Studies in diction and style, practice in composition.

MATHEMATICS. College algebra and geometry. Four hours. Mr. Wilcox.

HISTORY. History of England. Four hours. Miss Hinsdale.

BIOLOGY. Simple forms of animal and plant life. Lectures, recitations and laboratory work. Four hours. Miss Ellis, Miss Stearns.

PHYSICS. Mechanics, sound and heat. Four hours. Mr. Smith.

LATIN. Four hours. Miss Jones.

GERMAN. Four hours. Miss Christ.

The classes offered in foreign language will depend upon the number of students requesting the work. In making elections students are requested to indicate their first and second choice of language and the year (first, third or advanced) desired.

(**Figure 3**) Central High School, n.d. (Grand Rapids History and Special Collections, Archives, Grand Rapids Public Library, Grand Rapids, MI 178-1-11 Neg# 4091)

words were "'Now, Davis, I was once principal of that high school and I propose to treat you as I wish I might have been treated but was not.'"[2] Thus began a 13-year partnership and life-long friendship. Greeson was true to his word in every way.

New High School—First Junior High School in Michigan

As Central High principal, Jesse Davis's immediate agenda was the high school building itself. Finding it overcrowded and unsafe, he undertook a campaign to build a new high school. He sold to the community the need to broaden the curriculum to include vocational programs—one of his passions—especially in a city known as the furniture capital of the country. He argued that this sort of innovation could never happen in a building lacking the necessary facilities. A fire in a chemistry lab became the deciding factor in the minds of many citizens, who approved a state-of-the-art high school to accommodate 1,500 students, with an auditorium seating 1,760, a gymnasium, modern science labs, and classrooms for woodworking, automobile repair, and household arts. At Davis's urging, the board of education modified the old high school building and established Strong Junior High School, the first junior high school in the state of Michigan.[3]

The Junior College Movement

The idea to establish a junior college might never have entered Jesse Davis's mind had not an unusual local situation occurred. The creation of Strong Junior High had reduced the Central High School population by 400 ninth-grade pupils. Yet when the new high school opened for the 1910-11 school year, the building was crowded. This situation sparked an unprecedented expansion of secondary facilities in Grand Rapids. In 1912, Union High School became, by adding a twelfth grade, a six-year junior-senior high school; soon after, a new six-year school, South High, opened on the southeast end of town. Each took pupils from the Central district. Central, capable of accommodating 1,500 students, found its numbers reduced to around 900. Davis was now principal of an expensive new school with empty classrooms and a talented faculty with too few students to teach.

The junior high school movement was only one of many educational innovations that caught Davis's interest. He was equally intrigued by the junior college movement. The idea of offering the first two years of a college education in municipal centers scattered around the state had originated in 1852 in a rather left-handed way with President Henry P. Tappan of the University of Michigan. His thought was that the University needed to differentiate between upper and lower division college work and give its full attention to the much superior upper division.[4] In 1902, President William Rainey Harper of the University of Chicago along with J. Stanley Brown, Superin-

tendent of Joliet Township schools, had founded Joliet Junior College in Joliet, Illinois, the nation's first junior college, which they chose to locate in the high school building. The purpose of the junior college was to extend a general and liberal arts education through grades 13 and 14, yet with a more important collegiate function of providing the first two years leading to transfer and a baccalaureate degree. Harper eventually came to be known as the father of the junior college movement.[5]

Alexis Lange of the University of California and David Starr Jordan of Stanford University helped further define the mission of junior colleges: to provide open access to higher education by means of college transfer programs, occupational (terminal) programs, adult and continuing education, and college-preparatory remedial programs.[6] Later, because of the diverse and adaptive ways in which junior colleges served their communities, they began to be known as community colleges. There have been few more important developments in American higher education than the junior college movement.

Davis knew both J. Stanley Brown of Joliet and William Rainey Harper and was well acquainted with their ideas. Why not try something similar to their experiment and establish a junior college to fill the empty spaces in the new Central High School? (Figure 3) He took the idea to Superintendent Greeson who was enthusiastic. At the same time Greeson was quite certain that Grand Rapids taxpayers would never approve the extra expense of a college. Davis argued that running a high school at much less than full capacity was already wasting taxpayer money. He could start a two-year college using empty classrooms and their present high school faculty as instructors. There would be no extra expense, no additional taxes necessary. He proposed a nominal tuition fee to cover the cost of any new equipment.

1914-20

1914

Course offerings included mathematics, history, rhetoric and composition, German, Latin, biology, and physics. A two-year normal course in public school music was offered.

Enrollment for the first year was 49 students.

THE JUNIOR COLLEGE

Adrianse, Raymond H.
Allen, J. Milton
Alten, Eleanore
Austin, C. Leroy
Baxter, E. Ray
Barendson, Alban
Blake, Isabel F.
Bonnell, Ralph I.
Broene, Frances
Cobb, Myra
Craw, Ethelyn
Crosby, Rosamond
Culver, Imogene
Davis, Mildred E.
DeRuiter, Martin
Dunnette, Marian

Fitch, Ada
Gilleo, Avery
Hawley, Loretta
Hedrick, Walter A.
Hinyan, Vena S.
Holt, Rex
Hompe, Lorraine
Jacobs, Vivian
Jasperse, Cyrus
Kickintveld, Jeannette
Kortering, Florence
LeClear, Ethelyeen
Lindeman, Harold
Lindsley, Will
Marsman, Clarence
Marvin, Ruth

Miller, Bertha
Mitts, Jansen
Northrup, Dorotha
Perschbacher, Olga
Powers, Emma
Prange, Meta
Reed, Fay Allen
Riley, Joseph
Scott, Gatha
Smith, Raymond H.
Strong, May
Thatcher, Adaline
Vandermeulen, William
Vinkemulder, Blake
Wood, Clad W.
Zink, Gladys

Roster of students who attended 1914-15. (Helios, 1915, pg 67. Grand Rapids History and Special Collections, Archives, Grand Rapids Public Library, Grand Rapids, MI #316)

Resident tuition was $60.00 per year.

$1,800 budget for the school came entirely from student tuition.

Men's basketball team established.

Junior College

The Junior College—another of Mr. Davis' ideas—has materialized, as his ideas have a way of doing. It opened on the twenty-first of September with an enrollment of forty-two pupils, and these first weeks have held the promise of a successful year and a splendid future.

It has been the endeavor of the Board of Education to make the course as broad as possible, considering the size of the school. The following subjects are offered this year: rhetoric, mathematics, modern history, physics, biology, and first and third year German. The heads of the High School departments compose the college faculty, and Mr. Beattie has charge of a special department of public school music. Other subjects, Latin, French, etc., will be added as the demand for them increases.

(**Figure 4**) *Helios,* November 1914, pg 36. (Grand Rapids History and Special Collections, Archives, Grand Rapids Public Library, Grand Rapids, MI 178-11-10)

Greeson, though not convinced, said good-naturedly, "'Go ahead, if you think you can get away with it. I won't stand in your way.'"[7]

Records, reports, and newspaper articles from the time indicate no public interest in such a college. No citizens' committees had studied the issue or made recommendations. Michigan laws giving boards of education the authority to support junior colleges would not even exist until 1917.[8] These facts did not deter Davis. With only the guarded blessing of Greeson for support, he travelled to the University of Michigan with his curriculum plans, essentially duplicating the first two years of the University's Arts and Sciences program. He also had a list of his proposed faculty (the best of his Central High teachers) and their qualifications. Meeting with President H. B. Hutchins and the University Senate, he encountered no resistance to the curriculum but much uncertainty about the qualifications of his faculty. Davis had one teacher with an M.A., one with a Ph.D. The rest were without graduate degrees, though some were department heads and all were exceptional teachers. When the University's dean of the graduate school insisted that all faculty have doctor's degrees, Davis's heart sank. But the head of the philosophy department, a fiery Scotsman named Dr. Robert M. Wenley, came to Davis's rescue. He told the Senate it was "'none of their damned business'" how Davis chose his teachers. The University would judge the Grand Rapids Junior College faculty by the quality of students Davis sent to

it. This blunt assertion carried the day. Davis returned to Grand Rapids with the blessings and support of the University. "Thus fortified," Davis later wrote, "I had little difficulty in securing the enabling action of the Board of Education."[9]

First Junior College in Michigan

Davis had quickly gained allies in the business community by joining the Grand Rapids Board of Trade and developing a close friendship with Board of Education President George A. Davis, a successful furniture manufacturer (Stowe & Davis). The trio of Superintendent Greeson, Principal Jesse Davis, and Board President George A. Davis formed what historian Z. Z. Lydens referred to as "the Greeson triumvirate," three like-minded, strong-willed men working together for the improvement of the public schools. George A. Davis, an important force in the expansion of city high schools and a strong supporter of vocational and technical education, laid the cornerstone in 1922 of Davis Technical High School, named for him.[10] The building would later become the Grand Rapids Junior College Main Building.

Jesse Davis, from the beginning of his work in Grand Rapids, enjoyed the favor of both local newspapers. Edwin Booth, editor of *The Grand Rapids Evening Press*, had been a childhood friend. Arthur H. Vandenberg (who managed *The Morning Herald* and would become a distinguished U.S. senator) had been Davis's fraternity brother at the University of Michigan. Though neither newspaper actively promoted a junior college at Central High School (since there was no public appeal for such an institution), both papers reported the opening of the college in cautiously positive ways. *The Grand Rapids Evening Press*, in particular, was careful to note that the $1,800 budget for the school would come entirely from student tuition.[11] Both news-

PURPOSE OF THE JUNIOR COLLEGE.

The purpose of the Junior College is to offer to the students of Grand Rapids and Western Michigan the advantages of the first two years of the Department of Literature, Science and the Arts at the University of Michigan or at a standard college. The demand for higher education is growing rapidly. Our state institutions are finding it a serious problem to handle properly the greatly increasing numbers who are annually entering their doors. Other states have already established junior colleges in connection with the larger high schools. It is in accordance with the policy recently announced by the faculty of the University of Michigan that the Central High School of Grand Rapids is offering the work of a Junior College.

REASONS FOR ITS ESTABLISHMENT.

By inaugurating a collegiate department in the Central High School the Board of Education is bringing many advantages to the city of Grand Rapids. The records of past years will show that our interest in education ranks far above that of the average city of its class. The last report of the United States commissioner of education shows that thirty-five per cent of the high school graduates of the country plan to go on with their education, while in Grand Rapids an average of over fifty per cent of our graduates continue their education in some higher institution of learning. It is estimated that over two hundred and fifty thousand dollars are spent annually by Grand Rapids parents to send their children away from home to complete their education.

Most boys and girls at graduation from the high school are too young and immature to leave home and to assume the responsibilities of independent living. Parents appreciate the fact that when the son leaves home to enter college he will never return to it in quite the same capacity. A new life of the individual is begun and the old ties are broken. The opportunity to keep our boys and girls at home a little longer and to give them the advantages of two years at college will be most welcome. It will afford the needed time for securing greater maturity of thought and judgment, for establishing habits of work and character, and for obtaining a better knowledge of one's definite aim in life before he leaves the shelter and influence of the home.

ADVANTAGES.

We have been assured that students completing the two years' work prescribed for the Junior College with satisfactory standing will be admitted to the junior year at the University of Michigan with full credit for the subjects completed. The action of the State University will secure the same privilege in other colleges and universities throughout the country.

Those intending to take the six-year combined literary and professional courses will be able to meet the literary requirements at home. Such

papers made clear
that the college was
intended to be
a self-sustaining
institution, financially
independent of the
Grand Rapids Board
of Education, at no
cost to the Grand
Rapids taxpayer.
And for the first year,
at least, that was true.

(**Figure 5**) *Bulletin of the Grand Rapids Junior College,* August 1914. (GRCC Archives)

The newspapers further noted that the first junior college in the State of Michigan, though established in a local high school building, occupied its own separate area and functioned distinctly apart from the public school work at Central High School. The separation of college and high school student life, however, would prove a problem never entirely resolved until the college moved into its own building in 1925.

The college opened in September of 1914 (**Figure 4**) with 49 students who paid tuition of $60 per year and were held to the same admissions requirements as the University of Michigan. In the second year of operation, to encourage enrollment, the board of education reduced tuition to $40 per year for residents of the city and $50 for nonresidents and approved a second year curriculum. The course offerings, based on University of Michigan offerings and in many cases employing the same course numbers and examinations, were as follows: mathematics, history, rhetoric and composition, German, Latin, biology, and physics, all focused on college transfer. From the start, Grand Rapids Junior College students were highly successful transfer students, achieving as well or better than students who had begun their educations at four-year colleges and universities. According to Davis, "the academic rating of the Junior College was quickly established. Graduates were readily accepted with full credit by all standard colleges, even in New England."[12]

Davis insisted on excellence, and his exceptional faculty was up to the task. The first board-published *Junior College Bulletin* (**Figure 5**), directed at parents, argued that Grand Rapids Junior

1915

To encourage enrollment, tuition was reduced to $40 per year for residents of the city and $50 for nonresidents.

Teacher prep course in public school art established.

1916

Art and Industry Program established.

Students who attended in 1916-17. (*Helios,* 1917, pg 100. Grand Rapids History and Special Collections, Archives, Grand Rapids Public Library, Grand Rapids, MI #316)

(**Figure 6**) *The Grand Rapids Junior College Catalog*, 1918-19, cover and pg 11. (GRCC Archives)

College would save them significant amounts of money for college education—without any compromise of educational quality. Furthermore, money spent for higher education at universities would stay in the city, and the junior college would provide a safe and familiar environment for those students not ready to leave home. All of this proved highly persuasive to Grand Rapids families and provided encouragement to many for whom a university education was financially out of reach.

That first *Junior College Bulletin* also included a story describing the establishment of a two-year normal course in public school music, with plans for students to do their practice teaching in the Grand Rapids Public Schools. In a June 7, 1915, report to the board of education, Davis pointed out the savings to be realized by the use of unpaid practice teachers in city music departments. Davis's financial arguments provided the strongest rationale for the Junior College continuing beyond the first year. He would be forced to come to the college's rescue more than once in his tenure as president.

Expanding Curriculum, Expanding Problems

Davis never wavered in his dedication to a transfer curriculum and pushed for conferring a title of Associate in Arts, Science, Business Administration, Pedagogy, or Fine Arts to those successfully completing the transfer requirements; Greeson approved. Yet in the 1915-16 and 1916-17 school years, sensitive to the needs of the community, Davis began to urge the college into terminal, occupational programs—programs to which he, Superintendent Greeson, and George A. Davis were deeply committed. To the two-year course in music he added a teacher prep course in public school art. In cooperation with the furniture and printing industries in Grand Rapids, he helped establish an Art and Industry Program. When the effects of World War I began to be felt in an increased demand for nurses, Davis worked out a program for nurses' training in cooperation with the three large city hospitals. Sixty nurses took their academic courses at the college and their medical training at the hospitals. This would eventually result in a permanent cooperative Junior College School of Nursing that would become a model for the state.

Responding to another pressing community need, Davis in 1917 opened an Evening Institute for those who worked days but

(**Figure 7**) 1914-15 Grand Rapids Junior College basketball team. (GRCC Archives)

College received its initial accreditation from the North Central Association of Colleges and Secondary Schools.

The Evening Institute opened for those who worked days but wanted study beyond high school.

GRJC introduced the Students' Army Training Corps (S.A.T.C.) program administered by the U.S. War Department, to train recruits in various technical skills.

Program cover and credit page from *On Leave,* a musical program the S.A.T.C. held at Powers Theatre December 6-7, 1918. (Grand Rapids History and Special Collections, Archives, Grand Rapids Public Library, Grand Rapids, MI #216-8.8-18)

wanted study beyond the high school level. The Evening Institute offered the same courses as the day college, but also included Kalamazoo Normal Scholar (later Western Michigan University) and University of Michigan Extension courses. The Institute attracted both transfer and occupational students, among them many older adults. The *1918 Junior College Catalogue* (**Figure 6**) listed seven transfer curriculums: literary, pre-med, pre-law, engineering (the mirror image of U of M's program), teacher's normal, business administration, and home economics; it also included seven occupational curriculums: commerce and finance,

secretarial work, mechanics, art and industry, public school music, library training, and nursing. All the terminal/occupational programs were subject to less stringent entrance requirements and involved part-time work in the fields being studied.

In an effort to expand campus life, a Women's League was formed to foster "a democratic spirit among the women of Junior College and to sponsor social interests for the members." A weekly student newspaper, *College News*, came into being. A basketball team competed in the 1914-15 school year (**Figure 7**), a football team in 1918-20. The one-room college library was

The first regular meeting of the Women's League of the Grand Rapids Junior College was held Tuesday, June 27, 1919.

At this meeting the constitution of the organization was read and adopted.

The election of officers then took place with the following results:
President: Lucille Meyering.
Recording Secretary: Marjorie Shepard.
Corresponding Secretary: Mattie Ingersol.
Board of directors: Anna Broene and Hazel Whitting, representing the Sophmore class; Geraldine Troy and Helen Anderson, representing the Freshman class.
Advisory board: Miss Hinsdale, Miss Ellis, and Miss Rourke.

It was voted that the Recording secretary act as treasurer until a treasurer is elected.

Women's League Song

Words by Agnes Crips, '34

For the Women's League of Junior College
Let us raise our voices high
Let us work and play and strive together
Make her spirit live forever.

Chorus:

Let us keep her purpose ever foremost
Always lend a helping hand
And give a cheer, here, for everything
that's dear —
For the Women's League we stand.

For ideals of those who went before us
Let us proudly carry on,
Let us keep the torch of service ever,
Make our goal by strong endeavor.

The Women's League of Grand Rapids Junior College

The Women's League was formed in 1919 with the purpose of fostering "a democratic spirit among the women of Junior College and to sponsor social interests for the members." Over the years the League was one of the most active student organizations on campus. The League sponsored many events including teas for the alumni, faculty, and the senior girls of the city high schools, as well as yearly Mother-Daughter and Father-Daughter Banquets. It also awarded merit cups to the sophomore boy and girl who best exemplified the ideal Junior College student.

The League was involved in activities that reflected civic and social responsibilities. During World War II members of the League volunteered for the Red Cross, sent letters to Junior College men in service, bought war bonds from their treasury, and donated to the relief of Chinese children. In 1967 the Women's League sponsored an "International Night," hosting foreign students who discussed the ways in which their native countries differed from the United States, their impressions of the United States, and the adjustments required during their stay here.

In 1977, the Women's League, for 65 years one of the most popular and productive of student organizations, ceased as an active group. Their elegant suite in the Main Building became a student study area. The records of the Women's League are kept in the college archives located in the GRCC Library.

(**clockwise from top left**) Minutes from the first regular meeting of the Women's League. (GRCC Archives); Lyrics to the Women's League Song. (GRCC Archives); Lucille Meyering, Women's League first president. (GRCC Archives); Women's League room, ca. 1950s. (GRCC Archives)

(**Figure 8**) Rev. Fr. Robert W. Brown, 1914. (Courtesy of the Archives of the Diocese of Grand Rapids [ADGR])

greatly enhanced by a pact of cooperation with the Grand Rapids Public (Ryerson) Library. In 1917, the college was fully accredited by the North Central Association of Colleges and Secondary Schools. It has remained fully accredited ever since.

The first year of the Junior College cost the Grand Rapids Board of Education nothing. After that, financing the college was not as easy. Increasing enrollment required a larger budget. When the college's request for money reached $35,000, Mayor Philo C. Fuller stepped in and vetoed the appropriation. It took a public hearing before the City Commission to save the college. The fact that Davis had expanded the curriculum into occupational areas serving community needs helped the cause. Rev. Fr. Robert W. Brown (**Figure 8**), head of the Catholic Parochial Schools, argued eloquently that the Junior College had provided an opportunity for higher education to many Catholic school students whose parents could not afford to send them away to college. By the end of the evening, the Commission voted unanimously to override the mayor's veto.[13]

A College for the Community

The *1918 Junior College Catalogue* (**Figure 9**) stated that, although the first purpose of the college was to provide a transfer

PURPOSE OF THE JUNIOR COLLEGE

THE Junior College completes the most advanced work offered by the public school system of Grand Rapids, and is located in the Central High School building. Special classes in which certain equipment is needed are conducted in the other high school buildings. The faculty has been carefully selected from the heads of departments in the high schools and from the faculties of the University of Michigan and other higher institutions.

The purpose of the Junior College is two-fold; to afford two years of training beyond the high school for those who would prepare to enter professional schools or to complete their educations in higher institutions, and to afford an opportunity for those who do not intend to go to any further institution to fit themselves through practical courses for definite life careers.

Special Courses for Women

The War has made it necessary for women to fit themselves to take the places of men in almost every occupation. This demand for trained women has prompted the introduction of a number of special courses in an attempt to help those who would respond to the call to fit themselves for such service.

JUNIOR COLLEGE EVENING INSTITUTE

IN ORDER that the advantages of the Junior College may be open to those who are employed during the day and to those who may find it more convenient to attend classes in the evening, special night classes will be formed. The experience of the past two years has shown that there are many people who wish to take up the study of some subject which will be of immediate advantage to them in their vocations, or which they were unable to pursue when in school or college. When these subjects are given on one evening each week for eighteen weeks it offers a two-hours' university credit with the least possible inconvenience or sacrifice of evenings. Each class is conducted for two hours at each session, usually from seven fifteen to nine fifteen. Any subject taught in the Junior College will be offered in the evening classes if a sufficient number of students are enrolled.

The EVENING INSTITUTE will appeal to young men and women who desire better positions in business and in industry, to those who failed to find their aptitudes and abilities while in school, but who now have a desire to fit themselves for more congenial employment, to those who wish to improve themselves in their professions, and in gen-

page three

(**Figure 9**) *The Grand Rapids Junior College Catalogue* 1918-19, pg 3. (GRCC Archives)

1917

1916-17 GRJC Basketball Team. (*Helios,* 1917 pg 99. Grand Rapids History and Special Collections, Archives, Grand Rapids Public Library, Grand Rapids, MI #316)

1918

The college catalog listed seven transfer curriculums: literary, pre-med, pre-law, engineering, teacher's normal, business administration, and home economics. In addition it included seven occupational curriculums: commerce and finance, secretarial work, mechanics, art and industry, public school music, library training, and nursing.

(**Figure 10**) Students' Army Training Corps (S.A.T.C.) induction ceremony on Central High School lawn. (*The Grand Rapids Press*, Saturday, October 12, 1918.)

curriculum, a second purpose was "to afford an opportunity for those who do not intend to go to any further institution to fit themselves through practical courses for definite life careers." An earlier *Catalogue* stated, "It will be [the college's] policy to meet the demands of the public as rapidly as its needs are manifested." From its beginnings, Grand Rapids Junior College has kept a finger on the pulse of community needs. Not until 1991, however, would the school officially become known as a community college.

The record clearly shows that in the early years, support of the board of education sustained the college through its difficult times. The college needed the K-12 system behind it.

President Davis and Superintendent Greeson were close friends, both progressive educators and outstanding leaders, of the same mind on most issues. A unified school district worked well for them. Over time, the relationship of college president and superintendent would become less comfortable. As college enrollment and physical presence grew larger, as superintendents came and went, some with personalities attuned to the college, some not, the college president (for a period demoted to the title of dean) would feel at times like a poor relation in a K-12 system that saw to its own needs first. The superintendent and board made most major decisions involving the college—including financial ones. Seventy-seven years would pass before this situation found resolution.

The President Joins the War Effort

When America finally entered the war in 1917, the War Department announced a plan to establish a system of military training called the Students' Army Training Corps with help from American colleges. Grand Rapids Junior College responded to the call, turning the Central High (**Figure 10**) lunchroom into an Army mess hall for 109 recruits and Houseman Athletic Field into a military drill facility. Jesse Davis felt a strong pull to serve his country, though he was too old to enlist. The board of education provided him a leave of absence to do "hut service" for the Army, organizing recreation for the soldiers in Michigan's Camp Grayling and then in Waco, Texas. He also did war work for the U. S. Department of Labor, the Y.M.C.A., and, following the war, the Interchurch World Movement. In what little time he had to spare, he promoted the vocational guidance movement. Though he would return two weeks each month to run Central High School and Grand Rapids Junior College, the absence of the college's sole administrator (with the exception of a registrar, named in 1919) very likely created difficulties.

In 1920, beset by a restlessness he described as common to those returning from wartime service, Davis began to consider new challenges. When he was offered the office of supervisor of secondary education for the State of Connecticut, he—with regret—resigned from his duties in Grand Rapids. An editorial published in the *Grand Rapids Herald* shortly after his resignation expressed the sense of loss felt all over the city:

> *Mr. Davis has left his mark upon Central during his years of teaching and leadership here, but Junior College was peculiarly his baby. He sat up nights with the now lusty youngster and guarded and defended it…but perhaps even above his value to the city as an educator with vision was his worth as the earnest, all-around citizen.*[14]

In Davis's competent hands, a foundation had been laid—one firm enough to support a college for a hundred years, solid enough for others to build upon. When he left after six years as college president, the total enrollment had climbed from 49 to 401. Could he have imagined an enrollment of 18,000 students less than a century later?

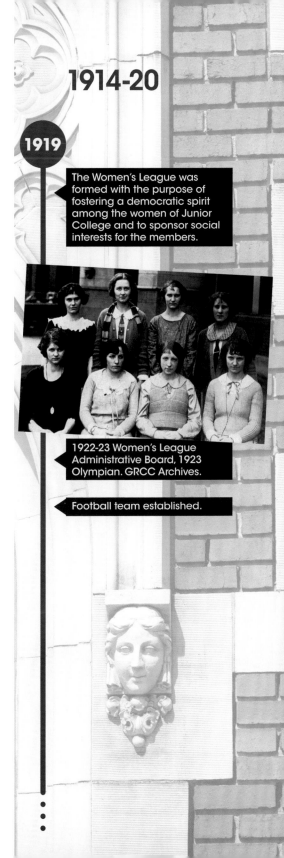

1914-20

1919

The Women's League was formed with the purpose of fostering a democratic spirit among the women of Junior College and to sponsor social interests for the members.

1922-23 Women's League Administrative Board, 1923 Olympian. GRCC Archives.

Football team established.

1924-25 freshman class. (GRCC Archives)

The Andrews Era—Act One
The 1920s

Gould Arthur Andrews

The resignation of Jesse Davis was reported in the *Grand Rapids Herald* on January 18, 1920. On January 22, the Grand Rapids Board of Education met and chose Gould Arthur Andrews (known as Arthur Andrews) President of the Junior College and Principal of Central High School at a salary of $3,300 per year. (**Figure 11**) At the same meeting the board considered a petition from Junior College students requesting that the college be separated from Central High School and provided its own building.[1] The end of World War I had seen increased interest in higher education; junior college enrollment continued to expand. Though sympathetic to the student request, Superintendent Greeson and the board felt that the community was not ready at this time to approve the idea. *The Grand Rapids Press*, reminding readers of the near demise of the college in 1918, supported that conclusion:

> *It is not very long ago that Junior College was so lightly considered by members of the city commission that citizens appeared before that body in order to prevent its appropriation from being cut off entirely....In due time Junior College, if it continues the even tenor of its ways, will have a separate building....We must avoid any danger of extravagance in ideas and operation that would tend to react against the college's continued usefulness and even its existence.*[2]

(**Figure 11**) Gould Arthur Andrews, second president of Grand Rapids Junior College. (GRCC Archives)

Arthur Andrews would eventually—by 1925—have a building for the college; he would cease being a principal and become solely the president of Grand Rapids Junior College. Having coached football and taught psychology and public speaking for Jesse Davis at the high school, sociology at the junior college, he would continue a partial teaching load into his presidency.

Andrews was a native of Canada, born in 1889 in Exeter, Ontario; when he was very young, his family moved to Holly, Michigan. He would later attend the University of Michigan, graduating with an A.B. degree in 1913 and an M.A degree in 1917. In his long, distinguished career, Andrews would receive honorary doctorates from Wayne State University and the University of Michigan, as well as a Centennial Award from Michigan State College for distinguished service.

For 35 years, from 1920 to 1955—a longer tenure than any other junior college president—Andrews guided, with a singular sense of mission, the growth and development of Grand Rapids Junior College. He outlasted a number of superintendents, each providing him new challenges. He became a pivotal figure in the development of junior colleges throughout the state and nation. In 1922, he co-founded and was named first president of the Michigan Junior College Association. In 1933 he co-founded and chaired the American Association of Junior Colleges.

1920

Arthur Andrews became the second leader of the college. He would go on to serve as president of the college for 35 years and become a significant figure in the junior college movement.

The college yearbook was first published in 1920 and called the *College News Annual*, renamed the *Olympian* in 1925 and published until 1950. (1928 *Olympian*. GRCC Archives)

1921

The Men's Union was established to promote a spirit of fellowship and sociality among the men of the college.

The Classical Club, dedicated to classical antiquity, was organized. In 1926, it was renamed Phi Alpha Gamma.

1922

The Physical Education Department, established this year, began offering such courses as dancing, swimming, hockey, basketball, volleyball, and other activities.

(**Figure 12**) The GRJC Building, formerly Strong Junior High School, on the corner of Ransom Avenue and Lyon Street became the college's home in 1925. (GRCC Archives)

The College Gains a Home

From the start, Andrews devoted himself to maintaining the college's high scholastic standards for transfer students. Admission standards remained the same as those of the University of Michigan. Superintendent Greeson, in his 1923 report to the Grand Rapids Board of Education, noted that "not a single student who had gone from Junior College to other colleges and universities had ever failed in a single subject—a most remarkable record." Strongly favoring a separate building for the college, Greeson added "The time is coming soon…when the Junior College will either crowd Central High School out of the building, or the high school will crowd out the Junior College." On December 15, 1924, the board, with an eye to continued university approval, recommended that a University of Michigan

representative be invited to inspect Strong Junior High School and determine its suitability as a GRJC building. (**Figure 12**) That representative was sent, responded favorably, and an engineer was hired to prepare remodeling plans.[3]

Gymnasiums for both boys and girls had been added to Strong Junior High in 1922 in response to the development of a physical education curriculum in the public schools. The college had introduced a Physical Education Department in 1922, so the timing was propitious. Included in the package was a nearby three-story structure, soon to be converted into a facility known as the Engineering Building, equipped with drawing rooms, labs for materials testing, metal processing, engineering mechanics, welding, and surveying. (**Figure 13**)

The Junior College moved into its refurbished quarters (later renamed the GRJC East Building) at the opening of the 1925-26 school year, both president and student body taking great pride in this new sense of identity. Strong Junior High students were transferred to Central, Ottawa Hills, and South High Schools. Andrews had been offered his choice of principal of Central High School or president of Junior College. He unhesitatingly chose Junior College. Superintendent Greeson, replaced in 1924 by Leslie A. Butler, head of the Ann Arbor schools, went to work at the age of 71 as a Latin and math instructor at the junior college he had helped to found. He would continue teaching through the 1929 school year.

Out of the college's early days at Central High School there had developed a widely-held student perception that Junior College was essentially an advanced high school. Arthur Andrews was passionately opposed to any thinking that characterized Grand Rapids Junior College or the junior college movement as an extension of high school. His transfer curriculum was as demanding as the University of Michigan's. His close cooperation

(**Figure 13**) The Engineering Building (on the left), was located behind the GRJC Building. Photo taken in 1971. (Courtesy of Al Sellers)

with the University of Michigan and strict adherence to North Central Association accrediting requirements had assured high standards. Andrews insisted that the terminal-vocational curriculums of the college, though less rigorous in their admissions standards than the transfer programs, be something far superior to those offered in the high schools. His greatest emphasis, consistent throughout his presidency, was quality. The junior college, now housed in its own building, was not a high school in any respect—it was a college and an exceptional one.

A Solo Administration

From the outset, Andrews was more actively involved in the workings of the college than most presidents. He continued teaching sociology through much of his tenure. He unilaterally initiated a summer school in 1924 and revived a lapsed Evening Institute in 1925. For a brief time he helped coach the baseball team.[4] An Athletic Board of Control managed sports for the college; he presided over it. He made a practice of personally recruiting West Michigan high school students as well as counseling all candidates for graduation about college choices and goals. According to his closest associates, he was a driven perfectionist who had difficulty delegating authority or trusting his vision of excellence to others. He hired a full-time registrar yet kept the position clerical in nature.

A later GRJC registrar, Dr. Robert Riekse, would make this observation: "the chart of the Andrews administration, had there

1922

President Andrews co-founded and was named first president of the Michigan Junior College Association.

The Aesculapian Club (a pre-med group) was founded.

The Swastika Club was organized among the girls in the Physical Education Department to further social activities and to foster friendships. (1923 *Olympian*. GRCC Archives)

1923

The football team won the state championship and would repeat this feat in 1924, 1926 and 1928.

1924

Summer school started and the orchestra was established.

Enrollment was 570 students.

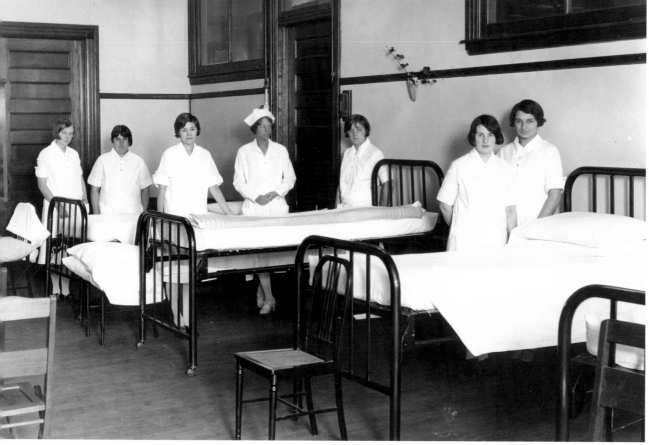

(**Figure 14**) Nurse training class, 1928
(Grand Rapids History and Special Collections, Archives, Grand Rapids Public Library, Grand Rapids, MI 43-2-3 #483)

been one, would have been very simple. Andrews, as administrative head of the college and high school, was responsible for all administrative details and responsibilities."[5] He made the important decisions at every level. Even as the college expanded, he held firmly to the reins of control. Those few who assisted him had little to do with the actual governance of the college.

Every Student a Personal Mission

At the same time Andrews was no Captain Bligh. He had a satisfying personal life with wife and three children. He gave himself to the betterment of those who might never have had the chance for an excellent higher education. Every student became his personal mission. He helped keep resident tuition at $50 per year, though nonresident tuition rose to $100. When the college needed a bookstore manager, he took on the job, donating his bookstore salary to the library for the purchase of a Lincoln collection, which grew to be one of the finest in West

Michigan.[6] He loved gardening and, in suit and tie, did much of the planting and weeding around the GRJC Building. The *Proceedings of the Board of Education* for the 1920s and 1930s show frequent approved leaves for Andrews, who traveled the country advancing the cause of junior colleges.

His professional life (and he was the first to admit it) was wholly dedicated to the well-being of the college. The continued success of Grand Rapids Junior College, in spite of regular threats to its survival, had much to do with Andrews' strong leadership and will.

Students referred with pride to their new college building as "Junior on the Hill," and in the 1920s there was much to be proud of. Follow-up national surveys of junior college students who transferred to senior institutions showed better records than those who entered the universities as freshmen, and, in Andrews' words, "the very best records were made by students who transferred from the Grand Rapids Junior College."[7] Andrews took special pride in GRJC being first in establishing patterns and programs later adopted by others: the first junior college in Michigan, the first junior college in the country to establish nurses' training teamed with community hospitals (in the 1924-25 school year, 120 nursing students were enrolled), the first in Michigan with a Department of Engineering, the first to establish a Practical Nursing Program (1948), the first to establish terminal education in many fields,[8] the first in number and variety of programs, both transfer and terminal.[9] (**Figure 14**)

A Music Department

In 1923, Andrews appointed Karl Wecker, a young German musician (whose impressive talents had also caught the eye of Jesse Davis), as the sole full-time member of the GRJC Music

(left, Figure 15) College production of the light opera *The Marriage of Nannette.* 1927 *Olympian* (GRCC Archives) (below, Figure 16) The Junior College Orchestra, 1928-29. 1929 *Olympian.* (GRCC Archives)

Department. At the time of his appointment, Wecker was conducting an all-male orchestra that in 1929 would become, under his leadership, the Grand Rapids Symphony. Starting with 10 students, Wecker, through his inspired teaching, prompted a steady growth in Music Department enrollment. The majority of his music students in the early 1920s were females pursuing the two-year public school music certificate. Within a few years, the student base would broaden. Wecker introduced light opera to the department, directing his students in such works as *Fire Prince* and *The Marriage of Nannette.* (Figure 15) He established a student orchestra, directed the first year by Glenn C. Bainum, Supervisor of Music for Grand Rapids Public Schools, and thereafter by Wecker himself. (Figure 16) In time he

1920-29

1924

Men's Glee Club established. (1925 *Olympian.* GRCC Archives)

1925

The college took occupancy of the former Strong Junior High School facility on the corner of Ransom Avenue and Lyon Street. This facility later became known as the East Building. The gymnasium of this facility exists today as part of the Music Center.

Andrews revived the lapsed Evening Institute.

GRJC participated in its first intercollegiate debate against Calvin College on April 15, 1925.

The college collaborated with Central High School in the production of the comic opera *Miss Cherry Blossom.*

Girl's Glee Club organized.

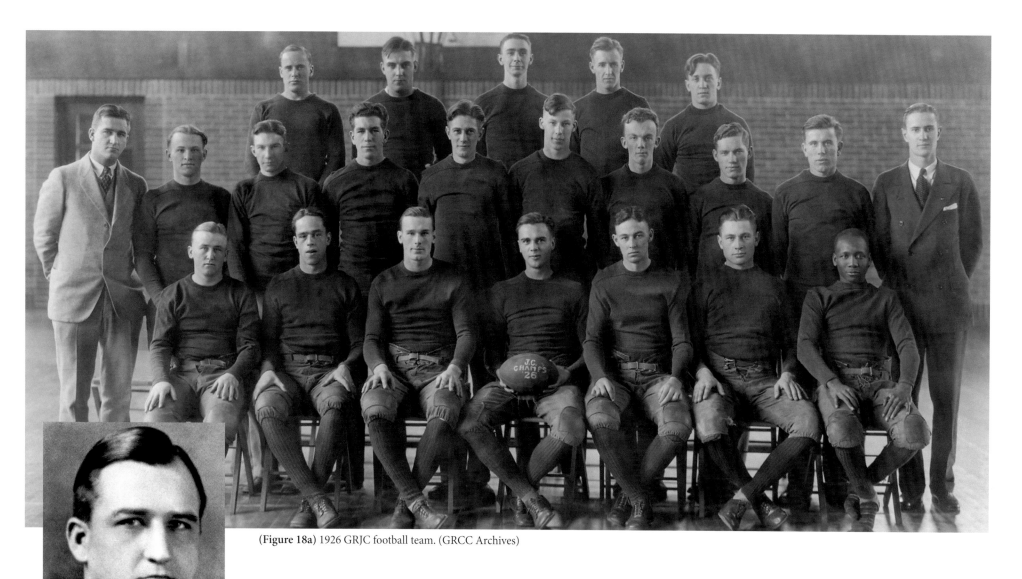

(Figure 18a) 1926 GRJC football team. (GRCC Archives)

(Figure 17) John Bos. 1931 *Olympian.*
(GRCC Archives)

Rapid Expansion of Athletics

Throughout the 1920s, the college experienced a remarkable growth in the area of athletics, as a procession of yearbooks has recorded. Sports teams proliferated. The college Physical Education Department expanded, thanks to the new facili-

began drawing on other talented community musicians and teachers as part-time staff, a practice that continues to this day.[10]

ties. Ruth Dunbar directed women's physical education, and women's sports teams included field hockey and basketball. Men's PE was headed by an amazing athlete and teacher named John Bos. (Figure 17) Bos, a man of high expectations, became a legendary iron man of the school; by the mid 20's he was coaching all men's sports teams—football, basketball, baseball, swimming, tennis, and track—and somehow doing it with astonishing success. There were state championships in football in 1923 and 1924 seasons and again in 1926 and 1928, state basketball championships in 1924-25, 1926-27 and 1927-28; a state tennis championship in 1927; and a state swimming championship in 1928. **(Figure 18a & b)** The teams became known as the "Bosmen," and did most of their winning against four-year colleges. Arthur Andrews took great pride in these accomplishments. An athlete himself, he was described in the 1924 college yearbook, *Olympian,* as "the best supporter of athletics we have."

(**Figure 18b**) 1926 track team (GRCC Archives)

Student Life

Student clubs and organizations abounded. Members organized dances, speakers, carnivals, drama productions, mixers, banquets, field trips—a student social life noticeably more organized and active than we find at the college in 2014. Each year new organizations appeared in the pages of the *Olympian*: Women's League, Men's Union, *The Exhaust* newspaper staff of 1920-22 (thereafter called *The Collegiate*), the yearbook staff, the Engineers Club (rivals of Lits and Laws), Lits and Laws (literary and law students, rivals of Engineers), Delta Sigma (the drama society), Phi Alpha

Gamma (formerly the Classical Club, dedicated to classical antiquity), Men's and Women's Glee Clubs, Varsity Club, Swastika Club (women's athletics), Aesculapian Society (a pre-med group), College Y (affiliated with the YMCA), Business Ad Club, the Social Science Club, Le Cercle Francais (French Club), Deutscher Verein (German Club), Attic Artists, and Feature Club (a writers' group). As a result of a lively debate staged between the Engineers Club and the Lits and Laws, a debate team was formed that won its first two intercollegiate debates—

1925

Basketball team won the state championship and would repeat this feat in 1927 and 1928. (1924-25 men's basketball team. GRCC Archives)

1926

Biology Club organized.

Social Science Club established.

1927

Tennis team won state championship.

The college put on a production of the comic opera *The Marriage of Nannette*.

Clubs established included: Der Deutscher Verein, a German club; the Secretarial Club; and the Science Club.

1928

The bookstore opened with President Andrews serving as manager.

Artist Extraordinaire—Lumen Martin Winter

Lumen Martin Winter, who gained a reputation as one of America's foremost muralists, graduated from Grand Rapids Junior College in 1928. Born in Ellery, Illinois, Winter moved at the age of three to western Kansas with his family. The family ranch was located along the Santa Fe Trail where the young Winter could gaze out and see the wagon paths made from years of passage on the trail.

While a student at GRJC, Winter created cartoons and art that enriched the 1927 and 1928 college yearbooks. He went on to study at the Cleveland School of Art and the National Academy of Design in New York City. In 1939 Winter settled in Santa Fe, New Mexico, working as a cartoonist and designer. He would serve as artist with the U.S. Signal Corps in the Army in World War II.

In 1969, Winter was commissioned to design a mural and the official medallion for the Apollo 13 mission. Entitled *Steeds of Apollo*, the mural depicts four racing horses of Apollo, mythological god of the sun. Winter's most lasting contribution to GRJC became the frieze he designed and sculpted for the front of the Gerald R. Ford Fieldhouse. He created the piece known as *The Legend of Grand Rapids* at his studios in New York and Italy, using marble from Italy's famous Mount Altissimo. Winter completed the commissioned work (depicting Michigan history, mythology, industry, education and culture) for the 1976 dedication of the fieldhouse, attending as a distinguished guest along with President Gerald R. Ford. That year the college further honored Winter with a Distinguished Alumni Award.

Murals by Winter grace the U.S. Air Force Academy Chapel in Colorado Springs, the National Wildlife Federation Headquarters Building and the AFL-CIO Headquarters in Washington, D.C., the Church of St. Paul the Apostle in the Lincoln Center in New York City, and other prominent sites.

Winter died on April 5, 1982, in New Rochelle, New York.

(**clockwise from top left**) Lumen Winter (left) inspecting the outside wall of the Gerald R. Ford Fieldhouse where his frieze is now installed, 1976. (GRCC Archives); *The Legend of Grand Rapids*, the frieze Winter designed and sculpted for the Gerald R. Ford Fieldhouse.; 1928, *Olympian* (GRCC Archives); Lumen Winter cartoon, 1928 *Olympian* (GRCC Archives)

against Calvin College and Central State Normal at Mt. Pleasant. By the 1928-29 school year, the team would win the State Junior College Debating Championship. (**Figure 19**)

1920s graduates who would go on to distinguished careers included Arnold Gingrich, co-founder and Editor of *Esquire* magazine, Dr. John A. Hannah, President of Michigan State College (and University); Edward N. Cole, President of General Motors Corporation (**Figure 20**); Dr. Jay Pylman, Superintendent of Grand Rapids Public Schools; and Lumen Winter, who gained a reputation as one of America's foremost artists and muralists. Winter's cartoons and art enriched the 1927 and 1928 *Olympian*. In 1976, the dedication of the college's new Gerald R. Ford Fieldhouse would feature along the building front a Lumen Winter frieze entitled *The Legend of Grand Rapids*.

Besides Greeson, Wecker, Dunbar, and Bos, 1920s luminaries among the thirty-some faculty included Marie McCabe (zoology), Wilma Marlowe (anatomy), Clarence Meyer (English), James Shew (engineering and math), Harry Kurtzworth (industrial arts), Tudor Lanius (English) and E. Ray Baxter (psychology).

The continued growth and success of Grand Rapids Junior College under Arthur Andrews seemed assured—until abruptly, on a dark day in 1929 known as Black Tuesday, Wall Street crashed and most assurances were off.

(**Figure 19**) 1928-29 GRJC Debate Team. 1929 *Olympian* (GRCC Archives)

(**Figure 20**) Edward N. Cole, 1928 GRJC alumnus, would later become President of General Motors Corporation. (Courtesy of General Motors)

1928

Men's swimming team won state championship. (1928 Men's Swim Team. GRCC Archives)

Men's basketball team defeated Calvin College 44-13 on January 6, 1928.

The football team finished the season 5-1 and outscored their opponents 205-27.

1929

Business Administration Club was established.

Debate team won the Michigan Junior College Debating Championships.

Delegates were sent to the Intercollegiate Model Assembly of the League of Nations for the first time. (1929 *Olympian*. GRCC Archives)

1937 Spring dance in the gymnasium. (GRCC Archives)

The Andrews Era—Act Two
The 1930s

Expansion and Contraction

Starting in 1924, the Grand Rapids Public Schools, under the leadership of Superintendent Butler, had experienced a rigorous seven-year expansion of the system. Ottawa Hills, Creston, and Davis Technical High Schools were built and dedicated before the 1920s were done. Butler oversaw the construction of Harrison Park, Burton, Aberdeen, Alger, and Eastern Avenue Schools. The 1929 stock market crash had only slowed his progress. Butler's approval level soared, and in 1930 he was reappointed to a three-year term. A new South High auditorium was dedicated in 1931.

At the same time, after five years in the GRJC Building, (according to Andrews' June 19, 1930, *Report to Superintendent Butler*), Grand Rapids Junior College was the neglected child of the system, needing Central High School's auditorium and sports fields for its programs. (**Figure 21**) Andrews' 1931 *Report to Superintendent Butler* would describe a building already taxed to capacity by increased enrollment. His hopes were that Butler's expansion plans might eventually touch the college. Such lavish facilities as Burton Junior High School must have bewildered him.

The same report presented evidence that a lean college administration was not entirely of Andrews' choosing. The President pointedly asked Butler for more administrative help, indicating that doubling administrative staff would still put the college well below the average of a junior college the size of GRJC. These requests for staff resulted in no measurable change. A three-person administrative staff, besides being economical, might well have provided the superintendent an edge in a subtle game of control.

Grand Rapids waited for an upturn of economic conditions, but it was not to happen. The ambitious school building

THE GRAND RAPIDS JUNIOR COLLEGE
GRAND RAPIDS, MICHIGAN

Mr. L. A. B. -3

taken since. While there is perhaps some question about the building of an auditorium on the present site, the need is urgent.

The Junior College problem is a distinctive one. One of the difficult aspects is presented in trying to create college morale. Many students come reluctantly. Many have a natural desire to attend some large or famous university. Feeling as they do, it is difficult to arouse their enthusiasm to a point where they do their best work. The fact that students feel that they are missing attractive features of college life, and in some instances an attitude of indifference, does not bring out the best. I appreciate that college activities may easily be overdone, but such is not the case in Junior College. Whenever the student body has activities, it is generally necessary to go to Central High School. This results in inconvenience to them as well as to us. Further, since the large high schools have a tendency to overshadow the Junior College, it is particularly desirable to have these functions in the college building.

(**Figure 21**) 1930 annual
Report to the Superintendent of Schools. (GRCC Archives)

program was put on temporary hold in late 1931—and would not resume for 20 years.[1]

1931 was the year the schools began to feel the suffocating squeeze of the Great Depression. Salaries were cut by 10 percent,

1930

Men's track team won state championship. (1930 track team GRCC Archives)

The International Relations Club was established for the purpose of studying and discussing national and international events and issues. (1930 *Olympian*. GRCC Archives)

Club Hispanoamericano, a Spanish club, was formed.

Debate team won the State Junior College debating championship and would go on to win it again in 1935 and 1938.

Resident tuition was $50.00 per year.

THE JUNIOR COLLEGE JOURNAL

UNDER JOINT EDITORIAL AUSPICES OF THE AMERICAN ASSOCIATION OF JUNIOR COLLEGES AND THE SCHOOL OF EDUCATION OF STANFORD UNIVERSITY. . . . MEMBER THE EDUCATIONAL PRESS ASSOCIATION OF AMERICA

Vol. III   FEBRUARY 1933   No. 5

Significance of the Junior College Movement

[EDITORIAL]

It is significant that after President Henry Philip Tappan, of the University of Michigan, first advanced the junior college idea, more than half a century elapsed before this educational development took place. With public junior colleges, at least, it was not a statement of educational philosophy that resulted in reorganization, but rather a theory that waited upon practical considerations which did not make themselves felt until the early part of the present century. It was only when secondary education had experienced a remarkable growth, when universities had reached unprecedented size, and when high schools were filled with postgraduates, that the junior college idea was given widespread attention. This fact explains much that otherwise leads to controversy and confusion.

It is well to remember that many junior colleges were established because of the demand of students for advanced training and that the organization was worked out under the guidance of a high-school principal whose heavy administrative responsibility left little time or energy for this new educational appendage. In other instances the junior college was a separate unit within the high school, with a division of responsibility and ensuing jealousy and misunderstanding. In meeting the immediate situation, in many instances it was hardly conceived that a junior college could mean other than the first two years of regular university work. Many newly appointed heads of junior colleges with commendable zeal immediately were called upon to take courses in education to learn something of the unit they were already administering. Under such conditions it was natural that policies in regard to junior colleges were tentative.

In the meantime junior colleges were making remarkable growth, and universities and senior colleges became vitally interested in the movement. Perhaps some saw in this educational innovation an undesirable rival. A large number were more particularly concerned because they were being asked to accept junior college transcripts. A number of factors led to a feverish attempt to analyze and define the proper educational status of the junior college. Some insisted that the six-four-four plan only could hope to endure, and others that the six-three-three-two had unquestioned advantage. Educational experts saw in the junior college an attempt to destroy American cul-

[233]

234   *The Junior College Journal for February 1933*

ture. Some were fearful that a lowering of the standards might be the inevitable result, while others welcomed the junior college as a dumping ground for those who wanted to go to college and should not. While junior college administrators were made to feel that the institution was definitely on trial and investigations were being made to see how the junior college graduates progressed in universities, it was argued that the junior college must not be merely a preparatory institution. During the same period the colleges developed in nearly every state in the union and something had to be done about them.

It is not meant to suggest that the movement proceeded without sympathy or leadership but rather that the growth was so rapid and under such greatly varying conditions that the task of evaluating and guiding has been a difficult one. More particularly, there is danger in trying without sufficient experience and experimentation to define the status of the junior college and the rôle it is to play. Fortunately progress has been made. As Secretary Campbell said recently: "It is true that the junior college, having to meet both the secondary standards below and the higher standards above, has found it difficult to serve two masters. However, there are even now indications that this difficult amphibian existence will not always be demanded."

There is evidence that the university may feel assured that the junior college graduates will not be a liability. With this assurance, it will be possible to let experimentation and experience lead to conclusions rather than to have somewhat uncertain conclusions lead to policies. A highly respected educator who some years ago ardently espoused the six-four-four plan now concludes that under certain conditions the six-three-three-two organization more nearly fits the need. Moreover, as has been suggested, with the amount of experimentation which has been going on, it is strange that a three-year junior college unit has not been tried more seriously and extensively.

In the curriculum of the junior college, there is a question whether emphasis shall be placed upon the preparatory function or upon the terminal courses, since there may be conflicting standards between the two. The student interested in occupational education confined to the "middle level" may not function in such general courses as are alike required of those in terminal curricula and those meeting the requirements of the first two years of standard university work.

Arbitrary statements will not answer these questions. They await experience and experimentation. The writer feels that those who deal most directly with the problems of the junior college will in time make their contribution. They will do well to keep an open mind. Where there is so much vigorous assertion of a contradictory nature, there is danger of becoming advocates of an educational theory rather than education. There are no "charmed" plans of organization; and it is the challenge of those associated with the junior college movement, while considering suggestions of friends and critics, to face their own problem thoughtfully and courageously.

ARTHUR ANDREWS

(**Figure 22**) Andrews, Arthur. "Significance of the Junior College Movement." *The Junior College Journal* 3, no. 5 (February 1933): 233-34. (Courtesy of American Association of Community Colleges)

ers were paid in tax anticipation warrants (short-term IOUs from the city).[2] Some schools closed, though Arthur Andrews found ways to keep Grand Rapids Junior College's doors open. In 1936, Superintendent Butler, butting heads with the board on economic policies, resigned and went to work for Michigan State Normal College in Ypsilanti. Arthur W. Krause, principal at South High School, was named acting superintendent; within a year he was awarded the job outright. Krause, a no-nonsense disciplinarian, seemed to possess the strength to guide a faltering system through a dark and difficult time.

The Michigan Degree Racket

Economic conditions continued to deteriorate; the starting salary for teachers in Grand Rapids dropped to $900 per year. In some Michigan school systems, including those of Junior College faculty. In 1932, the cut was 25 percent. By 1933, 110 teachers had been released from the Grand Rapids system and salaries were 37.5 percent lower than they had been in 1930. During the bank holiday of 1933, teachers pay for teachers fell as low as $25 a month. Times grew desperate—more than most of us can imagine. In education, only men and women with college degrees kept their jobs; all non-degreed teachers were being released. Many who had earned terminal teaching certificates felt a real sense of panic. They began scrambling for baccalaureate degrees, to the point of offering to pay for honorary degrees. The scene was ripe for fraud, and unscrupulous people began appearing to take advantage of suffering. Michigan became, during the depression years, an open playing field for the racket of selling degrees. Laws simply did not exist to regulate an underworld of educational con men peddling phony degrees for a price. Anyone with $15 could charter a college, and though such bogus colleges often never opened, their "staffs" could confer degrees for the price of a graduation essay and a cash gift to "the endowment fund."[3]

It took a new organization to put an end to the chicanery. In 1934, a group of concerned educators gathered in Lansing's Olds Hotel. Arthur Andrews, President of Grand Rapids Junior College, was one of the seven men who would on that evening create the Michigan College Association. The mission of the organization was "to collect evidence of shady practices, and to seek the cooperation of college and other leaders in Michigan" in putting an end to educational fraud.[4] The group compiled multiple examples of fraudulent degree-granting by legally chartered "colleges." Though the process took until 1939 to complete, the Michigan College Association at last presented a bill to members of the Senate Education Committee, who, stunned by the breadth of the problem, passed the bill without changing a word. It was the beginning of the end of a practice that had disgraced Michigan for a decade. Arthur Andrews would serve on the original Executive Committee, then as the group's treasurer from 1940-42, and as its president from 1951-53 (the first junior college president to serve in that position).

Not an Extension of High School

Andrews again and again proved himself a leader of courage and vision, willing to do battle with anything threatening the integrity of the junior college movement. In the 1930s, there was much speculation about the direction the movement would take. Should junior college course work be maintained at college level, or simply considered an extension of high school? When the University of Chicago School of Education proposed a 6-4-4 educational plan, with six elementary grades, four junior high grades (7 to 10), and four senior high grades (11 to 14), Andrews rallied the American Association of Junior Colleges to do battle against "this attempt to downgrade junior college education."[5] (**Figure 22**) Their successful efforts helped more clearly define the nature and purpose of the junior college in America.

Keeping the College Alive

Against unusual difficulties, Andrews worked to maintain the highest standards in both transfer and terminal curriculums. His own words express his ideals well:

We have been interested in presenting real educational opportunity to serious minded students…As I look back upon my association with thousands of fine young people, it is a great satisfaction to feel that we have tried to appeal to the very best that was in them, and to give them the background that would make it possible for them to render distinguished service to their fellows, and be able to share in the finer things of life.[6]

Inadequate finances, however, would persistently handicap these high ideals. During the depression, nearly every financial crisis of the school system threatened the existence of Grand Rapids Junior College. The board of education, under immense pressure to reduce expenses, looked often—as a natural solution—to the closing of the college, where per-student costs were higher. Andrews agreed to tuition increases three times

1931

As a result of the Great Depression, salaries at GRJC were cut by 10 percent in 1931, and then by an additional 25 percent in 1932.

Pi Lambda Kappa, pre-law, was organized and renamed the Law Club by 1937. (1931 *Olympian*. GRCC Archives)

The basketball, track and tennis teams all won state championships. (Tennis team, 1931 *Olympian*. GRCC Archives)

THE GRAND RAPIDS JUNIOR COLLEGE

GRAND RAPIDS, MICHIGAN

June 20, 1933.

Mr. L. A. Butler,
Supt. of Schools,
143 Bostwick Ave., N. E.,
Grand Rapids, Michigan.

Dear Mr. Butler:

Complying with your request in regard to adjustments in the Junior College made necessary by decreased enrollment, I am suggesting the following facts for your consideration.

1. With the new arrangement in music, it will not be necessary for us to have the services of Miss Silsby. We can, according to our tentative plans, take care of the group of third year music students by having one course taught by Miss Kunsman or some one else Mr. Morgan may suggest. The course is in comparative methods. Miss Silsby has been teaching it and if her schedule can be arranged to have her teach this course conveniently, this would be very satisfactory, I am sure. There would be, of course, a saving in the cost of the Junior College if it could be taught by Miss Kunsman, as Mr. Morgan has suggested.

2. We will be able to take care of the work in engineering without the services of Mr. Teele.

(Figure 23) 1933 annual *Report to the Superintendent of Schools.* (GRCC Archives)

to keep the college going. There were pressures on him to lower college standards with the intent of attracting more students. Andrews stood firmly in opposition to diluting programs. His June 20, 1933, *Report to Superintendent Butler* expressed his pain at having to cut staff. **(Figure 23)** In 1930 enrollment had stood at 987, and faculty numbered 50. By 1934, enrollment was down to 735, and faculty count was at 35, but the college was holding its own through the worst of the depression. Andrews fought on for GRJC, his determined arguments often all that kept the college open. On one occasion, when the board was considering closing the college, he stated, "'We may go down; but if we do, we will go down with our colors flying.'"[7]

Loss of Programs, Publications

The depression years saw a diminishing of terminal/occupational courses because of changes in the fortunes of local industries, particularly the

furniture industry. It was difficult to determine the occupational needs of a community in survival mode. In the early 1930s, the highly successful normal school program in public school music was threatened by a rivalry with state senior institutions, most notably the University of Michigan, whose leaders saw teacher training as their jurisdiction. When in 1935, the Michigan Legislature determined that four years, not two, were necessary to certify public school music teachers, the Junior College program abruptly ended. The Junior College Music Department, with the heart of its curriculum cut out, was in danger of dying.

The school district had no resources to put into new programming. Andrews loved music, wanted to build a distinguished music program, but his energy was entirely focused on keeping the college alive. He hoped that his ties to the U of M might result in GRJC providing the first two years of the University's four-year music curriculum, so he encouraged Karl Wecker to pursue the matter. Wecker's interests, however, lay in a growing Grand Rapids Symphony.[8] One observer close to the college noted that there was "evidence that Wecker and Andrews were not compatible. No doubt, the authoritarian patrician that was Arthur Andrews found the creative musician that was Karl Wecker difficult, if not impossible to live with."[9] In 1937, Wecker left the college, continuing as conductor of the Grand Rapids Symphony. For a brief period, the college's Music Department existed in name only.

The grip of the depression was felt in all areas of GRJC. The yearbook, *The Olympian*, depending on support from the athletic fund and advertising, went on hiatus for four years, from 1932-35. The men's sports teams, numbering six in 1930-31 (football, basketball, swimming, track, tennis, and golf) were reduced to three (football, basketball, and track) from 1932-34.

(**Figure 24**) 1930-31 basketball team and star player Webb Marris (first row far right). (GRCC Archives)

1930-39

1933

President Arthur Andrews co-founded and became the first president of the American Association of Junior Colleges.

1934

Enrollment was 735 students.

President Arthur Andrews co-founded the Michigan College Association.

1936

The college yearbook, *Olympian*, was published again after a four-year hiatus due to the depression.

1937

Quill Club established. (1939 *Olympian*. GRCC Archives)

The Bosmen managed to perform well in spite of severe belt tightening. The administrative structure of the college continued lean, made up of President Andrews, Registrar Iva M. Belden, and Assistant to the President Felix E. Wilcox (who also taught math).

Making the Best of the Worst of Times

At the same time, clubs went on sponsoring dances and students went on working hard, striving for a more hopeful future. GRJC won state championships in debate, track, tennis, and basketball in the course of the 1930-31 season. The basketball team went 15-1, with star Webb Marris setting a GRJC individual scoring record. (**Figure 24**) In 1936, thanks to a new subscription-based yearbook organization and donated proceeds from Delta Sigma's benefit drama productions (staged in the Central High School auditorium), the *Olympian* once again resumed publication. The debate team won state championships in 1935 and 1938.

The depression years of GRJC were times of wild student support for intercollegiate sports events. Pep rallies led by student "Yell Masters" could whip enthusiasm into frenzy. In 1937, the basketball team began calling itself—appropriately—the

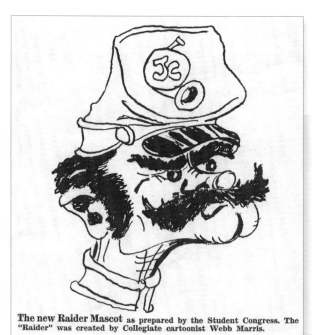

The new Raider Mascot as prepared by the Student Congress. The "Raider" was created by Collegiate cartoonist Webb Marris.

What Is a Raider?

The 1930s were a highly successful decade for the GRJC basketball teams, with state championships and strong fan support. Pep rallies led by "Yell Masters" could whip enthusiasm into a frenzy that spilled over into the games as well as into the streets afterwards. In 1937, the basketball team began calling itself the "Raiders," expressing the wild spirit they seemed to inspire in their fans after they had sacked the opposing teams. In 1938 the football team adopted the name as well, and soon all sports teams were JC Raiders, wearing the blue and gold colors they had acquired from the U of M in 1914.

It would take 24 years before anyone tried to imagine what a Raider looked like. *Junior Collegiate* cartoonist Webb Marris, Jr. created an unofficial mascot, a grizzled-looking Union soldier with heavy sideburns, moustache, and a Buddy Ebsen look. Student Congress President Bill Woodson and *Junior Collegiate* Editor George Graeber recommended to Dean Visser that this mascot and a Civil War theme officially embody the spirit of the college. Though there is no clear record of Visser blessing this idea, the baseball team adopted the Union soldier and wore his image on their caps for the next 50 years and more, even after a new mascot was commissioned in 2001.

GRCC's marketing department, at the urging of President Juan R. Olivarez, hired Stevens Advertising of Grand Rapids to create a new Raider mascot and logo. The firm contracted with illustrator Kevin White, who created an Indiana Jones-looking raccoon with a fedora hat and an attitude. The process cost the college $7500, but Olivarez was pleased with the outcome. *Grand Rapids Press* writer (and GRJC alum) Tom Rademacher was less enthusiastic. He wrote that a raccoon simply was not the kind of warrior figure you would want emblazoned on your football helmet. Alas, the Raider raccoon, never warmly received by students, fell out of use and was quietly retired at the end of the 2011-12 school year. Though a new official GRCC logo has been created for the college's 100th anniversary, a new sports mascot/logo has not yet appeared on the scene (momentum, however, may be gathering to fill that void).

For the first time in the history of Junior College the J.C. Raiders lost an athletic contest; for the first time in history the "Raiders" played in an athletic contest. It would seem that the acquisition of the name "Raiders" threw the Junior College basketeers off stride in their opening game, for they dropped it (the game) to Calvin by a 26-14 score. For an opening performance, however, the Raiders played well, and they gave indication of better things to come later in the season. Bishop showed signs of having eaten Wheaties, for he played like a champion by ringing up eight points and turning in a great defensive game. We feel that Mr. Bishop will be quite a help when he gets his full growth. Adams also performed well as did the pugnacious Mr. Challa, who did not get into the game until the second half. Harold Green was ejected from the game for committing four personals — foul play suspected!

It's funny (peculiar, not ha-ha) what a few days of vacationing will do to some people. At least we'll say that some of the blame for a 30-25 defeat at the hands of Kalamazoo can be attributed to Junior's early Christmas vacation. We apologize for failing to be facetious about Kalamazoo, but we feel that that city has been the butt of more than its share of wisecracks; but we might say that when you are Raiders in a Hornet's own gymnasium, you should

(upper left) Webb Marris, Jr. Raider Mascot drawing. (GRCC Archives)
(left) Article on the new sports team name, J.C. Raiders (*The Junior Collegiate*/1937 *Olympian*. GRCC Archives)
(upper right) Raider Raccoon. (GRCC Archives)

"Raiders." **(Figure 25)** After important games, police sometimes had to be called in to restore order. Victory celebrations were known to expand into snake dances down Monroe Avenue. Students were making the best of the worst of times.

Federal Help

When the Federal Emergency Relief Act was passed in 1933, the government made welfare a national concern. Up to that point, the city had been the only source of aid to impoverished families. By 1935, 8,000 Kent County men were working on Works Progress Administration (W.P.A.) projects. A similar program, the National Youth Administration (N.Y.A.), provided student aid ($15 a month to college students) and work for 18-to-25-year-old students from relief families. Hundreds of young men and women found employment on N.Y.A. projects in Kent County.[10] GRJC employed a substantial number of them, some gathering alumni information, others assisting as clerical workers. As a result, many were able to continue as GRJC students.

Turning the Corner

By the later 1930s, as the economy slowly began to improve, the outlook of the college's terminal/occupational programs began to improve as well. Arthur Andrews, in his 1938 *Report to the Superintendent*, made the following observations:

(**Figure 25**) 1949 baseball team with "Raiders" nickname on uniform. (GRCC Archives)

The demand for industrial chemists and those with secretarial training has been such that at times the positions available have exceeded the supply of candidates. The college continues to seek the advice of citizens in the community in building and revising the curricula. A group of ten physicians cooperated in revising the curricula for those preparing for positions as physicians' assistants. Contact has been made with industrial leaders in planning the curriculum for junior engineers. Several conferences have been held with merchants in the city in planning a program of merchandising to be organized under the George-Dean Act. There are a great many opportunities for the college to be of service to the community without any great expense to the community.

Later in the report, Andrews announced a new program for Dental Assistants beginning in 1939.

1938

Baseball reappeared as a major sport (1938 *Olympian*. GRCC Archives).

Mr. A. W. Krause - 4.

Already conferences have been held with over three hundred students and newspaper advertising will be started within the next few weeks. As suggested by the Junior College Committee of the Board of Education, a camera has been purchased to take moving pictures of college activities and these will be used during the coming year. Practically all the cost of publicity work thus far has been taken care of from the earnings of the bookstore. On another page I am listing some of the talks given during the present college year.

During the present college year, reports have been made as to size of classes, teaching load and other details in regard to the management of the college. If there are ways in which the college can be more economically operated, suggestions will be gladly received. While dealing with these matters may I quote two paragraphs from North Central Association standards:

"Faculty--Service. The number of hours of classroom work given by each teacher will vary in different departments. To determine this, the amount of preparation required for the class and the amount of time needed for study to keep abreast of the subject, together with the number of students, must be taken into account. Teaching schedules, including classes for part-time students, exceeding 16 recitation hours or their equivalent per week, per instructor, will be interpreted as endangering educational efficiency."

During the depression I believe the North Central Association allowed a teaching load of eighteen hours, but I understand that this was meant as a ruling to cover an emergency. I am calling attention to the fact that we have an eighteen hour teaching load, that I may not carry the full responsibility of "endangering educational efficiency".

For many years a great deal of emphasis has been given to Junior College musical organizations. This year, however, the glee clubs disbanded at the close of the first semester and other units suffered somewhat. The plan of having a director come into the college for two short rehearsals a week is not satisfactory. Since no one period can be set aside for such work, the directors should be here before the rehearsal is called in order to promote the activities. Moreover when concerts are given, directors should take some time for general supervision. It has been surprising that we have not lost musical instruments in the past and this is certain to occur in the future unless greater care is taken. These things warrant a larger remu-

(Figure 26) 1937 annual *Report to the Superintendent of Schools.* (GRCC Archives)

(Figure 27) Harold Steele. (GRCC Archives)

A weakness in the occupational area of the college had always been the lack of a professional placement office working to connect graduates to available jobs. Though money did not yet exist for a full-time placement officer, in the 1938-39 school year (and for several years thereafter), faculty members were given released time for this work.[11]

Guidance counseling (Jesse Davis's passion) was something Andrews had done almost single-handedly for years. As the college grew, the job became increasingly difficult, so Andrews established a system of faculty advisors, each responsible for the constructive guidance of 25 students. Further improvements were planned as money became available.[12] Andrews' yearly reports to Superintendent Arthur Krause

in the later 1930s contained requests for administrative help in any of the following areas: a placement officer, guidance counselors, a dean of student activities, deans of men and women, a supervisor of personnel, a records keeper, an attendance officer, a public relations officer, and more. The requests were heard but apparently not heeded. GRPS had staff, after all, to handle many of these matters. When a North Central report delivered a low rating in the area of financial support of the college, Andrews was hardly surprised. Each year he had spent much of his energy pleading for such basic things as adequate instructional space, equitable teaching loads, and expanded administrative help, but his requests more often than not went unmet. When in his 1937 report to Krause, he said, "If there are ways in which the college can be more economically operated, suggestions will be gladly received," one senses exasperated irony. (Figure 26)

Bosmen Become Steelemen

1938 marked the end of the John Bos era in GRJC athletics. Bos took the job as head of Grand Rapids Parks and Recreation, and Harold O. Steele, a football star with an A.B. and M.A. from University of Michigan, took over as GRJC Director of Athletics. (Figure 27) The Bosmen now became the Steelemen, and the sports programs continued to thrive. Steele coached the football, basketball, track and tennis teams, but chose to delegate some of the coaching responsibilities to others: faculty members Dwight Packard (English) took over baseball, and J. H. Geurkink (German) coached golf. Carroll Sweet, a former wrestling star from U of M, introduced wrestling as a new sport in '38, but it lasted only a year. In 1939, Steele further delegated responsibilities by securing Al Veenboer to take over the tennis team, and former U of M star fullback and punter John Regeczi to serve as his assistant football coach.

Silver Jubilee—Still Alive at 25

1939 marked Grand Rapids Junior College's Twenty-Fifth Anniversary, the Silver Jubilee year. **(Figure 28)** With the depression lingering, with Hitler invading Czechoslovakia and Poland, with Britain and France declaring war on Germany, the Silver Jubilee was a somber occasion. The female athletes of the Swastika Club (named for a Greek symbol of good luck and health), dismayed by Hitler's use of the symbol, reluctantly gave it up. The 1939 *Olympian* reported: "Hitler can no longer claim any Nazi followers among the JC students, for the Swastika Club, after much criticism, has finally agreed to change its name. It is now known as the Women's P.E. Club." **(Figure 29)**

1939 brought a significant alteration in the college's administrative staff. E. Ray Baxter, a GRJC alumnus and psychology teacher, a close friend of Andrews, was selected to replace Felix E. Wilcox as assistant to the president. Baxter had been a member of the college's first graduating class. Baxter and Andrews would enjoy a fruitful partnership through the rest of Andrews' presidency.

(Figure 28) 1939 Silver Jubilee banquet program. (GRCC Archives)

(Figure 29) Women's Physical Education Club, 1939 *Olympian*. (GRCC Archives)

Times remained hard, and war threatened to make them harder. Ten million were still out of work in the country. Yet the 1930s had offered Grand Rapids a few optimistic signs: federal money from the Civil Works and Works Progress Administrations had made possible the Civic Auditorium, the Grand Rapids Public Museum, sewer renewal, and construction of the Lake Michigan pipeline. The city also managed to build Grand River flood control walls, rebuild bridges, and widen and pave streets.[13] The downtown could boast three large department stores, the Ryerson Library, a symphony orchestra, and another presence that would grow more significant over the years. Grand Rapids Junior College, still alive at 25, would one day become a major force in keeping the downtown area thriving and vital.

1930-39

1938

The Men's and Girl's Glee Clubs were merged to form a College Choir. (1939 *Olympian.* GRCC Archives)

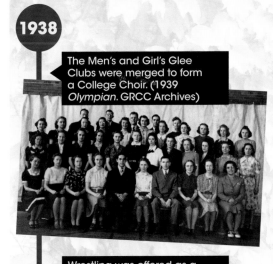

Wrestling was offered as a sport for the first time. (1938 *Olympian.* GRCC Archives)

1939

The college celebrated its twenty-fifth anniversary.

Golf team won state tournament.

Students studying in the GRJC Library, ca. 1950s. (GRCC Archives)

The Andrews Era—Act Three
1940-55

Taking Stock

By 1940, Grand Rapids Junior College had an enrollment of over 900. The GRJC Building contained gymnasiums for men and women, classrooms and labs, all running at close to capacity. It also housed the library, containing 12,000 volumes with the added blessing of the Grand Rapids Ryerson Library nearby. There was a student-managed bookstore, its profits directed to a loan fund for needy students. Twenty-five student scholarships were now available. The cafeteria of the Davis Technical High School, located a block away, furnished meals at a reduced price to Junior College students, who lacked such a facility. A makeshift Engineering Building, located to the immediate southeast of the GRJC Building, housed drafting rooms and engineering labs. The college boasted an extensive and successful athletic program (the football team was the only undefeated college football team in Michigan in 1940), in spite of having no athletic fields to play on but those belonging to the high schools. (**Figure 30**) As early as 1930, Andrews was expressing to Superintendent Butler his embarrassment at having to compete with high schools for field use.

Hoping for their own performing space some day, Delta Sigma, the college's active drama group, along with the college's Music Department (now led by Don Armstrong, Supervisor of Music for the entire GRPS system), had to be content with scheduling the Central High auditorium for productions and concerts. Commencement exercises, for lack of appropriate

1940

Olympian subscription drive (1940 *Olympian*, GRCC Archives)

Resident tuition was $100.00 per year, nonresident $140.00.

Enrollment was over 900 students.

Football team finished the season undefeated at 7-0.

Thirty academic transfer programs and 14 terminal/occupational programs offered.

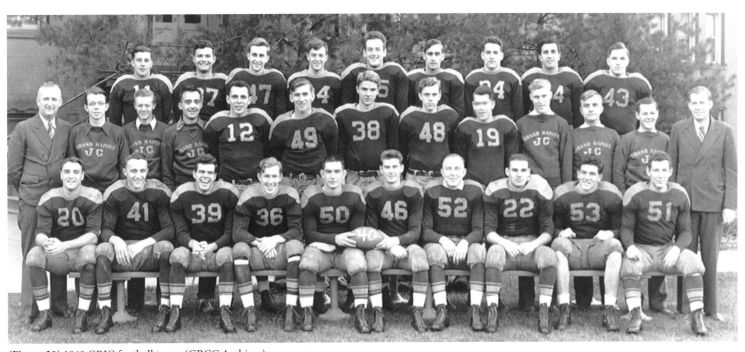

(**Figure 30**) 1940 GRJC football team. (GRCC Archives)

(top, Figure 31a) Elizabeth Wilson, freshman in 1941.
(top right, Figure 31b) Elizabeth Wilson (left) served as the speech student manager for the Speakers' Bureau, 1941 *Olympian*. (GRCC Archives)
(above, Figure 31c) Delta Sigma, the dramatic club, 1941 *Olympian*. (GRCC Archives)

space, were held at various off-campus sites, usually in downtown churches. [1]

1940 resident tuition was $100 per year, nonresident $140. The college, still mainly a transfer institution, offered 30 academic transfer programs and 14 terminal/occupational programs. Students were not permitted at the time to organize into social fraternities or sororities that could select and exclude members. Instead, the Men's Union and Women's League were, in the democratic spirit of the college, open to every student. New social groups came into being or replaced old ones: Choir, Quill Club (a writing group), the International Relations Club, the Home Economics Club, the Forestry Club, the Secretarial Club, the Biology Club, the Chemistry Club, and the Camera Club…each adding to the variety of student life.

One knowledgeable observer of the college wrote in 1940 that a three-person administrative staff was clearly insufficient for the size of the institution. He suggested that "the President should be relieved of all teaching and personnel work and be allowed to devote his time to purely administrative functions."[2] Within the space of the next 15 years, however, Arthur Andrews would add only a treasurer (1941) and a director of vocational guidance (1949)—both college instructors on partial released time—to the administrative team and would continue his teaching (two sections of sociology per semester) and guidance counseling work. Stories of his micromanaging abound: on Sundays, for instance, after attending Fountain Street Baptist Church, Andrews and E. Ray Baxter (who understood his perfectionist nature as well as anyone) would walk over to the college and carefully review attendance records of every GRJC student.[3] Yet, remembering Andrews' frequent and rarely heeded requests for administrative support, one gains a somewhat more balanced sense of the man.

From Crisis to Crisis

Thanks to Andrews' leadership, the college had navigated the aftermath of World War I and the worst of the depression. 1940 seemed to offer a moment of breathing space. It was impossible, however, not to be aware of a new crisis rumbling on the horizon. When the 1941 Japanese attack on Pearl Harbor swept America into war, the city joined the war effort with a stunning unity of purpose. Scrap iron drives began in earnest; citizens turned in cooking fat and old tires for the war cause; the government began issuing food stamps and rationing food and gasoline. Women went to work for the war effort, and families planted Victory gardens to supplement the food supply. On the very day of the Pearl Harbor attack, a local unit of the Michigan State Troops was sworn in to patrol the Kent County Airport, a Civilian Defense unit was opened to volunteers, and action was taken to protect industries gearing for war production. Japanese planes had reached all the way to Hawaii; the threat to the American mainland seemed very real. Within a year, the city had gathered 6,000 auxiliary police, 4,000 block wardens, and 2,000 auxiliary firemen.[4]

In spite of the clouds of war, 1941 was a banner year in sports for GRJC, with both tennis and golf teams winning state championships. The debate team added a state championship as well. The choir presented the light opera production of *The Mikado*. Delta Sigma staged a production of *The Royal Family* featuring Elizabeth Wilson, who would go on to star on Broadway, television, and in the movies, perhaps most notably as Dustin Hoffman's mother in *The Graduate*. (**Figure 31a, b & c**) From the start of 1942, however, the better portion of the male population on-campus began to depart for Europe and the Pacific. By 1943, enrollment had fallen by more than half, and all sports events were discontinued for lack of players and coaches.

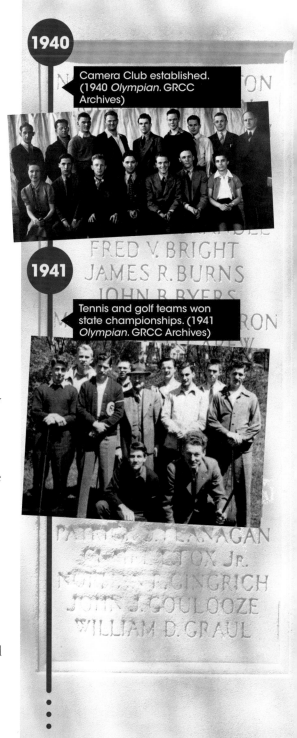

1940

Camera Club established. (1940 *Olympian*. GRCC Archives)

1941

Tennis and golf teams won state championships. (1941 *Olympian*. GRCC Archives)

(above, Figure 32) Stamp sale in support of war effort, 1944 *Olympian*. (GRCC Archives)
(right, Figure 33) Dedication, 1942 *Olympian*. (GRCC Archives)

Athletic Director Harold Steele would spend several years in the Navy, stationed in Alaska. Faculty members George Kremble, Ben Gregory, and Lowell Wingerd (the new college treasurer) also would be called into the armed forces. Most of the math and engineering instructors were serving the government (no calculus would be taught for two years). No *Olympian* yearbook would be published from 1943 through '45, though the Women's League put out a slim paper version as a brave gesture toward "keeping the home fires burning." The student newspaper, *The Collegiate,* disappeared for nearly two decades, the reasons now clouded by time.

The War Effort Builds

Grand Rapids school children began drilling for air raids starting in 1942. In 1943, trainees of the Army Air Force Weather School took over the Pantlind and Rowe Hotels, the Civic Auditorium, and other downtown buildings for 10 months of operations. At the same time, Grand Rapids Junior College, already running a popular course in Civil Pilot Licensing, provided training for

over 200 recruits preparing to fly Army transports or to become instructors for the Army Air Corps.[5] Grand Rapids staged its first air raid blackout test in April, 1943. By August the city had adopted an ordinance for blackout violators: a $100 fine, or 90 days in jail, or both. The city manager purchased 10 air raid sirens, each with a range of a mile and a half. A number of local industries were transformed for war work, and thousands of local citizens trained for war production. The war effort was serious business—and the business of everyone.[6]

Grand Rapids Junior College, though drained by the loss of most of its male population, gave itself to the war effort. The Women's League sold war bonds and fashioned armbands for air raid wardens. The Student Council sponsored paper drives and sold stamps and bonds. **(Figure 32)**

(**Figures 34 & 35**) Air Cadet Training Center, March 11, 1943. (Grand Rapids History and Special Collections, Archives, Grand Rapids Public Library, Grand Rapids, MI Neg.# H009320)

Clubs donated profits to children's relief funds and the Red Cross.[7] The 1942 *Olympian*, the last hardbound, full-length GRJC yearbook until 1946, was dedicated as follows:

> *To our men now in the united forces we dedicate this book… expressing our gratitude for their immeasurable contribution; our pride in their intractable spirit; our faith in their strength to destroy intolerance and create world peace. May these fragments of former life heighten their desire to build again on the foundation of wisdom in the radiance of new tomorrows.* (**Figure 33**)

The slim, 12-page, 1944 "yearbook" published by the Women's League, expressed student feelings in words less idealized, more deeply touched by experience:

> *1944…a war year, and Junior College enlists…saying 'so long' to our men in service…'joining up' ourselves by buying bonds…partying in our gayer moments…burning the midnight oil in moments not so gay…USO-ing the Army trainees in the gymnasium…welcoming back our JC boys on furlough, who never forget to remember…*

Few publications of the college have been more poignant or meaningful than the 1946 *Oympian*, back in full operation and opening with a long (and not yet complete) "In Memoriam" list of 66 young GRJC men who died serving the cause of freedom. The names match photos of faces on the pages of the previous *Olympian* of 1942—faces full of youthful expectation and hope, lost to the cruel necessity of war—photos heartbreaking to families, to faculty, and to a president who made a point of knowing them all.

The College Survives Once More

During the war, when college enrollment fell to its lowest ebb, the board of education adopted a tentative resolution to close Grand Rapids Junior College and offer Andrews a principal's job in one of the city high schools. E. Ray Baxter (in a 1988 *Collegiate* interview) recalled that time with emotion: "[Andrews] wasn't concerned for himself. All he seemed to care about was what would happen to the college, to the students, and to me…he risked his life and career for the Junior College." Andrews refused the offer and moved into action. First, he acquired the previously mentioned Army Air Force group—200 young men—who used the college for training. (**Figure 34 & 35**) Second, his well-known dedication to the highest educational standards

1940-55

1941

The debate team won the state championship.

1944

The Main Building was added as a facility. Previously this building had been home to the Davis Technical High School.

Enrollment was 485.

1944 Student Council members (1944 Women's League yearbook. GRCC Archives)

1945

Enrollment was 1,457.

Veterans Club established (undated. GRCC Archives)

Join GRAND RAPIDS JC VETS CLUB

Memorial Campus

World War II had a profound impact on the GRJC student body. Not only were students actively involved in the war effort at home, but also 70 young GRJC males gave their lives in service to their country.

A campus with gardens had long been a dream of President Arthur Andrews. A Memorial Campus inspired and funded by students, who raised $15,000 to honor those who had died, was even more meaningful. On October 7, 1949, the Junior College dedicated its Memorial Campus on a small plot of land, formerly a parking lot, on the south side of the Main Building. The focus of the pleasant green space was a flagpole with tall stone base on which were carved the honored names. Andrews would become the chief caretaker of this small sanctuary.

In June of 1954, a year before Andrews' retirement after 35 years as president, the GRJC freshman class dedicated a newly constructed fountain and Shakespeare garden (planted with boxwood hedges and English flowers) on the Memorial Campus in honor of President Andrews. The fountain was inscribed with a fitting line from Emerson, "An institution is the lengthened shadow of one man." The Memorial Campus would thereafter be known as the Arthur Andrews Memorial Campus.

The eventual rearrangement of fountain and Shakespeare garden, along with later reconfigurations of the campus, have had the effect of displacing the war memorial as the focus of the sanctuary, an unfortunate consequence of change. (Compare 1981 and 2007 aerial views, left.) Though Korean War casualties were later added to the stone base, Vietnam losses were not, nor those of wars thereafter. The original reason for a Memorial Campus was to honor those students who had died fighting for their country. The memorial's present out-of-the-way placement—behind trees and off in a corner—sends an unintended message of forgetfulness.

(**top left**) Memorial Campus dedication, October 7, 1949. (GRCC Archives); (**top middle**) Memorial Campus dedication, October 7, 1949. (Grand Rapids History and Special Collections, Archives, Grand Rapids Public Library, Grand Rapids, MI Robinson Studio Collection (#125) Neg# H009400); (**top right**) Fountain dedication, June 1954. (GRCC Archives); (**middle left**) Memorial Campus, 1981. (GRCC Archives); (**left**) Memorial Campus, 2007. (GRCC Archives)

(left, Figure 36) The college's Main Building, 1950. (Grand Rapids History and Special Collections, Archives, Grand Rapids Public Library, Grand Rapids, MI 125-934-31-NN) (below, Figure 37) Laying the keystone to Davis Tech High School, now the College's Main Building, 1929. (Grand Rapids History and Special Collections, Archives, Grand Rapids Public Library, Grand Rapids, MI 43-1-3 #125)

1940-55

1946

Christian Fellowship organized —the longest continuing active student organization at the college. (1947 *Olympian*. GRCC Archives)

1947

Grand Rapids Junior College is named one of the top 100 best colleges and universities in the United States by *Look* magazine.

Campus Memorial committee (1947 *Olympian*, GRCC Archives)

inspired President Alexander G. Ruthven of the University of Michigan to intervene on the college's behalf, insisting it was one of the finest in the nation and that closing it would be a tragic blow to education. Andrews secured from Ruthven a commitment to locate the University of Michigan Extension Center in GRJC. Given the prestige associated with this move, the board quietly withdrew its resolution.[8]

A Two-Building Campus

The city was restricted by a severe, wartime 15-mill limit on taxes, which reduced the budget for schools to less than five mills. Superintendent Krause, like President Andrews, was oper-

ating on a shoestring. In 1944, Krause made the decision to close Davis Technical High School, return vocational education to the remaining high schools, and provide Grand Rapids Junior College another much-needed building—newer, better equipped, and renamed the Junior College Main Building. (**Figure 36 & 37**) The building was to be shared with GRPS administrators, who would occupy the fifth floor—perhaps the only drawback. Krause's decision did much to guarantee the

(**Figure 38**) Veteran's Club, 1946 *Olympian*.
(GRCC Archives)

ongoing existence of the college. It also provided JC students with a cafeteria and more classroom and library space.

Physical Education and Chemistry Departments opted to stay in the gymnasiums and labs of the GRJC Building, soon to be renamed the East Building. The psychology lab would remain there, too, as would the Music Department, though Music would shift to the Main Building in 1950. Most other departments moved down the hill, including the labs for anatomy and physiology, bacteriology, botany, dietetics, physics, and zoology. Within a year the engineering labs had shifted all

machinery and equipment to the basement level of the Main Building; the Engineering Building thereupon ceased to be a part of the college. The U of M Extension added many volumes to the Main Building library's collection and, being largely an evening operation, motivated an increase in library hours. The Grand Rapids Ryerson Library, always cooperative with the college, began buying books recommended by GRJC faculty.[9] The college library, directed by Augusta Borneman, was in the process of growing to a size the North Central Association would find acceptable.

(**Figure 39**) Men's Union officers, 1947 (from left) Jack Ripstra, president; Alphonso (Al) Brown, secretary; and Bob Kleiman, treasurer. (1947 *Olympian.* GRCC Archives)

As the war moved toward an end, Arthur Andrews played a significant role in developing the G.I. Bill of Rights, especially as it related to junior college students. He is credited, as a member of the Veteran's Administration Advisory Committee, with securing benefits for junior college students equal to those of four-year college and university students.[10]

The War Ends

On the day of victory in Europe, May 8, 1945, the city rejoiced, but only half the battle was won. On August 14, when Japan surrendered, officially ending World War II, the true celebration began. Downtown Grand Rapids filled with 50,000 joyful citizens. Churches all over the city held services of prayer and thanksgiving. The college prepared for a large influx of students in the fall of 1945, yet many vets failed to make it home even by Christmas. Coach Harold Steele would not return from his naval service until early 1947. In spite of delays for veterans, the war effort was over for Grand Rapids, and economic recovery charged the air.

By the 1946-47 school year, sports teams began reappearing at the college. Returning vets were joining up, though coaching was a matter of improvisation. Gil Powers of Creston led the football team until Steele returned. Wendell Emery, former coach and PE director at Davis Tech, filled in as coach of the JC baseball team. The following year, Russ Waters from Central High School took over both basketball and baseball.

The Music Department was patched together with several part-time people, including Don Armstrong, (already spread thin in the Grand Rapids Public Schools) who directed the choir, and George Davis, Band Director. Faculty, now back to 50 members, included such names as Merle Dawson (English), Cecil DeKraker (history), Mary Baloyan (English), Geraldine Masters (American government), Dorothy Sonke (English), Maurice Thomas (history), Theodora Quick (math), and Richard Wherity (chemistry). A Veterans' Club (**Figure 38**) appeared on campus, a Future Registered Nurses Club, and a Christian Fellowship group. Alphonso (Al) Brown, one of only a handful of black students enrolled, was elected secretary of Men's Union and sophomore class vice president, marking a significant shift in the homogenous nature of student leadership. (**Figure 39**) Brown, a top student, gained notoriety when he was refused admission to the U of M Medical School, the first GRJC graduate (in spite of high grades and strong recommendations) ever to be turned away. In a 1988 *Collegiate* interview, E. Ray Baxter told a story of John D. Hibbard, the president of Blodgett Hospital, intervening on Brown's behalf with the U of M president. The decision was reversed, and Brown became the first black student ever accepted into the program.

Other prominent students that year included Adrian Swets (later the designer of the College Park Plaza Building), Ray Boozer (eventual head of the GRJC Foundation), and John Steketee (later to be a Grand Rapids probate judge).

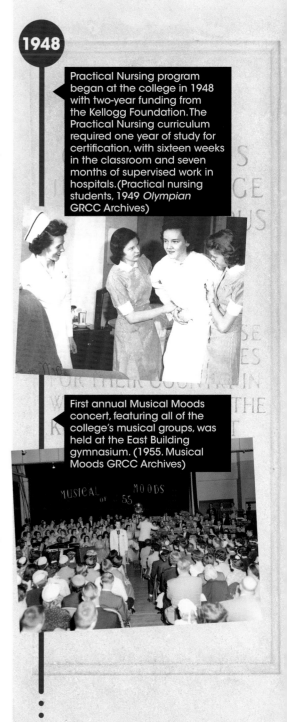

1940-55

1948

Practical Nursing program began at the college in 1948 with two-year funding from the Kellogg Foundation. The Practical Nursing curriculum required one year of study for certification, with sixteen weeks in the classroom and seven months of supervised work in hospitals.(Practical nursing students, 1949 *Olympian* GRCC Archives)

First annual Musical Moods concert, featuring all of the college's musical groups, was held at the East Building gymnasium. (1955. Musical Moods GRCC Archives)

(**Figure 40**) Albert P. Smith. (GRCC Archives)

Milestones

Arthur Andrews' ongoing dedication to excellence paid off once more in 1947, when the editors of *Look* magazine asked selected educators, among them college and university presidents and state superintendents of public instruction, to name the best 100 schools in the United States. Grand Rapids Junior College was selected as one of that elite group.[11]

An even more significant 1947 milestone was the hiring of Albert P. Smith, the 29-year-old Godwin Heights choral director and Grand Rapids Symphony violinist, as the single full-time member of the college Music Department. (**Figure 40**) Don Armstrong, who handpicked "Smitty," had the daunting task of convincing Superintendent Krause to hire someone from outside the district. Even more difficult was convincing President Andrews to take on someone so young, creative, and free-spirited, especially considering his earlier experience of Karl Wecker. Armstrong succeeded with both men, and Al Smith began what would become an illustrious 35-year-career with the college. In an interview, recalling his own sometimes over-exuberant nature, Smith revealed that Andrews had plenty of occasions to question his hiring decision:

> I was trying to explain what 'crescendo' meant to the choir… I stood on one side of the room, ran sliding across the floor and leaped onto the top of the grand piano. Just as I was executing my leap, Arthur Andrews popped his head into the room. My lack of decorum astounded him, and I was called into his office…and other times as well…to receive his fatherly lecture on teaching with dignity.[12]

Smith would, over time, attract an outstanding music faculty, the first hire being Joyce Verhaar, an accomplished pianist and his former student. By 1977 the Music Department would gain accreditation from the National Association of Schools of Music, to this day the only community college in Michigan to do so, greatly enhancing student transfer to four-year institutions.

Post War Expansion

In 1948, the city's 15-mill tax limit was lifted, and the schools began to breathe again. Superintendent Krause, who had led the school system through some its most difficult days, chose to resign. He was replaced by Benjamin J. Buikema, his assistant superintendent. (Figure 41) After 20 years of struggle, the schools would embark on a new era of much-needed modernizing and expansion. In a gesture of affirmation of the Junior College, the board of education authorized the annual awarding of GRJC scholarships, two to each of the city high schools, one to each high school in the county.

Enrollment numbers at GRJC shifted wildly in the war years and shortly thereafter, from a low of 485 in 1943-44 to triple that number (1457) the next year. 1946-47 saw a surge to almost 2,000

(**Figure 41**) Benjamin J. Buikema, Grand Rapids School Superintendent, June 29, 1949. (Grand Rapids History and Special Collections, Archives, Grand Rapids Public Library, Grand Rapids, MI Robinson Studio Collection (#125) Neg# H0022101.2)

(Figure 42) 1948 Campus Revue. (GRCC Archives)

students, thanks largely to the G.I. Bill, which began to rearrange the ethnic mix of the student body as well. A number of short-term instructors were hired to take up the slack. The surge of G.I.s had an immediate effect on curriculum. New developmental courses were created to aid veterans who wanted college but lacked the skills. That high enrollment point of 2,000 was followed by a gradual tapering off to around 1,000 students in each of the next six years, with a full-time faculty growing to nearly 60 members.

The *Olympian* staff, responding to complaints about the dull sameness of the old format, featured a brand-new look in 1949. Layout, design, typeface—everything was done with more flash and style, with staff introducing both formal and informal photos of student groups and photo advertising from community businesses. The yearbook celebrated new areas of college social life: the Pep Club, dedicated to maintaining school spirit; the Copper Carnival, a yearly event sponsored by the Pre-Medic Club, featuring penny games and club booths; and, the Campus Revue, a yearly variety show sponsored by the Student Council. (**Figure 42**)

The Memorial Campus: A Dream Realized
On October 7, 1949, the Junior College dedicated its Memorial Campus (now known as the Arthur Andrews Memorial Campus), located on a small plot of land, formerly a parking

1948 Commencement. (GRCC Archives)

The Memorial Campus was dedicated on October 7, 1949, in honor of the 70 students who died in World War II. The main focus of the memorial was a central flagpole installed on top of a tall stone base with the names of the honored students carved on it. The names of the three students who died in the Korean War were added in 1958.

1949 Honors Convocation program. (GRCC Archives)

(Figure 43) Arthur Andrews and dignitaries dedicating the Memorial Campus, built by student fund-raising. September 21, 1949. (Grand Rapids History and Special Collections, Archives, Grand Rapids Public Library, Grand Rapids, MI [#125] Neg# H009400)

lot, on the south side of the Main Building. (Figure 43) A campus had long been a dream of Arthur Andrews; a Memorial Campus inspired and funded by students was even more meaningful. Students had raised $15,000 in an effort to honor those 70 students who had lost their lives in the war. Though of modest size, this campus was a serene space of benches, gardens, ornamental fencing, and flagstone paths through expanses of grass, all focused on a central flagpole with tall stone base on which were carved the honored names. (Later reconfigurations of the campus would, unfortunately, diminish that memorial's centrality.) A reporter writing in the June 14, 1963, issue of *The Collegiate*, described the campus as "making up in beauty what it lacks in size." Andrews would, for the remainder of his presidency, act as chief caretaker of this small sanctuary.

Voice of the Faculty

Through the Andrews years, there existed no faculty organization or leadership, no department chairs. As faculty numbers grew in the late 1940s, members began to express dissatisfac-tion at having little voice in the workings of the college. In response, Andrews, in 1949, organized a Faculty Policy Committee, made up of seven faculty members and himself. The aim of the committee was "to study the functions of the Junior College faculty in regard to making policies pertaining to faculty-student relationships, inter-faculty relationships, improvement of the teaching process, and improvement of teaching conditions."

The seven committee members were handpicked by Andrews. This piece of micromanaging led to pushback from faculty about how members were chosen and how long they were to serve. Andrews' solution was to retain four members each year and drop three by lot. The faculty as a whole would then elect six potential members, from which Andrews would select the three he wanted. It was hardly surprising that his desire for control began meeting with resistance from the faculty. Out of the tension, however, would eventually develop a broader faculty involvement in college decision-making. The Policy Committee meeting of April 18, 1950, resulted in faculty committee members recommending that department heads be named for department organization, leadership, and improvement of instruction. Though the recommendation was approved by a six-to-one vote, it was not enacted until some years after Andrews' retirement.

A more immediate result of the Policy Committee was the creation of a Junior College Day at the city high schools. Andrews and faculty representatives scheduled a full day's visit to each high school, with Andrews addressing the senior class in the morning, followed by a group of GRJC faculty spending the remainder of the day presenting workshops in their fields and answering student questions. Junior College Day proved a vital connection to the public schools as well as an excellent recruiting device, earning glowing approval from Superintendent Buikema.

Practical Nursing Becomes a GRCC Department

The May 18, 1950, *Grand Rapids Herald* reported that the Practical Nursing School, begun at the college in 1948 with two-year funding from the Kellogg Foundation, had been recommended by the board of education to become an official GRJC department, led by director Leora B. Stroup. **(Figure 44)** The Practical Nursing curriculum required one year of study for certification, with 16 weeks in the classroom and seven months of supervised work in hospitals. GRJC was now a nursing school instead of simply a partner of the hospitals. Though practical nurses had originally been intended mainly for private care, hospitals began hiring away every graduate of the program.

Simpler Times

The *College Catalog* was shorter and simpler in 1950. As an example, the English Department's 1950 offerings numbered eight: English Lit. 31 (English fiction and poetry) and 32 (English drama and nonfiction), Freshman Composition 1 and 2, and EN 47 and 48, a two-semester sophomore Creative Writing class.

A specialized, two-part course called Engineering English was designed to teach engineering students the fundamentals of writing and public speaking. Those were simpler times. Today, the English Department course list has grown to beyond 30, typifying the expansion of more specialized subject matter throughout the college.

How did colleges manage without audiovisual or copy equipment, let alone computers? From a present perspective, it is difficult to imagine. Minutes of the Policy Committee meetings made frequent reference to Andrews' frustrated attempts to secure more mimeograph service for the college. Such minutes have been preserved in the college archives—often as faint, brittle

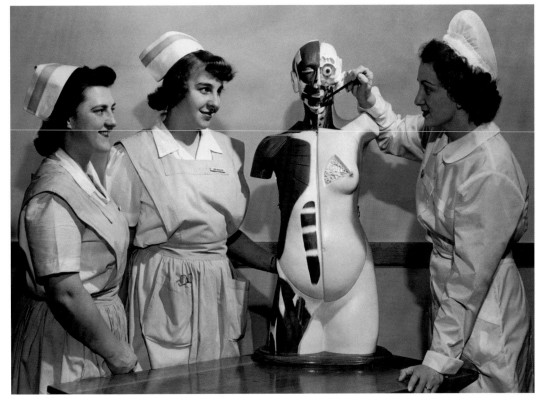

(**Figure 44**) Practical Nursing students 1951. (GRCC Archives)

1950

Resident tuition was $120.00 per year.

1950 Choir. (GRCC Archives)

1952

Mechanical Technology program started.

1953

1953 student dance. (GRCC Archives)

(Figure 45) Mechanical Technology Program, 1952 (GRCC Archives)

typewriter duplicates or yellowed mimeographed copies. Mr. Wherity, appointed the committee member in charge of developing audio-visual technology, reported frequently at meetings, but his progress appeared to be modest. Still, technological innovation was in the air, and the committee sensed it. The age of television was beginning—and this among other emerging technologies would forever change human communication and the delivery of education.

Voice of Students

Colleges sometimes grow too large to make publishing a yearbook a practical venture. But in the spring of 1950, college enrollment was only slightly more than 1,100 students—smaller, in fact, than the previous three years. The 1950 *Olympian*, a much more modest production than the imaginative 1949 edition, returned to the old format, making brief mention of student complaints and certain unspecified staff problems. The 1950 edition would be the final yearbook published at the college. The long-time publication would simply close its doors with little explanation. The loss of the *Olympian* proved significant to the college from both a personal and historical point of view. First published in 1920 by the *College News* newspaper staff and called the *College News Annual* (it became the *Junior*

College Annual in 1924, the *Olympian* in 1925), it continued for 30 years, with interruptions only for the depression and World War II. The photographic record of faculty, staff, student body, athletic teams, and social organizations over the years provided an invaluable sense of the history and spirit of the college. The loss of the yearbook, coupled with a protracted disappearance of the college newspaper, all but shut down a vital element of every college—the voice of students.

New Age, Old Template

In the final years of the Andrews presidency, there was a sense of a new age emerging within the framework of an outworn template. The Korean War, beginning in 1950, once again drained the college's male population, but it was offset by a substantial increase in the number of women attending. When Korean veterans began returning in '52, and Selective Service (in '53) began granting deferments to full-time college students, enrollment saw a steady rise. In response, Andrews established a Mechanical Technology Program and then a summer school. **(Figure 45)** From 1954-55, (the year of Andrews' retirement), GRJC's enrollment increased 18 percent, prompting the president to predict as many as 2,500 students by 1965; that figure would underestimate reality by 1,000 students. His solo administration no longer suited a rapidly-growing college; leaders who followed would be faced with the task of inventing an administrative structure appropriate to an evolving institution.

New leaders would also find that, though local school district control had been a necessity in the early history of the college, GRJC was now growing too large and complex for the board of education to manage efficiently. The board, in a number of ways, had actually begun to inhibit the growth and success of the college. President Andrews, feeling keenly his lack of control over college finances, knew he lacked full presidential autonomy in spite of a strong leadership style. Within the structure of the school district, Andrews functioned at the same level as a high school principal. The college, held to a salary schedule based upon the single, non-negotiable system used for the entire K-12 system, found it could not be competitive when it came to recruiting instructors.[13] The superintendent, who approved everything, including hires, inevitably had the last word.

A Retirement with Honor

In June of 1954, the GRJC freshman class unveiled a fountain and Shakespeare Garden (planted with boxwood hedges and English flowers) on the Memorial Campus, dedicated to President Andrews and inscribed with a fitting line from Emerson, "An institution is the lengthened shadow of one man." Andrews, who had cast the longest of shadows, was deeply touched. He would count the honor among his most cherished memories.[14]

In the spring of 1955, 300 students and colleagues gathered at the Pantlind Hotel ballroom to honor Andrews on the occasion of his retirement after 35 years as college president. (**Figure 46**) The room was filled with doctors, educators, musicians, artists, lawyers, judges, business owners—most of them apprecia-

(**Figure 46**) Arthur Andrews, undated. (GRCC Archives)

tive alumni of the college. Among honored guests were presidents and deans of a dozen colleges.

Attorney Gerald E. White, class of 1925, read a letter from General Omar Bradley, commending Andrews' important work on the G.I. Bill. Russell Christopher, a 1950 music graduate and later a member of the Metropolitan Opera Company, performed a musical tribute to Andrews. An even more lasting tribute came with an announcement of the board of education's decision to name the college library the "Arthur Andrews Memorial Library."[15] On this final note, the evening and the Andrews era came to a close.

But his legacy of integrity and academic excellence would serve as benchmarks for the future of the college. The man who had dedicated his life to Grand Rapids Junior College would live only 17 months beyond retirement. His funeral in November of 1956, presided over by Dr. Duncan E. Littlefair, new pastor of Fountain Street Baptist Church, was a final tribute from a caring community. Dean John Tirrell, Andrews' successor, cancelled morning classes so that students and staff might attend. Andrews' passing came just a year after that of his predecessor and mentor, Jesse Buttrick Davis.

1940-55

1954

Fountain dedicated on June 10, 1954.

Enrollment was 1,500.

1955

Arthur Andrews retired as president after leading the college for 35 years.

Recognition Dinner Honoring
Gould Arthur Andrews, M.A.,Sc.D.
President of the Grand Rapids Junior College
1920-1955

Given by the
Grand Rapids Junior College
Alumni Association

Pantlind Hotel   April 25, 1955

On April 25, 1955, a recognition dinner honoring President Andrews' long and distinguished career leading GRJC was held at the Pantlind Hotel. (GRCC Archives)

1964 commencement procession from the Main Building to Fountain Street Baptist Church. (GRCC Archives)

Years of Transition 1955-65

Dr. John Tirrell—The President Becomes a Dean

Arthur Andrews' tenure had been the longest of any junior college president in the country. When Dr. John E. Tirrell succeeded him as head of Grand Rapids Junior College in 1955, Tirrell became, at 29 years of age, the youngest college president in Michigan. **(Figure** 47) The only downside to his appointment was the fact that his title would be "dean" instead of "president." Four chief administrators of GRJC would be given the title "dean" within the space of 10 years.

Why had the college president been demoted to a dean? According to certain of Tirrell's staff and later college administrators, the answer was simple enough, though admittedly speculative. President Andrews had been a powerful presence for so many years in the constant push/pull of GRPS and the Junior College that Superintendent Buikema used the opportunity to trim the position down to size. If in the GRPS organization plan the head of the Junior College worked at a level equivalent to a high school principal, the title of dean seemed more appropriate than president—and it more clearly distinguished the superintendent's leadership. So "dean" it would remain for the next 21 years.

Tirrell, born in Muskegon in 1926, attended Holland High School and Hope College where he earned his Bachelor of Arts degree. After coaching and teaching science at Baroda,

(**Figure** 47) Dr. John Tirrell, third leader of GRJC. (GRCC Archives)

Michigan, he took the job of principal at Bridgeman High School. Next, with an eye to the world of higher education, he entered the University of Michigan graduate school, receiving his Master of Arts degree in 1951. Harvard was his choice for doctoral studies, and by 1954 he had earned his Doctor of Education degree. Tirrell quickly became one of the rising stars on the broadening horizon of higher education. He spent a year at Harvard as assistant director of the Center for Field Studies before accepting the job as dean of GRJC. Married, with a young family, his future was full of promise. He was named one of the "Five Outstanding Young Men in Michigan" by the Michigan Junior Chamber of Commerce in 1956.

Administrative Reorganization—A Beginning

It is no surprise that the first thing Tirrell discovered about his new job was the near absence of administrative structure. Throughout his first year as dean, he made do with the few administrators Andrews had in place, getting the feel of life under Superintendent Buikema and the Grand Rapids Board of Education. In his *Annual Report* for the 1955-56 school year, Tirrell proposed an administrative reorganization centered around the addition of several new positions: a coordinator of student affairs, a director of counseling, and a director of the evening program.

1955

Dr. John Tirrell became the college's third leader, and at 29 years of age, was the youngest college leader in Michigan. Tirrell worked to give the college the beginnings of an administration, promoted student engagement, sanctioned fraternities and sororities, encouraged the college newspaper to begin publishing again, and experimented with new technologies, especially television.

1955-56 basketball team. (GRCC Archives)

1956

The college newspaper, now called *The Junior Collegiate,* reappeared after a long absence on February 24.

Football team played in the inaugural National Junior College Championship game in Los Angeles on December 15, 1956. They lost to Coffeyville Junior College 46-6.

Delta Sigma To Give "Male Animal" Play

A young English instructor finds the question of academic freedom and the stability of his marriage are involved when he decides to read an anarchistic letter to his class.

This is the theme of "The Male Animal," a comedy farce by James Thurber and Elliott Nugent which will be presented by Delta Sigma Drama Society at 8:30 p.m. March 1 and 2 at St. Cecilia Auditorium.

Shown rehearsing a scene from the Delta Sigma play, "The Male Animal" are, left to right, Bob Wozniak as Ed Keller, trustee at Mid-Western University; Elinor Sedam as Ellen; Phil Hertel as Tommy, Ellen's husband, the English instructor; Mary Denton as Patricia, Ellen's sister; Boiten Plasman as Michael, outspoken young intellect, and Buzz Moxon as Wally, football hero and Michael's rival for Patricia's affections.

Tommy Turner (Phil Hertel) is a young, happily-married professor of English at Mid-Western University. The week-end of the Michigan game brings the former football hero, Joe Ferguson (Terry Green) back to the University and into the lives of Tommy and his wife Ellen (Elinor Sedam) who was once engaged to Joe. Tommy becomes involved with the opinionated Ed Keller, trustee of the University, (Bob Wozniak) over the question of academic freedom. Ellen tries to convince Tommy not to read the letter and Joe takes her side. In the end Tommy proves himself worthy of being a "male animal."

Other members of the cast are Boiten Plasman, Mary Denton, John Kooistra, Donna Snyder, Betty Skodsholm, Jean Huntley, Charles Moxon, Noel Cobb, and Archie Ghareeb. Mr. Stanley Albers, speech instructor, is directing the play. He is assisted by James Bronner, student director. Committee chairmen are Karen Parlberg, stage manager; Lillian Nabandian, business manager; Barbara Reeves, properties chairman; Margie Tappen, make-up supervisor; Edward Quirk, head electrician; Barbara Hansel and Annette Pehr, publicity chairmen. Tickets for both performances will be available to all Junior College students who present their activity cards in room 123. The room will be open from 10 until 3 o'clock every day next week.

The Junior Collegiate

Series II, Volume 1   Grand Rapids Junior College, Grand Rapids, Michigan, February 24, 1956   Number 1

Queen, Prizes, Booths Featured at Carnival

A $250 door prize, a contest for selection of a carnival queen, and a variety of carnival concessions will be combined to form this year's Copper Carnival, sponsored by the Pre-Med Club. The annual affair has been set for Friday, March 9, and will take place in the East Building Gymnasium of the college.

A gift certificate valued at $250 and redeemable at one of the downtown department stores will be raffled in the later part of the evening. Additional door prizes will also be given which include a desk lamp, Benny Goodman album, table lamp, and a silver turkey platter. Chances on the certificate may be purchased from any Pre-Med Club member for ten cents.

Many Booths Planned

Each college organization will be entitled to sponsor a contestant for carnival queen, each penny counting one vote toward the particular candidate. The winning queen and her sponsor will each receive a gift.

Plans have been made for a number of concessions sponsored by various college organizations including taxi dance, Future Teachers; fun house and popcorn booth, Women's League; carpet golf, baseball throw, penny pitch, and bean guess, Pre-Medic, and others which have not yet been decided upon.

Bruce Hilborn and Donald Rodgers have been selected as general co-chairmen for the carnival. The co-chairmen for their committees are tickets, Frank Duiven and John Kennedy; decorations, Inara Lieckskalnins, Mara Asaris, Judy Gerritsen and Ruth Verheule, arrangements, Sharon McGovern and Diana Ezergailis; prizes, Boiten Plasman and Jack Slot, construction, Fred Anderson, Bob Brown, and Dave Ellis, publicity, Paul Champion and Phyllis Hunter, queen contest, Velga Miske and Ilona Sergejevs, and clean-up, James Wielinga and Carl Branyan.

Engineers to Visit Chrysler, U of M

Tours of the Chrysler Motor Company and the University of Michigan will be the highlights of a trip planned by the Engineer's Club for April 2 and 3. An estimated 40 students under the leadership of Mr. James Shew will make the trip.

Along with the Chrysler tour, plans for the first day include a luncheon at the Plymouth division of the plant.

Tuesday the engineers will view the School of Electrical Engineering and the north campus at Ann Arbor. Luncheon will be served at the Union Building where Dean Brown, head of the School of Engineering, and two other speakers, whose names have not yet been announced, will talk on matters related to engineering.

The research projects now under way at the University will be of special interest to the visitors. There are over 250 of these projects under the direction of the Engineering Research Institute, which operates on a budget of over $3,000,000.

Some of the specific projects which the engineers may view have to do with automobile design, cosmic rays, electric motors, and natural lights.

Coming Attractions

Feb. 24	Basketball, Muskegon
Mar. 1, 2	Delta Sigma Play
Mar. 6	Skating Follies
Mar. 9	Copper Carnival
Mar. 16	Civic Play "Solid Gold Cadillac"
Mar. 31	Track Clinic
Apr. 6	Soph. Class Dance
Apr. 13	Style Show
Apr. 27, 28	Musical Moods
May 9	Art Open House
May 17	Honors Convocation
May 18	Civic Play "Of Thee I Sing"
May 26	John Bos Relays
May 29	Delta Pi Alpha Dinner

Young Student?

A rather bashful young man managed to keep Andrew Hansson's child psychology class engrossed as he illustrated some psychological points. Andy Jr., portrayed by Andy Sr. as a "little monster," refuted his father's claims as he sat quietly on his father's lap and munched crackers.

Annual Michigan Day Scheduled March 16

Students and faculty interested in visiting the University of Michigan are invited to attend the annual Michigan Day Conference, March 16.

Programs have been planned for each group, according to Mr. Richard Wherity, Junior College instructor.

Dr. James Lewis, Vice President of Student Affairs, will extend a welcome to the students at the morning session, followed by a general tour of the campus.

Representatives from each department of the University will be present to give information about admission requirements.

Junior College instructors attending have a choice of activities which include conferences with individual faculty of the University and discussion sessions.

A WORD FROM THE DEAN

Tirrell Encourages Activity Integration

Additional means of communication between the faculty and students, and among student groups is needed at the Grand Rapids Junior College. Better integration of our college activities is desirable and may be accomplished, at least in part, by the dissemination of information in a student publication.

Institutions require the responsible participation of all of its members. Our college, to be strong, needs the student view in regards to its problems and challenges.

As this publication will undoubtedly receive wide circulation in our community and across the state, I would encourage the editors to have student statements represent a thoughtful and constructive point of view.

Through this activity we can evolve another academic experience, particularly for those that are interested in journalism.

I pledge my support and offer congratulations to the staff of the Junior Collegiate.

John E. Tirrell

Pictured above is Dr. John E. Tirrell, dean of Grand Rapids Junior College, as he dictates to his secretary, Mrs. Kay Fifer in his office.

JC Council Studies Parking Problems

The major problem with which the Student Council is concerned at present is that of the parking situation. The possible solutions appear in the form of 4 to 6 hour parking meters to be located in the vicinity of Junior College and 12 cent bus-fare privilege cards.

These are intended to alleviate the frequent insertion of nickels in meters and to encourage the use of buses rather than of cars.

Parking survey blanks were in circulation last Wednesday. These will provide the city officials with some concrete evidence of the intensity of the parking problem.

Directory Planned

In state and regional affairs the council is now working with the United States National Student Association on a regional student government directory, to be located at Marygrove College, Detroit.

One or more representatives will be sent tomorrow to meet with the planning committee of the MJCSCA at Henry Ford Community College. The committee will plan and organize the agenda for the coming fall convention.

Stegenga Wins Sophomore Grant

James Stegenga has been awarded the Sophomore Class Scholarship for $100 on the basis of his scholastic achievement.

James is a graduate of Central High School and is enrolled in the engineering department. Next fall he plans to enter the University of Michigan Engineering School.

He is Vice President of the Industrial Club, and a member of the Engineering Club.

Ten years ago the sophomore class purchased a bond which came due this year. The Sophomore Cabinet decided to award this money as a scholarship to a sophomore student.

A registrar (Lyonne Riisberg) and assistant dean (E. Ray Baxter) would continue in their positions. All would report directly to Tirrell.[1]

Surprisingly, Tirrell got what he wanted from Superintendent Buikema—the modest beginnings of an administrative team. Richard Wherity was appointed coordinator of student affairs, a half-time position (he would continue as a chemistry instructor). Phillip Sidwell, an Air Force clinical psychologist, would assume the job of full-time director of counseling, and JC political science instructor Wendell Shroll would become half-time director of the evening program. Though in his plan Tirrell had made no recommendations for organization of faculty (particularly the appointment of divisional chairs), he would work to give the faculty voice by involving them more fully in committee work and decision-making.[2]

College Newspaper Resurrected

Shortly after Tirrell assumed the leadership of GRJC, the college newspaper, now called *The Junior Collegiate*, reappeared after a long absence. (**Figure 48**) John Van Krimpen of the English Department took over as the group's advisor, and Tirrell applauded the move. In volume one, issue one of this new series, in a column entitled "A Word From the Dean," Tirrell wrote the following: "Institutions require the responsible participation of all of its members. Our college, to be strong, needs the student view in regards to its problems and challenges…I pledge my support and offer congratulations to the staff of *The Junior Collegiate*." Tirrell firmly believed that colleges needed forums for student voices.

(**Figure 48**) February 24, 1956 issue of *The Junior Collegiate*. (GRCC Archives)

(above, Figure 49) Chi Kappa Phi members promoting a dance. (Grand Rapids History and Special Collections, Archives, Grand Rapids Public Library, Grand Rapids, MI Robinson Studio Collection [#125] Neg.# H007147.1) (right, Figure 50) List of GRJC Fraternities and Sororities from *Your Son or Daughter and Fraternities and Sororities at Junior College*, undated. (GRCC Archives)

A Greek Invasion

In a bold move, after years of such organizations being forbidden by Arthur Andrews, Tirrell and Wherity made the decision to allow fraternities and sororities to become official parts of campus life.[3] Wherity would, as a result of the decision, spend much of his time and energy trying to establish reasonable boundaries for these groups.

The Greek organizations were at first comprised of three sororities and three fraternities: the sororities were Pi Phi Rho, Chi Kappa Phi, Lambda Tau Omega; the fraternities were Sigma Kappa Theta (the Sigs), Delta Psi Epsilon (the Squires), and Phi Omega Sigma (the Saxons). **(Figure 49 & 50)** At one

JUNIOR COLLEGE FRATERNITIES AND SORORITIES

SORORITIES

Chi Kappa Phi

Pi Phi Rho

Lambda Tau Omega

Kappa Sigma Phi

FRATERNITIES

Phi Omega Sigma (Saxons)

Epsilon Xi Epsilon

Delta Psi Epsilon (Squires)

Sigma Kappa Theta (sigs)

Alpha Kappa Omega

For more information contact:

I. F. S. C. President

c/o Dean of Students Office

Grand Rapids Junior College

Grand Rapids, Michigan

point these organizations numbered as many as five of each. On occasion, the groups would run charity car washes or rummage sales, or even offer scholarships (the sororities tended to be much more conscientious about community service and better behaved than the frats), but in main their central activities ran to dances, drinking, and a fair amount of trouble. In fall and spring pledge seasons, the frats would have an Open Smoker, the sororities an Open Tea. Those interested in pledging would then attend a Closed Smoker or Tea. The fortunate ones selected as pledges could look forward to an eight-week period of enthrallment followed by Hell Week (culminating in Hell Night), during which they underwent traditional hazing rituals. If they survived them, they became Junior College Greeks without houses or even much time left to lord it over the next pledge group. The Greeks and GRJC were not a particularly happy fit. There must have been moments when Tirrell and Wherity (and deans who followed) realized all too clearly the wisdom of Arthur Andrews.

Student Appeal—Serving the Community

Tirrell's intent in most of his decisions was to make the college more appealing to students and the community. He wanted GRJC to be attractive to students and to function

1955-65

1956

The Adult and Continuing Education Program was established with 225 students enrolled that initial year.

1956 golf team. (GRCC Archives)

1957

Folk singer Pete Seeger performed at the fall convocation.

Spring 1957 Adult and Continuing Education brochure. (GRCC Archives)

1958

The college hosted the annual meeting of the American Association of Junior Colleges.

(**Figure 51**) 1956 GRJC Evening Program brochure. (GRCC Archives)

as a community college, serving community needs in as many areas as possible. The Evening Program was an instant success in that respect. (**Figure 51**) Wendell Shroll quickly built the program on day college offerings, yet he also developed such community-conscious ideas as short courses in management for local executives and programs for training of city fire fighters. Enrollment reached 225 in the first year of the Evening Program, including adults completing high school and foreign-born students taking "Americanization" courses in English and government.

Under Tirrell, the Salk polio vaccine was made available to students for a one-dollar fee. Both East and Main Buildings underwent partial renovation, though it was apparent to Tirrell that two buildings would soon be inadequate to serve a rapidly growing population. How timely it was that in 1956, as a result of a newly-enacted Michigan junior college state aid formula, the college experienced a modest upturn in fortunes. For the first time in Michigan history, separate state funding was earmarked for junior and community colleges. Thanks to this encouraging development, a number of new members were added to the faculty, among them Drs. Anne and Jerome Miller (life sciences), Leonard Anderson (business), Daniel Kovats (band and orchestra), Joanne Davenport and Helen Stacey (LPN), Jacoba Dalebout (English), and Tom VanWingen (math, swimming coach). Gordon Hunsberger, former JC football star under Harold Steele, was hired to replace Steele as football coach, with Steele becoming the director of athletics. In his first year of coaching, Hunsberger took the Raiders to the National Junior College Athletic Association football

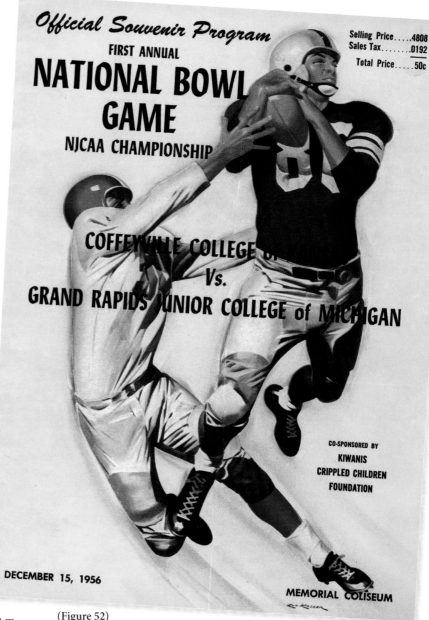

(Figure 52)
1956 National Bowl Game program. (GRCC Archives)

championship against Coffeyville, Kansas, in the Los Angeles Coliseum. (**Figure 52**) Though GRJC lost the game, it was clear that its football program had landed once again in competent hands and had secured a place in the national scene.

New Technologies and a Newspaper Change

The youthful dean was anxious to explore the educational possibilities of new technologies. He moderated a series of television programs on WOOD-TV on the subject of "Youth's Views on Teenage Subjects." He made use of closed-circuit television presentation when GRJC hosted conferences, and he encouraged a group of JC students, led by English Department advisor Jacoba Dalebout, to participate in College Omnibus productions at WOOD-TV with Aquinas and Calvin Colleges.

The November 22, 1957, *Junior Collegiate* announced that the newspaper advisor, John Van Krimpen, had taken ill and was being replaced by a highly-regarded fellow English Department colleague, Merle Dawson. *The Junior Collegiate* had struggled getting back on its feet, especially in assembling a willing and competent staff. The newspaper ran several writing contests with cash prizes in an attempt to discover potential journalists. The December 6 issue carried the story of Van Krimpen's death. It was a blow to the staff and the school as a whole, but Dawson was determined not to let the publication fail. By the following fall the paper was larger, more diverse, and measurably more energetic.

That first fall issue of 1958 carried a bombshell lead story: Dr. John Tirrell had resigned as dean to take the job of executive secretary of the Alumni Association at the University of Michigan, and he was being replaced by Dr. John E. Visser, a history profes-

(**Figure 53**) Dr. John Visser, fourth leader of GRJC. (GRCC Archives)

sor, head basketball coach, and dean of men at Hope College. Tirrell's stay at GRJC had been promising but brief. His higher education star was ascending. After several years at U of M, his next stop would be as first president of Oakland Community College—a new, independent community college with its own board of trustees.

Dr. John E. Visser

Dr. John Visser, like Tirrell, was young, bright, and destined for important roles in higher education. (**Figure 53**) A Grand Rapids native, he was a graduate of Creston High School, and a basketball star at Hope College where he did his undergraduate work. He was a World War II combat veteran who rose through the ranks from private to captain. He took his master's degree from the University of Iowa in 1947 and his doctorate in 1956. A married man with four young daughters, Visser had the immediate advantage of a good rapport with Superintendent Buikema, whom his wife and he knew well as fellow members of Central Reformed Church.[4]

Dr. John Visser's first year as dean (1958-59) saw a 28 percent enrollment increase to more than 2,000 students. Faculty numbers and classroom space were far from sufficient. New faculty members were hired, but the process for Visser shed light on the lack of faculty organization and input. Because both administrative and faculty structures were underdeveloped, and because a population boom of children born after the

1958

Dr. John Visser became the college's fourth leader. Visser established an open door admissions policy with an accompanying selective retention policy, undertook a detailed self-study resulting in a clear, systematic administrative structure and a faculty organized into five divisions with chairs chosen from divisional members. Visser gave student organizations freedom, but reined them in when it became necessary.

Dean Visser promoting Mechanical Technology program. (GRCC Archives)

1958 track team. (GRCC Archives)

Raiders in First National JC Championship Game

"CALIFORNIA HERE WE COME!" announce the '56 JC football team. Front row left to right: Assistant Coach Tom Van Wingen, Floyd Shepphard, Jim Emery, Frank Teeter, Roger Placeki, Preston Smith, Frank Brocato, Frank Major, Tom Cargill, Wally Wier, and Head Coach Gordon Hunsberger. Second row: Gus Unseld, Ed McCauley, Bill Friberg, Lyle Berry, Bill Czerwinski, Ed Grodus, Rex Smith, Henry Washington, and Cornie Bykerk, Head Manager. Third row: Manager Carl VanHeck, Larry Barcheski, John Welton, Earl Chellette, John DeBlaay, Don VandenBosch, Tom Miller, Lou Eggleston, Kevin Hanrahan, and Bill Piepers, trainer. Top row: Sherlyn Fetterman, Lee Harig, Fred Sauer, Irv Miller, Bob Coeling, Dave Stellema, Dave Krucki, and Bob Riggs.

Junior College Football Team Compiles Most Successful Record in 16 Years

(Continued from page 1) where two-a-day workouts will be held.

There is a possibility that a telecast of the game may be hand-

Raiders' Rumors

By Bob Ruster

Athletic Director Harold Steele announced that he needs a couple of men to help run off the intramural program. The job pays $1 an hour. Referees and officials are also needed. Anyone interested should notify Mr. Steele as soon

led by a local TV station, and it is almost certain that the same station will conduct a direct radio broadcast into Grand Rapids.

Not since 1940 has a Junior College football team had such an impressive season as this year, when the Raiders compiled a 5-1-2 record. The 1940 team went undefeated.

Beginning the year with new coaches, Gordon Hunsberger and Tom VanWingen, the Raiders first game was against North Park JC at Chicago, and they shut out the Illinois Conference team 9-0.

The most stunning victory of the year came against another top Junior College in the country on September 28, when Grand Rapids scored another shutout over Joliet, 32-0.

The victory over Joliet moved the Raiders into fourth place in the national ratings.

The next three games on the JC schedule were against four-year schools. The Raiders managed a win, a tie, and a loss in the series. The win was over Olivet, 14-12, the tie against Central Michigan JC, 19-19, and the loss was at the hands of Ferris, 19-13.

Grand Rapids tied Wilson JC, 12-12 on October 26 and then ended their three game winless streak by defeating four-year Manchester College, 19-13.

The Raiders closed the season with a 20-14 defeat over LaSalle Peru JC. Grand Rapids went into the game with a first place JC rating, but dropped to second in the final polling of the season.

Grand Rapids Meets Kansas Team In Post-season Grid Classic

By Bob Ruster

Grand Rapids Junior College took over the spotlight in the city this past week as a result of the selection made Monday enabling the football squad to play in a postseason football game.

The Raiders will represent the eastern division of Junior Colleges in the country in the first annual National Junior College Athletic Association football game to be played in the Los Angeles Coliseum on Dec. 15. The classic is expected to draw 70,000 fans.

"Grand Rapids Junior College's Christmas vacation will begin on Dec. 14 at 5 p.m. and only members of the football squad and managers will be excused before that date,"

stated Dr. John Tirrell, dean, in response to the many queries made.

"Other students missing classes before that date will be treated according to regular attendance rules," he added, "and the college will neither sponsor nor encourage any excursions or tours. If students want to go to California, they will be on their own."

The local college has been allotted 200 tickets for the affair, but Dr. Tirrell pointed out that if the school wants more they can have them.

Grand Rapids' opponent in the game will be Coffeyville, Kansas. Coffeyville compiled a 10-1 record during the season.

The Raiders received the final vote over Hibbing, Minnesota and Joplin, Missouri, by the three man committee of Hobart Bolerjack, secretary of the NJCAA, Charles Sesher, vice-president of the NJCAA, and Earle Holmes, director of the NJCAA service and statistical bureau. The squad is expected to head for the west coast on Dec. 8,

(Continued on page 4)

...llegiate

...higan, November 30, 1956   Number 4

(left) Ruster, Bob. "Raiders in First National JC Championship Game." *The Junior Collegiate, November 30, 1956. (GRCC Archives)*
(far left) "JC Students Travel to Coast." *The Junior Collegiate, December 4, 1956. (GRCC Archives)*

California Here We Come!
The 1956 National Junior College Championship

The GRJC/GRCC football program enjoyed a long and celebrated history. However, it was not until 1956 that the program gained national attention when it was selected for the inaugural National Junior College Championship. During the regular season, the Raiders finished with a record of 5-1-2, but their schedule included four games against four-year schools. As a result, junior college coaches chose them to represent the eastern division in the National Junior College Championship held on December 15, 1956.

Gordon Hunsberger, in his first year of coaching the team, received help from his in-state colleagues to prepare for the game. He took the team to East Lansing for a scrimmage at Michigan State's Stock Pavilion and received some tips from legendary coach Duffy Daugherty. Hunsberger was also able to secure blue practice uniforms from the University of Michigan.

The game was to be played at the Los Angeles Coliseum, requiring travel by air. The thirty-five players on the team were products of West Michigan high schools, coming from ten communities within 70 miles of Grand Rapids. For most of them this was a first-time experience. A crowd of approximately 500, including Mayor Paul Goebel, was on hand to wish them off at the Kent County Airport.

Weather conditions played havoc with both parts of the round trip. The flight to Los Angeles was delayed when one of the two airliners taking the team from Grand Rapids to Chicago was forced to land in Milwaukee due to a snowstorm hindering visibility over Chicago's Midway Airport. The other plane was diverted to Chicago's O'Hare Airport and buses were then used to transport the team to Midway to transfer to a larger jet. On the way back to Grand Rapids, an unscheduled refueling stop, a blown landing tire, and poor weather conditions again made it necessary for the team to travel by buses, this time from Chicago's Midway back to Grand Rapids.

In California, thieves broke into the locker room the GRJC team was using for practice at Compton Junior College and stole approximately $375 in cash and $495 in watches and other valuables. The Compton Junior College Student Council, Alumni Club and Boosters Club raised $375 to help compensate for the loss.

During the week leading up to the game, the team had a busy schedule of practices, banquets and visits to a movie studio and Disneyland, which had opened the previous year.

The trip received much attention in Grand Rapids due in part to four members of the local media traveling with the team to cover the event. *The Grand Rapids Press*, in the weeks leading up to the game, published an article nearly every day profiling the players, coaches, and preparations.

As for the game itself, Coffeyville Junior College (from Kansas) won by a score of 46-6, baffling the Raiders with their superior speed. In spite of the lopsided outcome, the game put GRJC football on the national radar, stirred interest in JC football in the Midwest, and created lifelong memories for the members of the team.

war was foreseen for the early 1960s, Visser quickly began a self-study to determine the college's most pressing needs.

Self-Study—Reorganization Plan

The North Central team that followed up on the self-study was deeply impressed with Visser's honesty and candor about the college's strengths and deficiencies. They found, as Visser did, that the college was under-administered in nearly all areas, that lines of authority were not clearly defined, and that faculty organization did not exist. Visser's plan for reorganization involved an increase in administrative staff he hoped would be economical enough to sell to the Grand Rapids Board of Education. Most of this staff would be half-time administrators, half-time faculty members.

First, his plan divided the faculty into five divisions, each with a divisional chair (responsible for curriculum development, teacher supervision, divisional budget, and academic counseling), a leader chosen from the ranks of that division (with released time from instruction) and answerable to a new assistant dean of instructional affairs, a position markedly different from the old assistant to the president. The new assistant dean was directly responsible for supervision of all faculty. The director of the evening college would also function at the level of assistant dean, as would an assistant dean of student affairs, to whom a new coordinator of business affairs, a registrar and director of admissions, a director of guidance and counseling, and a director of student activities would answer.

The five new divisions were organized as follows: the Division of Humanities was chaired by Dr. Clarence Meyer (replaced by Albert Smith the following year), the Division of Business and Technical Studies by Ralph Mowry, the Division of Social Sciences by Dr. Andrew Hansson, and the Division

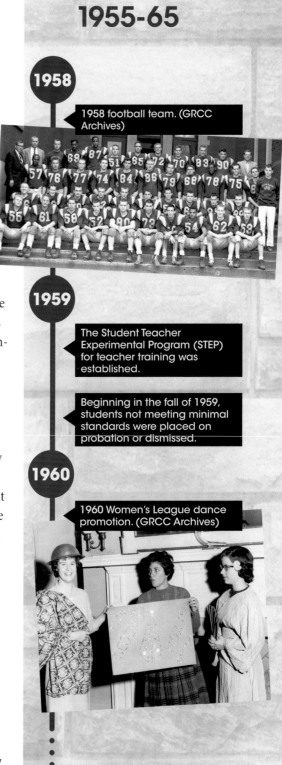

1958

1958 football team. (GRCC Archives)

1959

The Student Teacher Experimental Program (STEP) for teacher training was established.

Beginning in the fall of 1959, students not meeting minimal standards were placed on probation or dismissed.

1960

1960 Women's League dance promotion. (GRCC Archives)

(**Figure 54**) North Central Association of Colleges and Schools Report on the Visit to GRJC, March 22-25, 1959. (GRCC Archives)

of Applied Arts and Sciences by Carl Hofman. The fifth division, Engineering, Math, and Science, was co-chaired by Ben Gregory and Dr. Anne Miller (the latter replaced by Dr. Jerome Miller the following year). Dr. A. Martin Eldersveld was appointed the assistant dean of instructional affairs, Wendell Shroll was given the new title of assistant dean of the evening college, Richard Wherity became the assistant dean of student affairs, Leonard Anderson the coordinator of business affairs, Francis J. McCarthy the registrar and director of admissions, Dr. L. Harvey James the director of guidance and counseling.

Dean Visser would be responsible for the coordination and administration of the total college program, the development of long-range planning, and the hiring and firing of faculty and staff (with the superintendent's approval)—managing without micromanaging, delegating at least a portion of authority to a trusted team. To Visser's credit, he involved the faculty in every phase of this reorganization.

The North Central team, after finding Visser's plan a sensible one, went on to point out some problem areas in the college: a faculty teaching too many classes (often overloaded with 30 or more students); a recruitment policy that favored hiring area high school teachers over new graduates with advanced degrees, trained for college-level teaching; a library that, in spite of gains, was still too small; an aging East Building now only partially occupied; a lack of office space for faculty; neglected and inadequate physics labs (though refurbished labs for chemistry, botany, zoology, and dietetics earned high points); and, finally, the odd challenge of a collegiate program existing as part of a public school system. (**Figure 54**)

John Visser's reorganization proposal was approved and adopted, and the rapidly growing college began to function more efficiently. Faculty and administrative structures would adapt and further subdivide over the next few years and thereafter as conditions warranted. Yet Visser had laid the groundwork. Though he would spend only four years as dean of GRJC, his leadership would have a profound impact on the direction and well being of the institution.

A New Four Year College in Grand Rapids

Grand Rapids newspapers (including *The Junior Collegiate*) of the late 1950s carried stories of a college-age population explosion that would soon engulf local facilities. A pivotal report of Dr. John Dale Russell, Director of the U.S. Division of Higher Education, entitled *A Survey of Higher Education in Michigan*, made clear that a new four-year institution would be needed in the Grand Rapids area to meet a dramatic increase in students seeking degrees. Russell proposed three options (all assuming the continued existence of GRJC): a new branch of U of M or Michigan State University (MSU), a new independent state college, or an expansion of GRJC into a four-year college. In *The Junior Collegiate* of November 26, 1958, Dean Visser stated that he would support any of these options for meeting community needs. As time and circumstances would have it, option two was the popular choice; it resulted in the establishing of Grand Valley State College in 1960.

Open Door

Grand Rapids Junior/Community College has long been known as an "open door" institution. But "open door" is an elusive term, nearly always with an asterisk attached. Has the college from the start made higher education available to any student without qualification? During the presidencies of Jesse Davis and Arthur Andrews, transfer students were held to strict University of Michigan admissions standards (one obvious reason for JC student success after transfer). Some remediation was available to students who did not meet those standards. Special permission of the president was sometimes granted to students with unusual circumstances. Terminal students were held to less rigorous standards, but the door was not, by any means, open to all.

Under Deans Tirrell and Visser, admissions standards began to change. The University of Michigan requirements for transfer students disappeared from the college catalog during Tirrell's tenure. Those not qualifying for admission were still able to enroll on a probationary basis in a growing number of non-credit developmental courses designed to prepare the student for a regular college program. Unqualified older students and foreign students could request testing for proficiency and be admitted on a probationary basis.

Several in-house chronological histories of important college dates maintain that an open door admissions policy was adopted in 1956 under Tirrell, but there is no evidence of it in the college catalog. Dean Visser's 1960-61 college catalog described admission to GRJC as "a privilege extended to qualified students only," and went on the say "the college reserves the right to deny admission to students of questionable character or with past records of improper social conduct." Two years later, in Visser's 1962-63 catalog, the word "privilege" and all references to exclusion had been removed, with admission requirements summed up in this simple statement: "Because of its diverse curricular offerings, Grand Rapids Junior College is able to serve students with varying backgrounds and goals who are sincere in their desire to obtain a college education." This, for the first time, has the sound of an open door policy.

As positive and egalitarian as open admissions may seem, the policy is frequently problematic. John Visser was fully aware that GRJC had two buildings with a limited number of classrooms to accommodate a rapidly-growing student body. How does one manage open admissions within limited space? Over the years, deans and presidents of GRJC have had occasion to limit enrollments on the basis of both spatial and financial considerations.

Visser chose different paths to the same end: first, he set a late July cut-off date for enrollment, and, second, he developed a policy known as "selective retention." Beginning in the fall of 1959, JC students not meeting minimal academic standards would be placed on probation or dismissed. In the September 11, 1959, issue of *The Junior Collegiate*, Visser stated this was a practical, not a punitive measure. Disqualified students could be considered for readmission after the lapse of at least one semester. "The college," he said, "is caught between increasing enrollment and limited plant capacity. Therefore, it is necessary to adopt standards of retention." In a February 17, 1961, issue of *The Junior Collegiate*, after 358 students had been dismissed and another 333 placed on probation, Visser remarked that "since JC has an open door policy for admission, 12 percent disqualified and 12 percent on probation seems reasonable." To this writer's knowledge, Visser's statement was

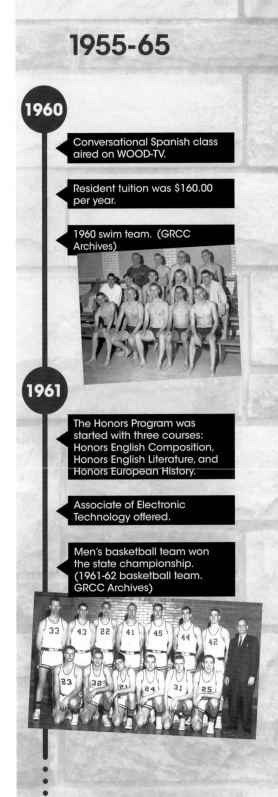

1960

Conversational Spanish class aired on WOOD-TV.

Resident tuition was $160.00 per year.

1960 swim team. (GRCC Archives)

1961

The Honors Program was started with three courses: Honors English Composition, Honors English Literature, and Honors European History.

Associate of Electronic Technology offered.

Men's basketball team won the state championship. (1961-62 basketball team. GRCC Archives)

(Figure 55) "358 Students Dismissed, 333 More on Probation" *The Junior Collegiate*. February 17, 1961. (GRCC Archives)

The newspaper front page (Figure 55) reads:

What's With Jack Paar? Criterion, p. 2

The Junior Collegiate

How Not to Get a Hot Dog page 4

Series II, Volume 6 — Grand Rapids Junior College, Grand Rapids, Michigan, February 17, 1961 — Number 8

358 Students Dismissed 333 More on Probation

Selective retention at JC has taken its toll. Of the 2574 students at JC the fourth week of the first semester, 358 have been disqualified, 333 are on probation.

The above figures include students enrolled in the evening college. Last semester, a thorough survey of all students enrolled in the evening college was made. All grade point averages were checked.

Several students who were not allowed in the regular college program had crept into the college credit evening college program. Those students, who did not have grade point averages necessary to maintain regular status, were either disqualified or put on probation.

The figure 2574 represents all students who remained after all voluntary withdrawals left class. Those who withdrew voluntarily before the end of the fourth week received a "W" grade. A few who withdrew after the fourth week because of illness or other valid reasons also received a "W". All others who left after the fourth week received either "N", equivalent to an "E" or an "E".

Dean Visser stated that he did not think that 385 disqualified and 333 on probation was inordinately large. The Dean stated that since JC has an open door policy for admission, 12% disqualified and 12% on probation seems reasonable.

Registration Moves Smoothly As 2231 Students Sign Up

Students, Faculty Assist in Roll

Comparatively short lines, simple instructions, few mistakes and rapid processing marked the most efficient registration seen at JC in recent years.

Under the direction of registrar Francis McCarthy, a handbook was published, from which students made out their own schedules and chose their own classes. On the three registration days, students ran the gauntlet of eighteen tables, pulling class cards, filling registration cards, residency cards, IBM cards, and tuition receipts. Twenty-three students were employed for the three day period along with the entire faculty.

Mr. McCarthy plans only one change for registration next September. Students with last names beginning with Z will be registered first.

Student assistants Dan Humphreys, John Geise, Diana Smith, Win Ferrell, and Bonnie Thomas help as Dorothe Cadman completes registration.

---

the first public acknowledgment by a GRJC president or dean of an open door admissions policy—predating his official catalog policy statement by over a year. (**Figure 55**)

Tightening the Reins

Visser's short tenure was productive but not without problems. As a rule, he gave students plenty of rope but sometimes had to rein them in. When *The Junior Collegiate* began to publish scurrilous humor and satire columns aimed at administration

and faculty, he threatened (as reported in the March 16, 1958, edition) to cut the columns if corrective action was not taken. The chastened *Junior Collegiate* staff immediately eliminated the satire column and upgraded the humor column. Legend has it that Visser shut down the newspaper altogether, but the real events were not so dramatic. By the following fall, Dr. Marinus Swets had taken over as the newspaper's advisor, with a staff determined to create a more professional news outlet. Under Swets' leadership—for the next 17 years—the newspaper would become one the best of its kind in the state. The character of Swets would set the tone of staff and publication. English Department instructor Sharon Wynkoop, a former *Collegiate* editor, described Swets as "unpredictable, slightly crazy, warm-hearted, brilliant, unconventional, inspiring, preposterous…but most of all [someone who] dares to care about the students."[5] Swets would leave an indelible mark as newspaper advisor, but also as teacher, chair of the Language Arts Division, and dean of Arts and Sciences.

John Visser's most persistent problem in his four-year tenure was student parking. The college had no parking ramps. Students competed for metered parking that they felt was unfairly time-limited and expensive. As the city doled out hundreds of parking tickets, student anger rose. The lead story in the March 1961 *Junior Collegiate* carried an anonymous student note addressed to the Grand Rapids Police and signed "Change or else," along with a photograph of smashed parking meters—65 of them in all—in protest of newly-hiked city parking rates. Besides on-street parking, a single private lot near the Main Building—with 300 spaces and exorbitant rates—had to serve well over 3,000 students. Though ramps would in time be built, the parking problem has never entirely gone away.

Visser tussled with the Student Council when it demanded more control of student activity funds. He eventually made students a part of the committee that administered those funds. The Greek problem intensified when, on March 3, 1961, Grand Rapids police raided a beer party sponsored by the Sigma Kappa Theta (the Sigs) Fraternity and 52 Junior College students were arrested. Visser suspended all of the arrested students pending a review, suspended the fraternity for a full year, and seriously considered ending fraternities and sororities on-campus altogether. That year and the following, in a scramble to clean up their act, the Greeks replaced Hell Week with Greek Week, during which pledges participated in community service projects rather than initiation rites. The Greeks would manage to hang around for another decade—until, in the 1974-75 school year, they disappeared without much notice, apparent victims of irrelevance in an age of social activism, Vietnam protest, Black Power, and women's rights[6]

(**Figure 56**) Arts Festival program, May 2, 1963. (GRCC Archives)

New Blood, New Energy

Under Visser, an already strong faculty was improved with the additions of Roger Walcott (Director of Library Services), Marinus Swets, Lela Johnson, James Hausman, and Jay Lieffers (English), James Bogdan (history), John Regenmorter (speech and debate), Allan Gerrard (Spanish), Esther Andreas (LPN), Charles Chanter (business), Robert Riekse and Harvey Olsen (political science), Antoinette Joiner (math and counseling), Donald McNeeley (physics), and Robert Breining (chemistry).

Visser gave his blessing to the Student Teacher Experimental Program (STEP) for teacher training. He supported Richard Chestnut's idea of expanding calculus to four semesters from two to improve the engineering program (Chestnut was thereafter known as "Mr. Calculus" of the college)[7] *The Junior Collegiate* began sponsoring a creative writing contest and publishing the winners in a Christmas literary edition. *Collegiate* cartoonist Webb Marris, Jr., (son of the JC baseball/basketball coach) created the Raider mascot, a caricature of a Civil War Yankee infantryman. The Humanities Division developed an annual spring Arts Festival, featuring music, dramatic readings, art, dance, and poetry presentations. (**Figure 56**) An Honors Council under the direction of Dr. Eldersveld, introduced an Honors

1955-65

1962

Counseling Center, 1962-63 GRJC Student Handbook. (GRCC Archives)

1962 Kappa Sigma Phi members. (GRCC Archives)

STATEMENT OF AIMS AND OBJECTIVES

Grand Rapids Junior College, in an effort to recognize, encourage, and reward able students, has established a two-year Honors Program in which participating students are given an opportunity to receive more instruction and counseling than is possible in regular classes. The new plan, which is entirely voluntary, may provide Honors classes of several types, such as new courses especially designed for Honors candidates, separate sections of existing courses, and special instruction within present courses. It is the college's answer to an urgent need to spur the best young minds to work toward the maximum development of their intellectual capacities.

The aims of the Honors Program are twofold:

1. To encourage intellectual independence; to provide and recognize work of greater depth, scope, and originality; and to allow for individual variations among students in the use of the college's educational resources.

2. To prepare the able student to enter senior college confident of his scholastic competence.

The general philosophy of the Honors Program at Grand Rapids Junior College is concerned with three major areas of responsibility, namely, (1) the student, (2) the college, and (3) the community.

The Student

1. To stimulate the able student to develop his talents by constantly associating him with his intellectual peers in classes which challenge his ability and maturity, and which will provide opportunities for exercising originality and resourcefulness.

2. To provide opportunities for more intensive and extensive study of regularly presented material which will enrich his background, and stimulate enthusiasm for learning those facets of knowledge normally beyond the reach of the average student.

(Figure 57) GRJC Honors Program "Statement of Aims and Objectives." (GRCC Archives)

Program in the 1961-62 school year with three courses: Honors English Composition, taught by Marinus Swets, Honors English Literature, taught by Merle Dawson, and Honors European History, taught by James Bogdan. (Figure 57) The Music Department's annual Musical Moods concert, featuring all of the college's musical groups, continued to grow in popularity and quality.

Then, unexpectedly, on April 23, 1962, the college community learned that Visser had resigned to accept an appointment as executive assistant to the president and full professor of social sciences at Ball State Teachers College in Muncie, Indiana. He would in time become president of Kansas State Teachers College.

Dr. Donald Fink

Dean Visser had made bold moves to modernize GRJC, but multiple executive turnovers created a degree of instability requiring frequent administrative adjustments. When, in August 1962, the board of education appointed a new college dean, 42-year-old Dr. Donald Fink, Director of Pupil

(Figure 58) Dr. Donald Fink, fifth leader of GRJC. (GRCC Archives)

Personnel for GRPS, the administrative staff of seven underwent a significant shuffle of personnel. (Figure 58) Former registrar and director of admissions, Francis J. McCarthy, became assistant dean for instructional affairs, replacing Eldersveld, who had departed for MSU, Dr. Robert Riekse replaced McCarthy as registrar and director of admissions, and Robert VanderMolen replaced L. James Harvey as director of counseling.

Fink, a Michigan native and Lansing Central High School graduate, had earned his A.B. degree from Alma College in 1942. After serving in World War II, he taught at Alma High School from 1945-48, returned to graduate school at MSU and took his M.A. degree in 1949. He was another whose star was ascending at a time of exponential growth in higher education, though to this point he had had no college or university experience. Several months before he accepted the job as dean of GRJC, he had received his doctorate from MSU. A Grand Rapids Board of Education insider, Fink appeared to be chosen to ease yet another administrative transition and provide Superintendent Buikema a close ally in the college. But as his leadership developed, Fink would prove to have a mind of his own.

From Five to Nine Divisions and More Changes

Under Fink, college divisions began to be more logically subdivided. By the 1963-64 school year, five divisions had grown to nine, each with a chair: Business Studies was led by Robert Duffy; Fine Arts and Foreign Language, Albert Smith; Health Education, Rosalyn Ghysels; Language Arts, Merle Dawson; Life Sciences, Roland Constant; Physical Education, Gordon Hunsberger; Physical Science and Mathematics, Albertus (Bud) Elve; Social Science, James Bogdan; and Technical Education, O. Stewart Myers. The chairs, all skilled leaders and teachers (Smith, Elve, and Bogdan would lead for decades), now participated in establishing their budgets, evaluating instructors, and hiring new faculty.

The same year, Fink was behind the creation of a Grand Rapids Junior College Foundation with $12,000 in seed money from alumni and friends of the college to develop scholarships for deserving students and study grants for faculty. In 1964, the Dental Assisting Program was established with Maureen Munger as director. **(Figure 59)** With Fink's blessing, Dr. Robert Rieske introduced a microfilm record-keeping system and IBM data processing equipment into the college's admissions and registration process.

NEW CURRICULUMS

Grand Rapids Junior College is constantly adding and revising courses to meet the changing needs of students in the metropolitan community. As this catalog is being compiled, curriculums in the areas listed below are in the final stages of development. The College will publish details of specific course offerings, requirements, etc., as they become available. For further information, contact the Dean of Instructional Affairs.

Data Processing Technology

The College is now offering instruction in electronic data processing. An electronic computer and related equipment is being installed to provide three basic instructional needs: (1) training in an area of knowledge which is fast becoming indispensable toward a comprehensive understanding of business, technological, and scientific processes; (2) opportunities for those enrolled in other curriculums to enhance and enrich their educational experiences through the research potential afforded by a computer center; and (3) training for those interested in becoming skilled operators of computers and related machines at less than a professional level.

Dental Office Assistant

In order that the increasing demand for qualified and competent individuals trained as dental assistants may be served, the college has been authorized to establish a two-year dental office assistant program consistent with the educational and professional requirements of the Council in Dental Education of the American Dental Association. Training in three major areas is being planned: (1) assisting in the dental operating room; (2) assisting with dental laboratory techniques including X-ray; and (3) office management and secretarial practice. In addition, experiences in general education consonant with the College's avowed belief that our modern society requires that individuals prepare themselves for a broad range of responsibilities and opportunities as well as for a specialized vocation.

(Figure 59)
Dental Office Assistant program description,
1964-65 *Grand Rapids Junior College Catalog.* (GRCC Archives)

Student Life

The social life of GRJC students proved diverse and energetic during this period, featuring homecoming celebrations with royal courts, political clubs and rallies, Miss GRJC contests

1955-65

1962

Dr. Donald Fink became the college's fifth leader. Fink subdivided college divisions more logically, creating nine divisions out of five. He organized the Golden Anniversary celebration of the college, establishing a GRJC Foundation and the beginnings of an alumni association. He was outspoken about the need for expanded facilities (including parking), but even more so about the necessity of separating the college from GRPS control. Fink would go on to expand occupational programs, make fuller use of citizen's advisory committees, and broker the purchase of the West Building as a short-term fix for overcrowded classrooms.

1963

Men's cross country team finished 2nd in the National Junior College meet. (1963 Cross Country Team. GRCC Archives)

The GRJC Foundation was established.

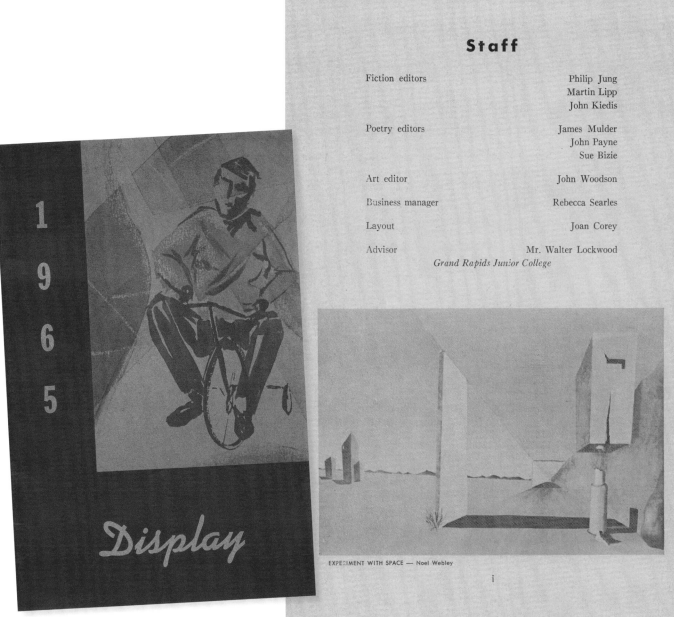

Staff

Fiction editors	Philip Jung
	Martin Lipp
	John Kiedis
Poetry editors	James Mulder
	John Payne
	Sue Bizie
Art editor	John Woodson
Business manager	Rebecca Searles
Layout	Joan Corey
Advisor	Mr. Walter Lockwood

Grand Rapids Junior College

EXPERIMENT WITH SPACE — Noel Webley

i

(Figure 60) First issue of *Display* magazine, 1965. (GRCC Archives)

the state championship in 1962. The debate team led by Coach John Regenmorter took top prize in the State Junior College Debate Tournament the same year. In the 1963-64 school year, *The Junior Collegiate* once more became *The Collegiate*, the name it would keep for the next fifty years and more.

In January of 1965, newly-hired Language Arts instructor Walter Lockwood was recruited to become advisor to a fledgling writing group called the Pens Club (organized by Lorene Wabeke), which in the fall semester had published a small, mimeographed literary bulletin they had named *Display*, containing winners of a departmental writing contest. Lockwood encouraged them to continue the publication and secured student activities funds to upgrade it to magazine form, with glossy paper, professional printing, and student editors. **(Figure 60)** Though the Pens Club would soon disappear, the student publication and its student staff would not. In the 1965-66 school year, a writing contest began accompanying publication of the magazine. In spite of having to weather early skirmishes related to freedom of expression, *Display* soon was recognized by the Michigan Collegiate Press Association as one of the best junior college literary magazines in Michigan. Lockwood would continue as advisor for 36

that sent winners to the Miss Michigan Junior College pageant, Copper Carnivals, Blossom Balls, Greek Weeks and rush seasons. Former JC star Webb Marris's men's basketball team won more years, 73 consecutive issues, with assistance from various members of the Art Department, particularly Glen Raymond, Joyce Kennedy, and Nancy Clouse.

The magazine has, as of 2014, appeared each semester for over 51 years, a total of 103 issues. Maryann Lesert (English), David Cope, (English), Julie Stevenson (English), Katie Budden (Art), Katie Croutcher (Art), Robin Van Rooyen (Art), and Jonathon Russell (Photography) have served or are presently serving as advisors. A number of successful writers have published their early work in the magazine, among them novelist and poet Joseph Dionne, fiction writer Philip Jung, Pulitzer prize-winning journalist Richard Cooper, non-fiction humorist (*Enslaved by Ducks*) Bob Tarte, columnist Tom Rademacher, poet/story writer David Montgomery, poet/novelist/editor Marlene Chase, poet/novelist Carmen Bugan, poets G. F. Korreck, Barbara Saunier, and Kim Wyngarden, and Grand Rapids Poet Laureate David Cope.

Buikema Retires

In April of 1964, Superintendent Buikema's massive building and renovation plan was reaching completion, yet soaring birth rates showed the need for even more school construction and expanded operations. The board felt it had no option but to seek approval of an additional four-mill tax levy for operating costs. When the millage vote failed, Buikema resigned, though a three-mill levy would be approved five months later. Deputy Superintendent Dr. Jay L. Pylman was named Buikema's successor.[8]

Golden Anniversary and Self-Study

The spring of 1964 saw a whirlwind of preparation for the college's golden anniversary. The college instituted a Distinguished Alumni Award to honor celebrated graduates. (**Figure 61**) The organizers also held an Alumni Luncheon and Alumni Weekend, with clear designs on an alumni association. Edward N. Cole, 1920s alumnus and Vice President (soon to be President) of General Motors, was the keynote speaker. A Founder's Day Luncheon was held at the Pantlind Hotel, where a model of a new Urban Renewal project

(**Figure 61**) 1964 Distinguished Alumni recipients. (GRCC Archives)

1955-65

1963

In the 1963-64 school year, *The Junior Collegiate* was renamed *The Collegiate*. (*The Collegiate*, September 24, 1963. GRCC Archives)

1964

Bookstore, 1964. (GRCC Archives)

Varied program marks 50th Anniversary year

The first Junior College Newsletter was issued in January. It is our intention to issue six of these informative bulletins during the year to all alumni and interested citizens. An attempt is being made to locate graduates and former students of the college. Be sure your name is on our mailing list. We have a great story to share with you.

A committee is at work writing a history of Grand Rapids Junior College, complete with illustrations.

An incorporated Foundation for the College has been established to receive contributions from alumni, business and industry, interested individuals and foundations. The income from this project will be used for student aid and faculty study grants.

The entire staff of Grand Rapids Junior College will devote a considerable amount of time during the next 18 months in a self-study of the entire program of the College, including the educational objectives, course content, community needs and others.

SPECIAL EVENTS

Kick-off Dinner .... January 28, 1964

National Junior College
Invitational Tennis and Golf .... June, 1964

Alumni Weekend .... June 12-13, 1964

Founders' Day .... September, 1964

Professional Leadership
Days .... October 4-6, 1964

(**Figure 62**) GRJC Fiftieth Anniversary brochure, 1964. (GRCC Archives)

(known as the Jefferson Connector-Junior College Project) was displayed. (**Figure 62**) Dovetailing with the local celebration, the July 2 passage of the Civil Rights Act marked a new era in the life of the nation, with profound long-term effects on its colleges.

In the midst of this whirl of activity, Fink and his staff were deeply involved in preparing a self-study for the North Central Association. Fink would mince no words in this study or in his *Annual Report to the Superintendent of Schools* dated July of 1964. He expressed to North Central his "unequivocal commitment to shared responsibility and authority, to total staff involvement in the on-going philosophy and operation of the college." He asserted that the college needed to abandon the crumbling East Building, to expand the physical plant and parking facilities to meet enrollment demands, and to commit itself to the downtown campus idea.

Advisory Committees—Linking College and Community

Fink also committed himself to the 1964 federally-mandated expansion of vocational education at the junior college level. GRJC had long been known as an academic transfer college with a modest terminal/occupational program. Fink acknowl-

edged fears of some staff members that vocational education presented a direct threat to the school's academic tradition. Yet he argued that such fears were groundless, even potentially destructive to the well-being of the college. He and his staff set out to assess the technological and occupational needs of area business and industry. Along with Assistant Dean McCarthy and occupational staff, Fink spearheaded the formation of multiple advisory committees from the community—in the areas of mechanical technology, data processing, drafting, electronics, dental assisting, practical nursing, and a police cadet program (introduced to the college in the fall of 1962)—to develop courses for job skill training wherever they were needed. The Mechanical Technology Advisory Committee, to illustrate with a single case, helped launch a new course in nonmetallic fabrication and secure the installation of a plastics injector molder at the college. GRJC was clearly functioning as a community college long before it officially became one.

The Dean Makes a Stand

If Superintendent Buikema had believed he was hiring an insider who would be cooperative and compliant, Jay Pylman found himself faced with a dean aggressively outspoken about GRPS mismanagement of college affairs. In his *Annual Report*, Fink told the Superintendent that a college must have freedom to make its own decisions in a timely manner. He noted that, though the decision had been made to expand the college's facilities, bungling and a lack of urgency on the part of the board had caused disastrous delays. The result would be construction of a classroom building three years too late for the high tide of enrollments. He complained of stagnant and uncompetitive faculty and administrative salaries. He fumed about two years of delays in adopting an Associate Degree

REPORT OF A REVIEW VISIT

TO

GRAND RAPIDS JUNIOR COLLEGE

GRAND RAPIDS, MICHIGAN

April 20-21, 1964

for the

Commission on Colleges and Universities

of the

North Central Association of Colleges and Secondary Schools

VISITING COMMITTEE

Donald A. Eldridge, President, Bennett College, Millbrook, N. Y.

Harold L. Bitting, Director, Lyons Township Junior College (Chairman)

2. The basic problem of financing and control of the junior college should be carefully and objectively appraised. Specifically, can any Board of Education which has responsibility for 68 schools devote the required amount of time and attention to a college which now enrolls more than 3,000 students and which expects to have an enrollment of 6,000 to 7,000 within a decade?

Should not the evolution of an independent Board of Trustees be carefully considered, to be coordinated with the Board of Education and the rest of the school system, but fiscally independent and autonomous? This seems to be a very pertinent question when it is realized that only about 15% of the financial support of the junior college now comes from the Board of Education, which yet has 100% control.

3. A careful study should be made of the long range constituency of the college. What are its obligations to the population outside the city limits of Grand Rapids? Outside the greater Grand Rapids area? The county? These questions obviously are closely related to Numbers 1 and 2 above and to Number 3 under Areas of Concern.

(Figure 63) Commission on Colleges and Universities of the North Central Association of Colleges and Secondary Schools *Report of a Review Visit to GRJC*, April 20-21, 1964. (GRCC Archives)

Nursing program, in spite of letters from local hospitals urging its immediate creation. He summed up his frustration as follows:

> *The Dean frankly feels a complete lack of freedom to recommend any study, innovation, addition, change or other movement that might result in the improvement of Grand Rapids Junior College. Under the circumstances, the fine spirit and favorable attention generated by the 50th Anniversary is empty… the college has no future without the freedom to rise and meet the new challenges of the day….This is not possible if Grand Rapids Junior College is to continue as the sixty-first of sixty-one school units in the Grand Rapids Public School system.*

Fink concluded his report by pinpointing the source of his frustrations: a college "attempting to operate within the loyalties and the restrictions of a public school district which is already short of funds, with an administrative line organization which provides for little self-determination or creativity on the part of the college staff itself."

From this point on, pressure to separate the college from the Grand Rapids Public School system seemed to come from everywhere, including *The Grand Rapids Press*. Both the North Central Accreditation Review Committee of 1964 and a local Citizens and Alumni Council Study Group, formed during the Fiftieth-Anniversary Celebration, recommended that GRJC widen its tax base from city to county, establish its own board of trustees to be elected county-wide, and separate from the Grand Rapids Public Schools' Board of Education. **(Figure 63)** Each year, larger numbers of GRJC students were arriving from outside of the Grand Rapids area. The proposed separation made solid sense. Even the superintendent and school board began to see the logic of it. The single remaining obstacle was convincing the voters of the Kent Intermediate School District to assume financial support of the college.

1964

Students Kay Willmering, Barbara Patton, Susan Walton, Wendy Hoeizley and Sandra Dieleman appear in period costumes in front of Central High School in honor of the College's fiftieth anniversary. (1964-65 GRJC Student Handbook. GRCC Archives)

The college purchased the former Lear-Siegler facility on Division and Fountain and renamed it the West Building. This facility was necessary for a growing student body and was used to house Language Arts and Music. West Building sign. (GRCC Archives)

The Need for Teaching Space

Fink, with an eye to expansion of facilities, forged ahead into a broader diversity of terminal/occupational offerings, including Manpower Training programs, making GRJC eligible for funds from the Higher Education Facilities Act of 1963. He also was aware that a new (1962) State of Michigan Constitution had made funds available for community college buildings and programs, particularly if the community college was based in a downtown area. Given that fact, a briefly-entertained idea of moving the college to the old Calvin College campus was put to rest. While a visionary collaborative plan for a downtown cultural center and parking ramp took shape, centered around the college but also involving the city, the Ryerson Library, the Grand Rapids Art and Public Museums, Park Church, and Butterworth Hospital, Fink and C. Robert Muth, the board's assistant superintendent for business, brokered a deal to buy an empty Lear-Siegler facility on Division and Fountain to be remodeled into a classroom building (the West Building) as an interim solution to GRJC's rapidly-growing student body. **(Figure 64)** Lear-Siegler gave up the aging structure for the gift price of $150,000. At the same time, the Evening Program led by Wendell Shroll, having expanded to more than 1,200 students, helped relieve some of the daytime crowding. The West Building had its problems: narrow stairways, unpredictable and inadequate elevators, a hazardous Division Avenue crossing for students, an unusable west half that did not meet fire codes (though later it would be remodeled to house extension centers for U of M, MSU, and WMU). Still, it served its purpose until 1984, when the Kendall School of Art and Design would take possession of it.

Though the collaborative cultural center as originally envisioned never came to fruition, Fink's tenure marked the genesis of significant college expansion, carried out by his next two successors.

In the spring of 1965, Dr. Donald Fink announced that he was leaving GRJC to become the founding president of Montcalm Community College, an independent institution with a countywide tax base and its own board of trustees. This move, given the depth of Fink's frustrations with board of education control of the college, seemed fairly predictable.

1964

During the college's fiftieth anniversary year the Distinguished Alumni Award was established and a number of events were held, including an alumni luncheon, an alumni weekend and a Founder's Day luncheon. (50th Anniversary brochure. (GRCC Archives)

Grand Rapids Junior College 50th Anniversary 1914-1964

Dental Assisting program established.

Enrollment was 3,500.

(left, Figure 64) West Building, undated. (GRCC Archives)

Students walking from the West Building (later Kendall College of Art and Design) back to the Main campus. undated. (GRCC Archives)

The Builders: The McCarthy Years 1965-75

Francis J. McCarthy

In the summer of 1965, Francis J. (Frank) McCarthy, Assistant Dean of Instructional Affairs, became the favorite of most faculty and administration to replace Donald Fink as college dean. **(Figure 65)** McCarthy had begun at GRJC as an English instructor in 1958, having taught English and Latin at Howe High School in Bellerica, Massachusetts, then English and drama at East Grand Rapids High School. He had earned both Bachelor of Arts and Master of Education degrees at Tufts University. A formal, gracious man, (a transplanted Easterner born in Salem, Massachusetts), McCarthy—along with his wife Lorraine—found Grand Rapids a positive environment in which to live and raise three children. He was appointed the college's registrar and director of admissions in 1959, worked in that position until 1961, when he took a leave of absence to do doctoral work at the University of Michigan. He returned to GRJC to assume the position of assistant dean of instructional affairs under Fink. When Fink resigned in the spring of 1965, the board's appointment of McCarthy as dean was no surprise.

Fink had laid some foundation for an era of building and expansion, but it was McCarthy who became the first important leader-builder of the college. Within his decade-long tenure as dean, he oversaw a dramatic increase of enrollment and

(**Figure 65**) Francis J. McCarthy, sixth leader of GRJC. (GRCC Archives)

full-time faculty, the construction of a classroom building, a parking ramp, a library/learning center, and most of the preliminary stages of a physical education facility. He also helped broker the purchase of the former Grand Rapids School of Bible and Music to provide even more classrooms.

Downtown Urban Renewal

"Urban Renewal" was in the air in Grand Rapids of the 1960s. Fed by federal dollars, the program came to be known by many local citizens as "Urban Destruction," thanks to the wrecking ball that laid waste to many of the city's historic downtown areas (128 buildings in all). The last of them to fall, the ornate City Hall, was saved for a time by protestors, but came down at last in 1969, in spite of the heroics of Grand Rapids singer Mary Powell, who made international news by chaining herself to the wrecking ball.

Rising in place of historical city blocks were areas like the stark new government complexes around Vandenberg Center. The wrecking ball had done its damage; the new interstate highway system through the city continued it. Suburban malls began to drain the life from the central city, leaving behind a drab, dying downtown that would be years in recovering. One sign of hope, however, was the 1969 Vandenberg Center dedication of artist Alexander Calder's inspired stabile, *La Grande Vitesse*,

1965

Francis J. McCarthy became the college's sixth leader. During his decade-long tenure, he oversaw a dramatic increase of enrollment and full-time faculty, the construction of the North Building, a parking ramp, a library/learning center, and most of the preliminary stages of a physical education facility.

Student Congress sponsored a "Bleed-in" blood drive in memory of the Americans who died in the Vietnam War.

Nuclear Chemistry was first offered in 1965.

1966

The first annual Miss Grand Rapids Junior College pageant was held in 1967. In 1968, Jean Reed won the pageant and went on to win the Miss Michigan Junior College pageant. In 1968, GRJC hosted the pageant. (GRCC Archives)

The Junior Collegiate newspaper clipping:

Flint Downs JC — Raiders Finish Second 12-4

| Eiko Takano page 3 | | Swim Team page 4 |

The Junior Collegiate

Series II, Volume 6 — Grand Rapids Junior College, Grand Rapids, Michigan, March 3, 1961 — Number 9

Dean Reiterates Cut Policy
Forum in Commons Poorly Attended

The first of a possible series of forums took place February 24 in the Student Commons. Representatives from the faculty and from the student body took part in a forum concerning JC attendance rules.

Dean Visser opened the program by explaining how he had settled on the present attendance rules. Dr. Visser stated that he was disturbed about the attendance when he first became Dean at JC. He believed the system then in effect needed a revision. The main features of the old system were these:

1. Students were allowed a number of cuts from class equal to one week of class time.

2. If a student took more than an allowable number of cuts, a warning notice was issued by the Assistant Dean's office and mailed to the student.

3. Students missing classes to an extreme excess were subject to disciplinary action.

4. An excused absence was granted only upon presentation of a doctor's excuse to the instructor.

Dean Visser said that he didn't believe this was a satisfactory system because he believes that allowable cuts are not justifiable. Students had gotten the notion that they were entitled to a free week of cuts in each class. Moreover, Dr. Visser feels the present policy of leaving attendance matters up to the prerogative of the instructor is more in keeping with the character of a college, and follows generally accepted college practices throughout the nation.

Following the address by the Dean the floor was open for comments by the students. Most of the comments subtly voiced the opinion that class cuts should be left to the discretion of the students.

Many absent

Dr. Visser, Dr. Eldersveld, the registrar, Mr. McCarthy, and the two faculty representatives who appeared (several more were invited but either had class or "cut") then commented on the student comments. (Of the 1600 odd students in school only about 100 were there. The rest were in class or "cut").

It seems that all the students there had a preformed opinion as had the faculty members. No opinion seemed to be altered one whit.

Continued on page 4

Letter to Police Hints of Meter Raid

An anonymous letter arrived at the desk of Captain Shippy of the Police Traffic Division at the same time the first meter damage was discovered (see lead story). A copy of the letter is printed below:

What in H is wrong with you guys. Can't your cops patrol downtown where there needed instead of around Junior College giving parking violations. Most of us kids barely get along as it is and can't afford tickets. There better be a drastic change or something drastic is going to happen. I hope you guys value your jobs. change or else.

Sixty-Five Parking Meters Smashed in College Area

... No ticket ...

$1000 Damage Follows Hiked Rate

Sixty-five parking meters were destroyed, sixteen of them beyond repair, in front of Junior College Thursday, February 23, between 9:30 and 11:00 a.m., the day after the price of parking was doubled. Officer Zahn remarked that "They said that they would get us when we put them (new meters) up. He was apparently referring to the heckling officers received when the ticketing a student vehicle.

Gerald Hanson, parking supervisor for the city, estimated damage at $1000. He said that the fine would be at least $100 plus 30 days in jail for each offense. Apparently a blunt object such as a tire iron or hammer was used to inflict the damage by striking the meter on the top and the window.

When a *Collegiate* reporter and photographer appeared on the scene, an officer shouted: "Why don't you take a picture of this and put it on the front page of your paper." He was referring to the picture in the January 13 issue of the *Collegiate* of an officer ticketing a student vehicle.

Several students witnessed the investigation of the incident by police, and one student reflected that the traffic squad in Grand Rapids was more efficient than the detective force. He went on to illustrate his point by telling of the precision with which the officers appear at 3:00 p.m. every day to ticket cars in violation of the 3-6 p.m. traffic lane ordinance.

A $50 reward is offered for information leading to the arrest and conviction of person or persons involved in this destruction of public property. (The *Collegiate* has no information on this).

The administration has promised full cooperation with law enforcement agencies, regardless of what the policy might be about the parking problem in general.

Rates Up
★ ★ ★ ★

City Installs 2-Hour Meters Here But Doubles Hourly Rate

Two hour parking meters have been installed in the vicinity of Junior College. This action was taken as a concession to Junior College students, who are no longer forced to use the old half hour or one hour parking meters.

However, the parking rates have been raised to five cents per half hour or ten cents per hour. The new parking rates are double the old ones.

Ed Matthews, head of the Student Congress Parking Committee, had asked the city parking supervisor to install four-hour meters in the Junior College area. He was told that this could not be done at this time.

The new parking meters are able to take up to four nickels, enabling students to park up to two hours. The meters will not accept dimes or pennies. From 8 a.m. to 7 p.m. the new meters may be used, according to Mr. Richard Wherlly.

According to Al Kypstra, city manager, the change is part of the city's long range planning. Eventually, the city plans removal of metered parking spaces. The long range parking plans of the city result from an independent survey by a research firm, Wilbur Smith and Associates.

However, the city had another reason for the changeover to the two-hour, ten cents per hour parking meters. The city is floating a bond issue of $2,385,000 to provide 662 off street parking spaces in the downtown area. The former parking rate of only five cents per hour reflected adversely on the city. The increased parking rate of ten cents per hour, which is city-wide, makes a difference of one-fourth to one-half per cent in the interest rate the city pays.

Therefore, the decision to raise city parking rates was largely based on the interest rate the city must pay on its parking bond issue. The installation of special two hour parking meters in the Junior College area, bounded by Ransom, Library, and Lyon Streets, is regarded by the traffic division as a concession to Junior College students.

Collegiate Promotes Two
Hoekstra, Humphreys Take New Posts

The *Collegiate* has two new editors. Because of the interest they displayed, Doug Hoekstra and Dan Humphreys have been appointed News Editor and Managing Editor, respectively. These students will serve next year as co-editors.

Both Hoekstra and Humphreys were graduated from South High in June, 1960. They joined the staff in September. Doug was a reporter and political analyst prior to his appointment. Dan writes a column which appears under his cartoon in each issue. He also sells advertising.

Doug plans to transfer to Michigan State and pursue a Journalism curriculum. Dan wants to go to the University of Michigan to take a Liberal Arts course, and major in English.

The Parking Problem

In 1914, the GRJC parking problem was solved with bicycle racks. Fifty years later, 3,500 students found themselves having to make do with metered street parking and one expensive 300-space private lot across from the Main Building. College enrollment increased dramatically through the 1960s, and so did the parking problem. The lead story in the March 3, 1961, *Junior Collegiate* detailed the destruction of 65 new parking meters installed on or near the college campus. The city had not only metered previously free spaces, but had doubled the per-hour rate. The mystery meter raiders left a note warning "I hope you guys value your jobs. Change or else."

Meanwhile, GRJC and the city were brainstorming ideas for a downtown cultural complex with the college and a new parking ramp at the center. Plans for the complex developed and changed; funding came and went. By 1965, Superintendent Jay Pylman was no longer fighting for a cultural complex but for the desperately-needed college parking facility. He met with resistance from Mayor Christian Sonneveldt who felt Civic Auditorium parking represented a greater need. In 1966, board of education member Robert Jonkhoff blasted the city for "the inexcusable delay" on college parking. GRJC students spent time picketing city hall. Parking had become the college's most pressing problem.

In 1972, the college and board of education, after years of

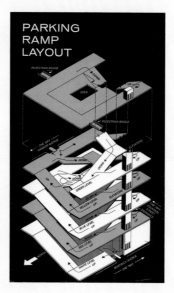

PARKING RAMP LAYOUT

(above) "Sixty-five Parking Meters Smashed in the College Area: $1,000 Damage Follows Hiked Rate," *The Junior Collegiate*. March 3, 1961. (GRCC Archives); (top center) Student discussing parking issue with police officer, undated. (GRCC Archives); (right) Bostwick parking ramp, undated. (GRCC Archives); (far right) Bostwick parking ramp layout. (GRCC Archives); (page 73) Lyon Street parking ramp dedication, 1994. (GRCC Archives)

wrangling with the city, dedicated a 1,600-space, multi-tiered parking facility in the center of campus, with "crossovers" leading to college buildings. The facility would be overcrowded within two years, but its presence helped cool what had been the hottest of student grievances.

As part of construction of the Student Community Center, 250 spaces were added to the parking facility in 1981. In 1994, with college enrollment at more than 14,000 students, a second parking ramp (750 spaces) was opened on the corner of Lyon and Bostwick.

commissioned by a panel of local citizens and international art experts. This soaring sculpture motivated, in 1970, the first Festival of the Arts centered on the work itself. A modest affair at the start, Festival exploded into one of the largest and most vibrant arts festivals in the country, hosting as many as half a million people over a long weekend.

Yet another sign of hope came from a growing GRJC campus (a blend of old and new, committed to downtown), with a student body of 6,000 and all its accompanying energy and diversity. Today, GRCC students (numbering close to 17,000), mingling with student populations of other downtown colleges and universities, fill the central city with as many as 25,000 students each day. Fully recognizing the area's promise, local philanthropists, arts enthusiasts, and entrepreneurs have for some years provided the vision, investment, and facilities necessary to a cultural and commercial renaissance.

Collective Bargaining, a New Era

McCarthy's tenure was marked by some profound changes in the relationship of faculty and administration. When in 1966, the State of Michigan granted public employees the right to collective bargaining, an existing Faculty Advisory Council (soon renamed the Faculty Council and, in 1974, the Faculty Association)—made up of representatives from the nine divisions—suddenly found itself in a position to effect changes in faculty salaries, benefits, working conditions, and college policy making. A negotiating team, appointed by the Council—now the legal representative body of the faculty—began hammering out improved contracts by means of direct bargaining with the board. Early Faculty Council leaders included Charles Chanter, Jack VanAartsen, and Dick Godfrey. Rollie Lubbinga, the industrial arts instructor who served as first chief negotiator

1965-75

1966

1966 Michigan public employees gain right to collective bargaining.

1967

Memorial Campus, 1966. (GRCC Archives)

American civil rights movement figure, writer, and political adviser James Meredith spoke on-campus.

The Women's League sponsored "International Night" where foreign students spoke and shared their native costumes.

Associate Degree Nursing program established.

1968

A Citizens and Alumni Committee, brought together by Superintendent Pylman, was charged with conducting a survey of past achievements and present status of the Junior College and then making concrete recommendations to the Board of Education concerning the college's future needs.

Grand Rapids Junior College
1914 ~ 1974

A
Self
Analysis

prepared for the
North Central Association of
Colleges and Secondary Schools
Commission on Institutions of Higher Education

(**Figure 66a & b**) *Grand Rapids Junior College 1914-1974: A Self Analysis.* (GRCC Archives)

Another break with tradition was the abolition of the bimonthly faculty meetings, a fact which, in all honesty, was applauded by both faculty and administration alike. The positive results of such a decision were freedom in scheduling, decentralization of some decision-making to the divisional level (each division now met once a month), a salutary sense of breaking with what had long been looked upon as a vestigal holdover from K-12, and freedom from what had become an admittedly artificial committee structure.

However, these changes -- collective negotiations with its adversarial character, and breaking with the traditions of the past -- were to result ultimately in a growing, ill-defined malaise. To be sure this malaise was not simply the result of these two factors. Growing problems associated with a decline in liberal arts enrollment with the corollary problems of possible staff reduction coupled with incursions by the state legislature into the arena of faculty load, and more particularly community college redistricting, exacerbated the malaise. This latter item, community college redistricting, is significant enough to be dealt with separately later in this narrative.

Suffice it to say, administrators and many faculty began to discuss quite openly as early as 1968 (although in a somewhat disorganized fashion) measures for dealing with some of the fundamental problems besetting the College. For example, regarding communication, various approaches were discussed; some were tried and discarded, others were retained. Faculty-administrative coffee klatsches, committees, faculty memos, newsletters, daily bulletins, monthly bulletins, and the like were promoted. Concerns vis-à-vis administrative-student relationships resulted in a monthly luncheon meeting with selected students and student leaders. Advertising ventures both sophisticated and unsophisticated resulted in greater faculty-

for the Council, proved so effective in crafting the initial contract that the board hired him away as its chief negotiator.

As reported in the June 2, 1966, *The Grand Rapids Press*, Junior College instructors and the Grand Rapids Association of Educational Secretaries were the first groups to settle contracts with the board. The JC faculty saw salary gains both in day and evening colleges, a reduction in increments, increases in remuneration for music directors, coaches, and *The Collegiate* advisor, health and retirement benefits, and the creation of a grievance procedure. These were significant gains and cause for celebration for the entire GRJC community. A 1974 GRJC self-study entitled *A Self Analysis*, (in a section written by McCarthy himself) spoke of the many positive effects of collective bargaining, yet made note of a "growing, ill-defined malaise" affecting the college, the result of what McCarthy saw as the increasingly adversarial nature of the bargaining process. (**Figure 66a & b**) As equitable as the process was, it would in time create something of an "us vs. them" relationship between faculty and administration, dampening a spirit of trust and cooperation.

That said, the common concern for quality education often resulted in strong cooperative efforts, particularly when reduced state revenues threatened the college's well being. According to those involved on both sides of the table, the first decades of the negotiating process were carried on with surprisingly little negative spirit.

Signs of the Times

The McCarthy years were a time of unprecedented growth

(**Figure 67**) Black Student Union office, 1978. (GRCC Archives)

and change for the college, but also a time of nationwide turmoil, of riots in prisons and cities (Grand Rapids included), of anti-Vietnam protest, of the gathering of Black Power and militant feminist movements, of student protestors occupying public buildings—a prevailing spirit of youthful revolt against entrenched values. Though Grand Rapids Junior College was no Berkeley, it was not untouched by national events. *The Collegiate* began publishing supportive editorials about the Black Panthers and Students for a Democratic Society, stories opposing the Vietnam War, letters taking Grand Rapids to task for discriminating against hippies, ads for Floyd Bloss's Capri Theater and its triple X films, with accompanying editorials defending Bloss's rights. *Collegiate* columnists representing the

interests of a rapidly-expanding Black Students' Union (225 members by 1972, with new Language Arts instructor, Pat Pulliam and, later, counselor Tempi Hoskins, serving as advisors) celebrated the beauty of blackness and the collective strength of the race. (**Figure 67**) In spite of (or because of) controversial material, the Michigan Collegiate Press Association named *The Collegiate* the Best Junior College Newspaper in Michigan for 1969. That year, GRJC students joined a nationwide Vietnam Moratorium, with a march down Fountain Street hill, followed by a teach-in opposing the United States' involvement in the war. In other arenas, GRJC students loudly picketed City Hall to protest foot-dragging about construction of a student parking ramp, and the JC Inter-Varsity Christian

1965-75

1968

GRJC students participated in the nationwide Vietnam Moratorium, which included a march down Fountain Street hill.

The football team won the Wool Bowl in Roswell, New Mexico by a score of 24-0 over Henderson Junior College on December 12, 1968. (1968 Wool Bowl billboard. GRCC Archives)

1969

The Collegiate was named best junior college paper in Michigan by the Michigan Collegiate Press Association for the first time in its history.

The token system was implemented for parking. This system would be in place for the next 35 years.

GRAND RAPIDS JUNIOR COLLEGE PARKING

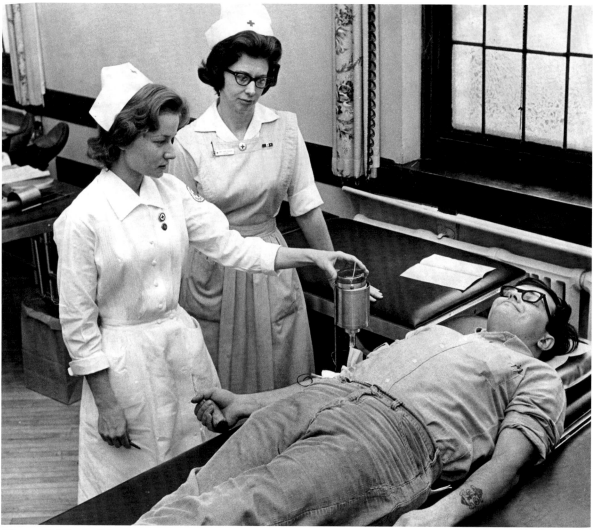

(Figure 68) "Bleed-in" for Vietnam War, 1965. (GRCC Archives)

Fellowship sponsored "Bleed-ins" to provide blood for those wounded in Vietnam. **(Figure 68)**

Growth and More Change

In his 10 years as dean, McCarthy saw enrollment increase from 3,600 to more than 6,000 students. With the establishment of 12 new occupational curriculums that attracted many adults seeking job training and retraining, a pioneer program for displaced homemakers called "Women in Transition" (the

college would become a haven for a growing population of women striving to improve their lives), the 1974 founding of a Laboratory Preschool inspired by Anne Mulder and Phyllis Fratzke (directed by Marilyn Kovach) as well as increased offerings in adult and continuing education, the average age of the GRJC student rose from 19 to 26. To accommodate this new population, evening and weekend sections were added to college offerings.

The McCarthy years saw a larger percentage of new faculty and staff hired than at any other period in college history. In 1965, Don Black became the assistant dean of student services, with Betty DeYoung assisting him. Gene Paxton joined PE as basketball coach, David Clark as swimming coach. In Language Arts alone, nine new full-time faculty signed contracts, in Social Sciences, five, in Physical Sciences, three, in Life Sciences, two.

In April of 1966, Tom Hofmann, an all-star baseball player at Aquinas College, took over the baseball team from Webb Marris. Language Arts instructor Bill Dix developed and introduced a two-course sequence of English Literature. The following fall, 25 more full-time faculty would join the college. Anthony LaPenna would replace Robert Riekse as registrar and director of admissions, and Emil Caprara became head wrestling coach, leading the wrestling team to state championships in his first two years.

The later 1960s saw several "firsts" for the college. A 1965 course in nuclear chemistry, developed and taught by Ron Edwards, was the first in a Michigan community college. In 1967, GRJC's first Director of Housing, John Boerema, was appointed—not to oversee campus housing, which did not exist, but to attempt to set housing policy for local landlords and the students who rented from them. The policy specified that "no member of the opposite sex will ever be allowed into a room or apartment,

(**Figure 69**) 1968 Wool Bowl program. (GRCC Archives)

except for members of the immediate family." It strictly prohibited drinking, drugs, gambling, and profanity.[1] As one might expect, the housing policy was largely ignored. In 1967, civil rights activist James Meredith spoke on campus; consumer advocate Ralph Nader and theologian Dr. Francis Schaeffer followed in 1968. John Ham, the gentle birdman of the Biology Department, began advertising for dead bird specimens in *The*

Collegiate. The same year, Jean Reed won the Miss Grand Rapids Junior College and Miss Michigan Junior College pageants; English instructor Elaine Clarke introduced a Children's Literature course; Fine Arts and Language Arts Divisions offered a team-taught Humanities course developed by English instructor Jay Lieffers, music instructor Charles Buffham, and art instructor Glen Raymond. The Hunsberger-led football team received an invitation to the Wool Bowl in Roswell, New Mexico, which they won by a score of 24-0 over Henderson County Junior College from Texas. It was the team's first win in a national bowl game. (**Figure 69**)

Despite these positive events, the McCarthy years revealed a slow, curious change in student participation in extracurricular activities. Interest in Student Congress, in college clubs (with the exception of the Black Students' Union) and organizations began to fall off. Sports events, once so enthusiastically supported, began to see attendance diminish. Some staff attributed it to a higher percentage of working students who lacked time for activities, some to an increasingly older student body with family and work commitments. Others felt it was the serious and cynical spirit of the times, the increasingly "commuter" nature of the college, or simply apathy. Whatever the reasons, the college was changing, and so were the activities its students pursued.

Growth continued at a dizzying pace. The fall of 1968 saw 20 more new faculty added, eight in Language Arts. New divisional chairs were named in Business (Charles Chanter), Language Arts (Marinus Swets), and Physical Education (C. Richard Smith). Within a few short years, both student body and faculty had nearly doubled in size.

1965-75

1970

The Black Student Union formally established to celebrate the beauty of blackness and the collective strength of the race (The Black Student Union dance, 1978. GRCC Archives)

Resident tuition was $210.00 per year.

1971

The North Building opened August 24, 1971. Located on the corner of Bostwick and Lyon, this was the first new structure in the college's history. Connected to the Main Building on Bostwick Avenue, the seven-story structure initially contained general purpose classrooms, technology and health education laboratories, library accommodations, a Student Center and Student Services area, and one floor devoted to the administrative offices of the Grand Rapids Board of Education.

Dental Hygiene program was established.

(**Figure 70**) North Building, 1971. (GRCC Archives)

Citizens and Alumni Committee Recommendations

In March of 1968, a Citizens and Alumni Committee, brought together by Superintendent Pylman, was charged with conducting a survey of past achievements and present status of the Junior College and then making concrete recommendations to the board of education concerning the college's future needs. Their first and most pointed piece of advice was this:

> *That the Grand Rapids Board of Education initiate by appropriate resolution the establishment of a community college district to be composed of all the school districts that make up the Kent Intermediate District with the contemplated expansion to include those school districts in Ottawa County serving the Jenison and Hudsonville areas.*[2]

Further recommendations went as follows: that the tax base for the new community college be the Kent Intermediate School District, and that a levy not exceed two mills; that the college remain downtown; and that it construct a student parking ramp as quickly as possible.

Referendum Crushed

Most board of education members were in agreement with the committee's conclusions. Yet in spite of that support, a redistricting referendum presented to the voters in 1974 was voted down by a crushing two-to-one margin. If the educational community was ready for the change, the voters were not. It would be 17 years before another redistricting vote was attempted. Yet as a result of the intensive airing of problems and recommendations, an unforeseen sea change, a deepened understanding between the Junior College and the GRPS, transpired. The board of education, now more fully-attuned to the college's needs, began to grant the college a greater independence.

The North Building— The College's First New Facility

Under the administrative leadership of Superintendent Pylman and Dean McCarthy, plans for the classroom building known as the Junior College North Building got underway in 1967. The $3.3 million price tag would be split evenly by the board of education and the state. By the time the building was dedicated in 1971, Pylman had resigned, Norman P. Weinheimer had spent a brief two years in the superintendent's job, and Dr. Phillip E. Runkel had succeeded him. Though Runkel would prove a dynamic leader with a deep interest in the college, McCarthy found him a more difficult presence than Pylman.[3]

Opening to students on August 24, 1971, the North Building was the first new structure in the college's 57-year history. (**Figure 70**) According to the *North Central Report of 1974*, the

(**Figure 71**) Bostwick parking ramp aerial, 1977. (GRCC Archives)

1972

The college signed the Michigan Association of Collegiate Registrars and Admissions Officers (MACRAO) Agreement to facilitate transfer from community colleges to baccalaureate colleges and universities.

The Bostwick Parking Ramp opened, providing 1,600 parking spaces in the center of campus, with elevated crosswalks leading to college buildings. An additional 250 spaces were added in 1980.

Radiologic Technology program started.

The college purchased the building that had previously housed the Grand Rapids School of Bible and Music at 226 Bostwick Avenue NE. This four-story building became known as the G Building and housed a food service area, 15 classrooms, and six offices. G Building. (GRCC Archives)

college's physical plant was "a mixture of the most modern and (almost) luxurious in buildings and equipment and…the most dilapidated and outmoded." Connected to the Main Building on Bostwick Avenue, the new seven-story structure contained 17 general purpose classrooms, nine much-needed technology laboratories, 14 health education laboratories allowing immediate expansion of medical training, 52 office spaces, 11 conference areas, library accommodations, a Student Center and Student Services area, two lower floors of parking, and one floor (the fifth) devoted to the administrative offices of the Grand Rapids Board of Education. The reinforced concrete structure with column, joist and pan construction, permitted future

modification by simple relocation of walls.[4] Over the years, as the campus has expanded and instructional departments have shifted about, the versatile building has been modified numerous times to accommodate them.

Parking at Last, the G Building, and the Learning Resource Center

In 1972, the college and board of education, after years of wrangling with the city, were able to build a 1,600-space multi-tiered parking facility in the center of campus, with "crossovers" leading to college buildings. (**Figure 71**) The parking facility would be overcrowded within two years,

(**Figure** 72) Learning Center, undated. (GRCC Archives)

housed the college library directed by John Lally, three audio-visual labs, a materials preparation area, a TV production area, a photographic lab, six offices and three general classrooms.[5] The East Building's 1922 gymnasium addition remained, to be used by the Physical Education Department until their new facility, already in the planning stages, could be built. The red brick building would continue standing beyond its scheduled demolition, eventually assuming an altogether different purpose for its existence.

The Health Division Expands

When the Associate Degree Nursing Program was established at last in 1967, (**Figure** 73) Dorothy Koelbl became its director, followed by Joan Berends, and the program flourished. Later directors of a combined ADN and LPN program would include Bobbi Schrader, Nicky Pelissier, Donna Adams, Sue Wombach, Marilyn Smidt, Dr. Margaret Bowles, and Michelle Richter. The Dental Hygiene Program was introduced in 1971, Maureen Munger directing, and the Radiologic Technology Program in 1972, headed by John Godisak. Each program found a home, modern laboratories, and state-of-the-art equipment in the North Building. As a medical complex expanded near the college, the Health Division would continue to grow in size and significance, and consistently place most of its graduating students. (**Figure** 74)

MACRAO Agreement, Celebrations, Honors, and More Changes

1972 marked a major step forward for the college's transfer programs—the signing of the Michigan Association of Collegiate Registrars and Admissions Officers (MACRAO) Agreement, greatly easing the transfer of credits from two-year to four-

but its presence helped cool what had been the hottest of student grievances.

In the same year, McCarthy and the board struck a deal for the purchase of a four-story classroom building that had formerly housed the Grand Rapids School of Bible and Music. It was named the G Building, and the facility proved as undistinguished as its name. In immediate need of remodeling, the G Building contained a food service area, 15 classrooms, and six offices.

After the parking facility became reality, a third new building, the Learning Resource Center (or simply the Learning Center), funded by the Grand Rapids Board of Education, the State of Michigan, and the U.S. Department of Health, Education, and Welfare, opened in the fall of 1973, located on the eastern perimeter of the campus where the East Building, now history, had stood. (**Figure** 72) The Learning Center

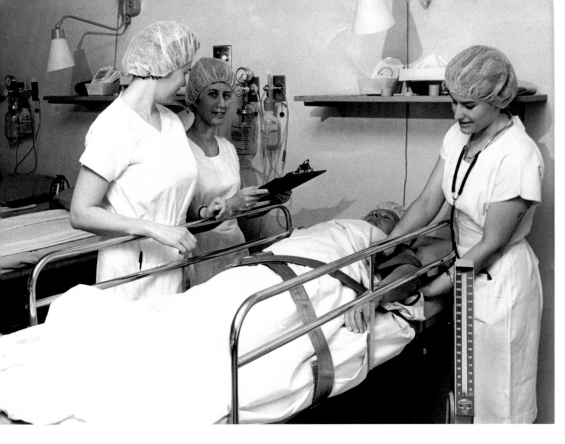

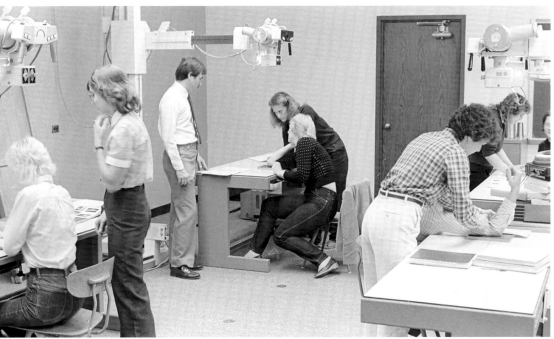

year colleges and universities. It provided and continues to provide for the full transfer of community college credits to meet the general education requirements of participating four-year institutions. (The MACRAO is to be replaced in the summer of 2014 by the new Michigan Transfer Agreement.)

In July 1971, passage of the 26th Amendment to the U.S. Constitution prohibited states and the federal government from setting a voting age higher than 18. In 1972, Michigan lawmakers lowered the legal drinking age to 18 (though a petition drive in 1978 helped return it to 21). New Title IX legislation gave women equal access to programs and sports. The long Vietnam War came to an end in 1973, followed by an end to the draft. Students heaved a collective sigh of relief and went out to vote and celebrate.

In the fall of 1971, speech instructor Peter Northouse introduced a course in interpersonal communications; Northouse soon left the

(**top, Figure 73**) Associate Degree Nursing, 1967. (GRCC Archives)
(**left, Figure 74**) Radiology Technology, 1983. (GRCC Archives)

1965-75

1973

The Learning Resource Center (LRC) opened in the fall of 1973, housing the college library, audiovisual labs, a TV production area, a photographic lab, and three general classrooms.

Two hospitality programs were introduced, a one-year Food Service Certificate and a two-year associate degree in Hotel and Restaurant Management.

Automotive Technology program started.

The Women's Resource Center was established.

Wrestling team won the Region XII championship and placed third in the national tournament where GRJC wrestlers Charlie Wells and Bob Ankney claimed individual titles and were named first team All Americans.

GRJC Cafeteria, 1973. (GRCC Archives)

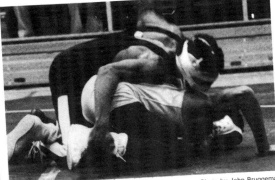

Photo by John Bruggema

Nat'l. Champ Charles Wells in action

Wells, Ankney claim titles

JC used four wrestlers to place third in the National tournament held in Worthington, Minn., on March 1—3. The third place finish was JC's best ever.

CHARLIE WELLS, AND Bob Ankney showed their prowess on the mats by winning five bouts apiece to claim National championships, and first team All-American status.

Wells pinned last year's run-nerup, in 7:41 while Ankney wrestled his tough opponent to an 8—5 decision.

Harold King lost a bout in the quarter finals, but wrestled back to win on an 11—6 decision for fifth place.

Terry Baer lost a first round match on riding time, and didn't receive an opportunity to wrestle back.

JC WAS THE only team which claimed two individual championships.

The Raiders highest previous placement was fourth in 1971 and last year the grapplers placed ninth.

Northern Iowa was the team champion with nine wrestlers tallying 72.5 points. Northern Idaho's eight wrestlers scored 44.5 points, to place second. Junior College with only three point producers, chalked up 41 points for a third place tie with defending champion New York.

Muskegon CC, JC's arch rival finished in tenth position.

Coach Emil Caprara's mat-

men scored a stunning upset win in the regional finals on Saturday, February 17th.

JC paced the meet with 54 points. Second and third place went to Cuyahoga West with 53.5 points and Cuyahoga Metro with 53 points. Both schools are from Ohio.

Muskegon CC, which easily dominated Junior College in the State meet finished a distant fourth with 37.5 points to further enhance the Raider victory.

JC brought only six men to the tournament, and wrestled five as Dave Vibber (118) became ill before the meet began.

The Raider grapplers trailed each of the Ohio schools by six points at the beginning of the championship bouts.

JC'S CHARLIE WELLS* headed for a possible National championship, got the Raiders on the move with decision in the 134 pound weight class. Terry Baer wrestled next, but lost (142) before Bob Ankney and Harold King won at (177) and (190), respectively.

King scored a win in a very close match by a 5-4 decision over his opponent to secure the meet for the Raiders.

Bob Ankney's match, a win by disqualification, also proved vital as it was scored as a "pinpoint", or, in effect, four points for the win instead of three for a decision win.

college and Ken Bultman took over the development and teaching of the popular course. In May of 1973, GRJC wrestlers Charlie Wells and Bob Ankney claimed the national wrestling championship and were named first team All-Americans. **(Figure 75)** In September of 1973, sax man Ray Gill joined the Music Department to lead the jazz ensemble, and Douglas Scripps, Director of Instrumental Music, became interim director of the Grand Rapids Symphony. In February of 1974, Dave Clark's GRJC swim team won the state championship. Clark was named Michigan's Coach of the Year, and soon after, the National Coach of the Year. In 1974, the Michigan Collegiate Press Association named *The Collegiate* to six first-place awards, *Display* magazine to a first-place for Best Layout and the award for Best Overall Literary Magazine. In the fall of 1974, the college also mourned the passing of Assistant Dean of Students, Don Black, who had suffered from leukemia.

The Orange Arrow

Language Arts would spend far longer than anyone anticipated (16 years) in the drab confines of the West Building. In 1973, Language Arts instructor Keith Longberg, in protest of the deadening sameness of the building's institutional beige color scheme, painted a bright orange stripe the width of

(**Figure 75**) "Wells, Ankney claim titles" *The Collegiate.* March 9, 1973. (GRCC Archives)

a paint roller from the sixth-floor elevator down 200 feet of hallway, around a corner where it became an arrow pointing to his office. Bill Siemion, the college's legendary plant engineer, who knew the workings of every dial, valve, and circuit breaker on campus—and who struck fear into the hearts of even upper administrators—was speechless at the sight of this desecration. When he at last found words, he delivered a short, unprintable speech, impressive in its power and clarity. Longberg was called into Frank McCarthy's office. The Dean was uncertain about an appropriate course of action. Longberg asked him if anybody besides Siemion had complained about the orange stripe. McCarthy had to admit that no one had. "Then it's no problem," Longberg reasoned. "Oh—and I won't do it again." Siemion had the last word, however. One of his crews quietly removed the orange stripe the following day, and Longberg received a bill for it. Language Arts friends, in the name of aesthetics, took up a collection.[6]

North Central Report and a Transformative Steering Committee

The *1974 North Central Report*, containing the accrediting commission's conclusions and recommendations after a visit to the college and close examination of GRJC's self-study, laid the groundwork for some transformative moments in board/college relations. The commission strongly recommended that the college and board set limits on faculty overtime, offer more extensive remediation to students with deficiencies in English and math, expand the Nursing Program, improve the outmoded and inadequate facilities of the Industrial and Mechanical Division (located in the basement of the Main Building), and vacate the "drab, inadequate" West Building. More important, though, was a suggested rethinking of the college's administrative make-up.

Though a redistricting referendum had recently failed and hope for another in the near future was dim, the commission still stated that the image of the college would be immediately enhanced by changing its name to "community college," by naming the chief administrator president rather than dean, and by renaming other administrative positions to align with the chief administrator's new title. "The image of the college," the Commission reported, "suffers from its 'junior college' name and the titles of the top administrators," as well as from its governance by a local board of education.

As a result of that report, Superintendent Runkel appointed a Faculty Steering Committee, charged with reviewing the entire North Central evaluation and making recommendations for change to the superintendent and the board. The Steering Committee was divided into subcommittees. One of them, with a focus on administration and made up of Jack VanAartsen (Chair of the Faculty Council), Dr. Robert Riekse, (now faculty), and Bob Chase (business faculty), carried in writing to Runkel a plan for a full reorganization of the college administration as well as the board and superintendent's relationship to it. Built into the plan was a college with a stronger say in its own destiny and a chief administrator with his hand (instead of the superintendent's) on the wheel.

It was not clear whether Runkel was happy with these ideas, but he listened, and (according to Jack VanAartsen) seemed grateful.[7] Runkel took the subcommittee's ideas to the board. He also sought the opinion of one of his closest associates, Assistant Superintendent Richard Calkins, who was impressed with the spirit of the document. What transpired thereafter—the realization of most of the Steering Committee's goals (except a change of the college's name)—amounted to a reinvention of the character of Grand Rapids Junior College.[8] To the surprise of nearly everyone, it also resulted in the appointment of a new college president.

1974

Swim team won state championship and finished second at the National Swimming and Diving Meet.

Enrollment was 6,054.

A redistricting referendum to separate the college from the K-12 district was voted down.

The Michigan Collegiate Press Association named *The Collegiate* to six first-place awards and *Display* magazine to a first-place for Best Layout and the award for Best Overall Literary Magazine.

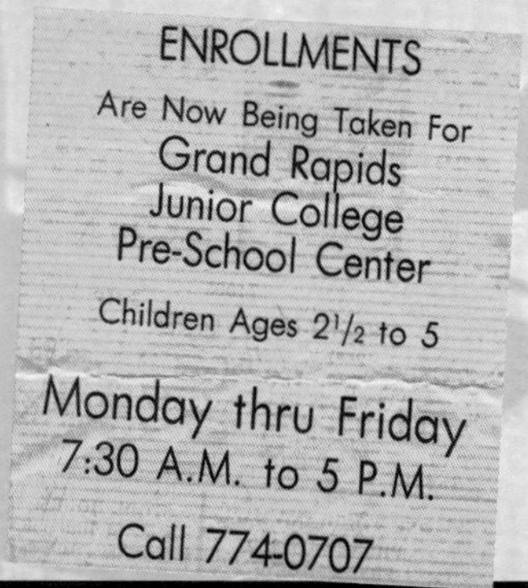

ENROLLMENTS
Are Now Being Taken For
Grand Rapids
Junior College
Pre-School Center

Children Ages 2½ to 5

Monday thru Friday
7:30 A.M. to 5 P.M.

Call 774-0707

The Pre-school opened in the First United Methodist Church located on the corner of Barclay and Fulton. The facility provided a quality center for the children of students, faculty, staff and community members and a practicum for students in the child care curriculum. (Preschool enrollment ad. (GRCC Archives)

Members of the GRJC jazz band and Director Charles Buffham (sitting far right) at Calder Plaza, 1973. (GRCC Archives).

The Builders: The Calkins Years—Part One 1975-84

Richard W. Calkins

Though more academician than visionary leader, Frank McCarthy had done nothing tangible to warrant being replaced as the college chief administrator. He had maintained positive relationships with faculty and staff, had grown the college dramatically, accommodating spectacular increases in enrollment. He had hired a great many able faculty, introduced a myriad of new programs, and calmly navigated the upheavals of student unrest. Yet Superintendent Runkel was not about to entrust broad new administrative freedoms to someone he did not know well. Richard W. Calkins, 36-year-old Assistant Superintendent of Personnel and Community Services, former vocal music teacher at Creston High School, had been one of Runkel's most trusted associates for five years. **(Figure 76)** Shortly after their discussion of Steering Committee recommendations, Runkel had looked at Calkins and said "How will you like being president of the college?" Calkins was stunned at this unexpected turn. The offer hung in the air. When he finally said yes, it was on one condition—that Runkel would give him the freedom to lead the college without interference. "Runkel agreed and never backed down on his promise. My years with him were very honest," Calkins said later.[1] It was a giant step toward self-determination, a movement Calkins would guide to full realization.

Within the space of a few days the board of education had approved Calkins' appointment as the seventh chief executive (once again president) of Grand Rapids Junior College. Frank

(**Figure 76**) Richard W. Calkins, seventh leader of GRJC. (GRCC Archives)

McCarthy, given the new title of executive vice president of academic affairs, was now second in command. The demotion was a bitter pill for McCarthy, who, within several months, left the college to become president of Grand Rapids Osteopathic Hospital, a position in which he again found fulfillment and success. Calkins, as it turned out, would lead the college for the next 23 years—arguably the most visionary and productive of GRJC presidents. Superintendent Runkel, it seemed, had chosen wisely and well.

Richard W. (Dick) Calkins was a native of Grand Rapids, a 1956 graduate of Creston High School. Earning his B.A. at Albion College and M.A. at MSU (where he also finished coursework for a Ph.D.), he returned to Creston High School with wife and family to become a highly successful vocal music director who traveled the country with his choirs and recorded their concerts to raise funds. In 1967, the Grand Rapids Jaycees named him the "Outstanding Educator of the Year." A singer and pianist himself, he served as director of music at Eastminster Presbyterian Church and the Schubert Club of Grand Rapids. He later would serve as president of the board of trustees for the Arts Council of Greater Grand Rapids. In 1969, Superintendent Runkel hired him to be the board's assistant director of personnel. He proved a highly competent administrator, closely mentored by Runkel in educational politics (both local and state), staff selection, fund-raising, and millage campaigns—yet few would have guessed Runkel saw in him the makings of a college president.

Richard W. Calkins became the college's seventh leader. He would oversee the establishment of numerous programs including Theater, Computer Applications, Photography and Culinary Arts. Under Calkins, building continued in earnest: the Ford Health and Physical Education Center, the Music Center, the Student Community Center, the McCabe-Marlowe house, and the Applied Technology Center. Calkins addressed diversity in both the student body and staff through the development of the Women's Resource Center, the Council for Minority Concerns, and the Handicapped Student Programs. Calkins also guided the college through the process of separating from the K-12 system and becoming an independent institution.

Women's basketball team won the state championship. (1974-75 women's basketball team. GRCC Archives)

The original Spectrum Theater opened in the former Violet Chapel located on Crescent Street.

(**Figure 77**) *The Collegiate* office with advisor Keith Longberg (center), 1977. (GRCC Archives)

Administrative Reorganization

By December of 1975, just four months into his presidency, Calkins had begun his reorganization, doubling the size of McCarthy's 11-person administrative staff. Among his new appointees were Cornelius (Corky) Eringaard, Administrative Assistant (soon to be executive vice president), who would prove a perfect second in command to Calkins. Calkins, the visionary, would focus on the administrative and planning side of the college; Eringaard, an academic with strong people skills, would capably lead a diverse faculty.

Other appointees included Don Maine, Director of Public Information and Development (soon to be dean of Occupational Education), Anne Mulder, Director of Community Services (soon to be assistant dean of Continuing Education), Bob Chase, Administrative Assistant to the President (soon to be acting dean of Continuing Education, following Wendell Shroll's retirement), Dr. Louis Murillo, Director of Career Planning and Placement

(soon to be assistant to the president), Andre van Niekerk, Director of Career Planning and Placement (soon to be assistant dean of Student Services), Dr. Allen Jackson, Dean of College Services, and Betty Robbins, Director of Student Activities. Within a year Calkins appointed three former GRPS employees to administrative positions: Darrell Weller, Registrar, Donald Shriemer, Director of Financial Aid, and Dr. Ray Boozer, Dean of Continuing Education.

In the fall of 1976, in a move demonstrating its understanding and support of the college, the Grand Rapids Board of Education formed a subcommittee known as Community Relations, made up of several seated board members meeting to consider GRJC business separate from that of GRPS.

The Collegiate Gets a New Advisor

In the spring of 1976, Calkins named Dr. Marinus Swets (Language Arts chair, *Collegiate* advisor) Dean of Arts and Sciences. Language Arts instructor Keith Longberg stepped forward to assume leadership of the journalism program and the college newspaper. Under his tutelage, *The Collegiate* continued its successful ways, in the process growing larger and more comprehensive in its coverage. (**Figure 77**) Lucille Thomas replaced Swets as chair of Language Arts.

Work to be Done

Calkins spent his initial months getting to know the college and its people. He was distressed that the engineering program was "in the bowels of the Main Building basement." The West Building was not only drab and inadequate, as the North Central report had expressed it, but it also was isolated from the Main campus. Since 1968, the Language Arts Division and Music Department had occupied the building. Music, especially—

located on the third floor—lacked satisfactory practice, rehearsal, and performance areas. Calkins was sensitive to those deficiencies. Both students and faculty felt separated from the Main campus by the great dividing wall that was Division Avenue. He made it a priority to move them onto campus as quickly as possible.

The Ford Health and Physical Education Center

Calkins had even more pressing matters to see to. A new $5 million physical education facility was in the works. Named after the 38th President of the United States, the Gerald R. Ford

(left, Figure 78) Gerald R. Ford Fieldhouse, late 1970s. (GRCC Archives)
(below, Figure 79) President Gerald R. Ford (left) and his wife Betty (right) with President Calkins, faculty member Dick Godfrey, and Superintendent Runkel at the Gerald R. Ford Fieldhouse dedication, September 1976. (GRCC Archives)

Health and Physical Education Center—with its Olympic-sized swimming pool in an attached wing—was scheduled for dedication in the fall of 1976. **(Figure 78)** One of Calkins' earliest challenges was to raise money to commission a five-by-sixty-foot bas relief frieze to be created by artist and alumnus Lumen Winter for the south exterior wall of the fieldhouse. Winter, sculpting in New York and Italy using marble taken from Italy's Mt. Altismo, conceived a series of scenes from Grand Rapids history. Thanks to grants, raffles, calendar sales, donations, and money from the college Foundation, both the college president and the artist managed to make their deadlines.

In September of 1976, President Gerald Ford was present to dedicate the building in grand style. **(Figure 79)** The facility marked the seventh building on campus and provided the PE Department one of the most comprehensive physical education complexes in West Michigan, serving not only the Junior College, but also Central High School, the Grand Rapids Recreation Department, and the general public. The multipurpose fieldhouse could seat up to 4,000 for large events such as basketball games or graduation ceremonies. The space could be used for an archery range, for three separate basketball courts, for four tennis, badminton, or volleyball courts. A one-tenth mile track encircled the entire fieldhouse area that also provided winter practice space for the baseball team. Besides the natatorium, the various levels of the building contained locker rooms, handball courts, weight training room, dance rooms, and a gymnasium room. After years of making do with

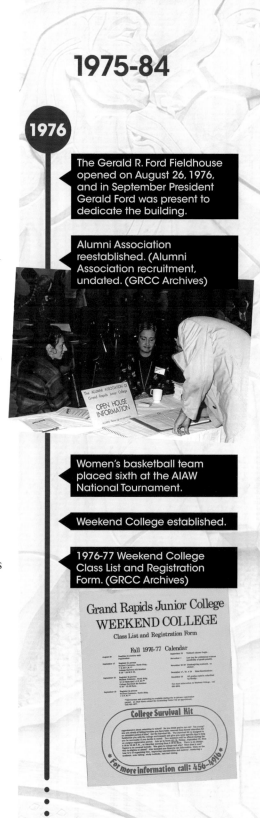

1975-84

1976

The Gerald R. Ford Fieldhouse opened on August 26, 1976, and in September President Gerald Ford was present to dedicate the building.

Alumni Association reestablished. (Alumni Association recruitment, undated. (GRCC Archives)

Women's basketball team placed sixth at the AIAW National Tournament.

Weekend College established.

1976-77 Weekend College Class List and Registration Form. (GRCC Archives)

Grand Rapids Junior College
WEEKEND COLLEGE
Class List and Registration Form

Fall 1976-77 Calendar

College Survival Kit

* For more information call: 456-4910 *

Great American Talk Festival

In the fall of 1976, Robert Wepman, Arts Coordinator of GRJC, suggested a college-sponsored lecture series as a project for utilizing the college's newly-completed Ford Fieldhouse to enrich student experience of American culture. Wepman's idea involved compressing into an intense six-day period a series of lectures featuring some of the best-known personalities in the nation.

This Great American Talk Festival began in 1977 and continued to 1984, hosting authors, actors, comedians, activists, musicians, journalists and politicians. Profits from ticket sales went directly to the Junior College Foundation scholarship fund—more than $20,000 over the eight-year run of the Festival. The Talk Festival became a hugely popular event in West Michigan and one of the largest and most successful lecture series in the United States.

The following is a list of Great American Talk Festival speakers (in order of appearance) over its eight-year run:

1977	1979	1981	1983
Paul Harvey	Mike Wallace	Morley Safer	David Brinkley
Art Buchwald	Ray Charles	Gerald R. Ford	Dr. Joyce Brothers
Judith Crist	Tony Randall	Edwin Newman	Terry Bradshaw
Dick Gregory	Cleveland Amory	David Brenner	Tom Sullivan
Ralph Nader	Alex Haley	Frank Abagnale	Robert Klein
Carl Bernstein	Ivor Richard	Jayne Kennedy	

1978	1980	1982	1984
			Vladimir Pozner
J. Allen Hynek	Dan Rather	William F. Buckley, Jr.	G. Gordon Liddy and
David Frost	Mark Russell	Pearl Bailey	Timothy Leary
Cicely Tyson	Donald Rumsfeld	Sam Donaldson	Coretta Scott King
Steve Allen	Ann Landers	Vincent Price	John Houseman
Jack Anderson	David Letterman	Steve Landesberg	David Frye and
Phil Donahue	Julian Bond	Irving R. Levine	Carol Leifer

(clockwise from top) David Letterman, 1980 Great American Talk Festival. (GRCC Archives); President Gerald R. Ford, 1981 Great American Talk Festival. (GRCC Archives); Coretta Scott King, 1984 Great American Talk Festival. (GRCC Archives)

(**Figure 80**) Original Spectrum Theater, 1981. (GRCC Archives)

(**Figure 81**) Spectrum Theater, 2012. (GRCC Archives)

borrowed facilities, GRJC students and teams found themselves in a sports paradise.

Spectrum Theater and a Theater Program

When Fred Sebulske began teaching English in 1967, the Delta Sigma theater group had been inactive for some years. Though his stage background was limited, Sebulske heard students expressing a desire for theater at the college. A opportunity soon presented itself in the form of a stage play entitled *Breakfast of Oranges and Blue Shade*, penned by talented creative writing student Joseph Dionne. *Breakfast* served as Sebulske's directing debut. It also planted a seed that would grow into a full-blown theater program.

Violet Chapel, just north of the G Building, had been purchased during McCarthy's tenure. It was a small, adjoining chapel of a Lutheran church the college had razed. Sebulske and fellow English instructor Karin Orr, having now teamed for several years to direct student drama productions on a volunteer basis in assorted cafeterias and lecture halls (and having persuaded Marinus Swets to run an Introduction to Acting class under the umbrella of Language Arts), approached the newly-appointed president with the idea of turning the chapel into a small theater

for college productions. Calkins liked the idea, and Spectrum Theater, opening in late 1975, was the result. (**Figure 80**) From that point, Sebulske and Orr took turns directing college productions in the new theater. By 1979, the two had established a Theater Program (part of the Fine and Performing Arts Division) with 14 theater class offerings. When Orr left the college in 1981, Sebulske became head of the program. He invited Robeson Players and other groups to share the Spectrum space and was the creative force (with the support and fund-raising savvy of Dean Anne Mulder) behind the establishment of Actors' Theater and Actors' Workshop, bringing cutting-edge contemporary theater to the college and community.[2]

In 1995, near the end of his tenure, Calkins would engineer the purchase of the Salvation Army Family Services Building on Fountain Street (formerly a Central Reformed Church office building transformed into an insurance office complex known as the Stoddard Building). Overseen by Sebulske and other knowledgeable theater people, renovations began on what would become the college's new Spectrum Theater—with a Culinary Arts Baking and Pastry Arts Program on the lower level. President Calkins dedicated the exciting new facility on September 18, 1997. (**Figure 81**) Over the years, the prospering Theater Program

1976

Volleyball team finished seventh in national tournament in Miami, Florida.

Fashion Merchandising, Interior/Furnishings, Office Management and Dental Laboratory Technician programs added. (Fashion and Design Club, undated. GRCC Archives)

1977

March 27 · April 1
GRAND OPENING FORD FIELD HOUSE
The great American talk festival

GRJC sponsored the Great American Talk Festival from 1977-84. This successful lecture series featured authors, actors, musicians, journalists, and politicians including Alex Haley, Cicely Tyson, Pearl Bailey, Ray Charles, David Letterman, Mike Wallace, and Dan Rather—48 in all. Profits from Talk Festival ticket sales went directly to college scholarship funds. (Great American Talk Festival bumper sticker. GRCC Archives)

(Figure 82) College television studio, 1980s. (Left to right) Mark Vogel, Tina Lockwood, and Bruce Lockwood. (GRCC Archives)

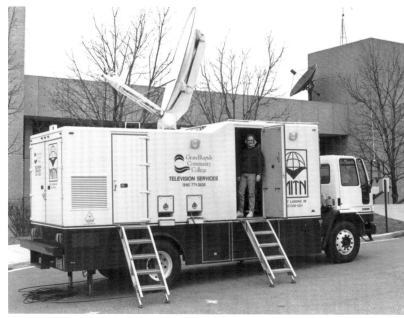

(Figure 83) Mobile Uplink Truck. (GRCC Archives)

has been enriched by the instructional talents of such people as Tom Kaechele (present department head), Michelle Urbane (present theater manager), Jean Reed Bahle, Duane Davis, Don Rice, Rich Rahn, Janet Simpson, Judy Kienitz and others.[3]

An Explosion of Technology—Media Services

The original Media Services staff at the college was simply library staff members who distributed audiovisual equipment to faculty. In 1972, to improve the system, Ron Hoogerwerf was hired as GRJC's first media specialist, replaced in 1976 by Bernice Whitley when Hoogerwerf became acting head of a new Photography Department. Soon Whitley was named director of the Learning Resource Center, and Rob Gutek took over as coordinator of Media Services.

In November of 1978, Superintendent Runkel resigned suddenly to take a similar post in Athens, Greece. His Deputy Superintendent, Dr. John Dow, was named to replace him. Dow was close friends with Calkins and would continue Runkel's policy of full cooperation with the college.

New ideas were in the air, and the President invited their development and actively pursued financing. Calkins proved to be a visionary with true financial acumen, orchestrating a golden age of college expansion. With every new program, he found excellent people, gave them freedom to create, expected no less than their best, and rarely was disappointed. His energy and decisiveness paved the way for rapid change. When Bruce Lockwood, with a background in commercial television, was

The Career Resource Center was established with the mission of helping students, alumni, and community members relate their academic pursuits and personal values to career goals and objectives. Services included career counseling, occupational exploration, career assessment surveys, and testing. The center merged with Counseling in 2006. (Career Resource Center display, 1980. GRCC Archives)

Associate in Photography established.

Handicapped Student Programs organized as the college sought to comply with federal regulations prohibiting discrimination against persons with handicaps.

A $210,000 grant from the National Science Foundation enabled the establishment of a Computer-Based Instruction Center, directed by Ray Hoag.

hired as the college's first television production coordinator, both Calkins and Dean Anne Mulder sensed that the role of Media Services was about to expand miles beyond the distribution of AV equipment.

Lockwood found the available college equipment outdated and inadequate. Calkins supported replacing it, and, helped by grants from the Wege and Grand Rapids Foundations and others, he managed to do just that. When Superintendent Dow suggested merging the GRPS and GRJC Media Departments to streamline services, Calkins approved. As a result, most K-12 equipment came to the college.[4] The merger would ultimately prove a success. Lockwood and his wife Tina, who was director of media for GRPS and became director of Media Services for GRJC/GRPS, began working together—with a young, creative staff (Mark Vogel, and later Klaas Kwant, Jim Schafer, and others) that was instrumental in developing a state-of-the-art studio for video production, cable television stations for both K-12 and higher education, a full range of college telecourses, and college-produced documentaries and television programs. **(Figure 82)** By 1992, Media Services was operating a mobile satellite uplink truck, participating in national television broadcasts. **(Figure 83)** Vogel, Kwant, and Schafer continue to guide Media Services in a role vital to the life of GRCC. Calkins looked upon this department as a shining example for other junior and community colleges.

The Computer Revolution

As the college was experimenting with educational uses of television, another technological innovation, the computer, began to make its presence more strongly felt on campus. Thanks to a $210,000 grant from the National Science Foundation in 1977, a Computer-Based Instruction Center, directed by Ray Hoag,

was established in the college's Learning Resource Center. **(Figure 84)** Eighteen faculty members from the science divisions stepped forward to be trained in computer technology. Excited by the educational potential of computers, the science instructors could not have imagined how vast that potential would prove to be. By 1982, the college, by means of federal vocational education dollars, would purchase 24 Apple computers and establish a new Computer Applications Division. An Academic Computing Center would provide training for faculty and staff. Within 25 years, computers would be vital tools for every student and GRCC classroom.

The Scientific Calculator

In the mid 1970s, Hewlett Packard introduced a hand-held scientific calculator that the Physical Science and Math Division adopted for students. Overnight, the slide rule would become an anachronism. The effect of such rapidly-developing technology

(Figure 84) Ray Hoag, Director of the Computer-Based Instruction Center. (Courtesy of Ray Hoag)

proved both a blessing and a curse to math instruction, according to John Dersch, present chair of the Mathematics Department. On one hand, students were now able to explore areas inaccessible before technology; on the other, they experienced a loss of number sense, a diminished awareness of process. "Though we have been blessed by technology, students are now simply less adept at basic computational skills," Dersch stated.[5]

Bob Wepman, Coordinator for the Arts

One of Calkins' earliest additions to staff was Robert A. (Bob) Wepman, who was given the title coordinator for the arts. Wepman, a flamboyant promoter of the arts in Grand Rapids, business manager for the Grand Rapids Symphony, was a young, supercharged, sometimes controversial figure, "a whirlwind of creativity," Calkins remembered. "Bob would come up with 75 ideas a week. The problem was trying to pick out the one or two that might actually work." With the President's blessing and the active support of Student Activities Director Joyce Hofman and Information Coordinator Mel VandeGevel,

(**left, Figure 85**) Great American Talk Festival. (GRCC Archives)

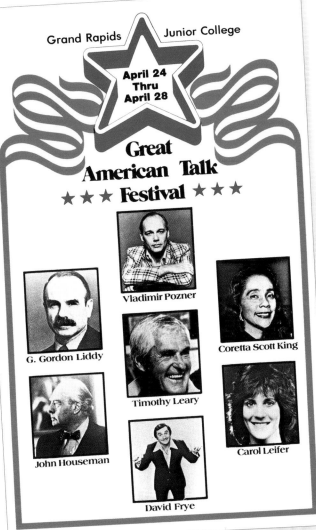

(Figure 86)
1984 Great American Talk Festival program. (GRCC Archives)

Wepman created the Great American Talk Festival, a highly successful lecture series that from 1977-84 packed the Ford Fieldhouse with audiences attracted by such celebrities as Paul Harvey, Alex Haley, Pearl Bailey, Tony Randall, David Letterman, Mike Wallace, Cicely Tyson, and Dan Rather—48 in all. (**Figures 85 & 86**) Profits from Talk Festival ticket sales went directly to college scholarship funds.

Granted broad creative freedoms and intent on making the college and community a mecca for the arts, Wepman promoted the building of a Magnum Opus harpsichord (the world's largest, a gift to the college from the Harry Samrick family of Grand Rapids), which attracted nationally-known musicians to campus. He also secured GRJC "artists in residence" status for the talented New World String Quartet, and was instrumental in bringing a company of New York's Joffrey Ballet to the city.

A Photography Program

September of 1977 marked the unveiling of a new Associates Degree in Photographic Technology, with Ron Hoogerwerf serving as acting head of the program, followed shortly thereafter by Jonathon Russell. Early on, the photography program was

1978

Genetics course offered addressing human heredity and related social issues such as cloning, birth defects, and transsexualism.

First annual Student Congress blood drive brought in 53 pints.

GRJC hosted the National Junior College Athletic Association Swimming and Diving Championship in 1978 and 1979. (1978 NJCAA Swimming and Diving Championships. GRCC Archives)

1979

Occupational Therapy program established.

(**Figure 87**) Culinary Arts students, 1980.
(GRCC Archives)

part of the Public Service Division, and then the Technology Division. When it landed in Fine and Performing Arts, it had at last found a home.

Russell, having just finished graduate school at the Institute of Design in Chicago, was approached by Executive Vice President Corky Eringaard to develop a full photography curriculum at GRJC. He said yes, even though it meant commuting from Chicago until he could move his family. Over the span of two years, with Hoogerwerf teaching beside him, Russell managed to develop materials for a complete photography program. When, in 1983, a millage election failed (the only

election Calkins, who ran millage campaigns for Runkel and succeeding superintendents, would ever lose), the photography program was dropped for budgetary reasons. Russell, who continued working in other media areas, never gave up on the program and within two years managed to have it reinstated.[6]

The Photography Program remains thriving and well to this day—with two full-time instructors (Russell in film, Fillippo Tagliati in digital photography), three adjunct instructors teaching introductory classes, and 300 to 400 students per semester. In time, the Photography Program outgrew the Learning Resource Center and moved to the Main Building to become the Visual Arts Department along with Art. The program is considered among the finest and most comprehensive of any offered by a Michigan two-year college.

A Culinary Arts Program

In 1973, during the tenure of Frank McCarthy, instructor Marcille (Pridge) Dalgleish introduced two hospitality programs, a one-year Food Service Certificate and a two-year Associate Degree in Hotel and Restaurant Management. By the start of Calkins' presidency, the program had grown to 65 students. Classes were taught in a renovated kitchen in the G Building, where a new Lunch on the Hill Cafeteria began serving meals to the public.

Both Calkins and Occupational Dean Dr. Till Peters, aware that the food industry was growing at an unprecedented rate, began a search for someone to lead a full Culinary Arts program. Twenty-six-year-old Bob Garlough, who was working as an executive chef and food manager in Florida, was one of the first to answer the college's ad for a chef-coordinator. The maturity, enthusiasm, and vision Garlough displayed during his interview with administration proved highly persuasive. Calkins told him the community was ripe for a culinary program if he was willing to work for it. "You can accomplish anything in this world if you don't care who gets the credit for it," Calkins said. "We'll help you get started, but you will need to earn our future support." Calkins also promised that the program would not become the college's private catering service. Garlough started work on June 6, 1980, determined to rise to Calkins' challenge.[7] (**Figure 87**)

Garlough quickly made curricular changes, wrote new courses, and opened the first Heritage Restaurant in the G Building (moving it to the new Student Community Center the following year). He hired Lynden Lewis as table service instructor, Jerry Benham as storeroom manager, and Carl Butenas as a chef-instructor. Garlough himself taught baking and pantry/garde manger while coordinating the program. When he also assumed the job of Food Service director, he was forced to give up teaching to become a full-time administrator, successfully shepherding both the Culinary Program and Food Services for the next 10 years. In December of 1981, with the program already gaining recognition, Culinary Arts added full-time instructor Henry VanderEnde, a Dutch pastry chef. After him, according to Garlough, there was a succession of other full-time hires with degrees and teaching experience from U.S. culinary schools (Bob Monaldo, Terry Dunn, Marcia Rango, and Bill Jacoby), degrees from hotel/restaurant management schools (Randy Sahajdack, Charlie Olawsky, and Jim Muth), and two master chefs from Europe (Gilles Renusson, France, and Angus Campbell, Scotland). Later instructional staff would include Dan Gendler, Bob Schultz, Kevin Dunn, Mike Whitman, and Audrey Heckwolf. Support staff included Carol Manciu, Marcia Arp, Mike Kidder, and Dale VandenBerg. Jerry Benham would become Food Service director.

Garlough's vision was to build the program into a national model for community colleges, and a regional center for all things related to food service. Within very few years, he had accomplished all of that and more. Generous federal Perkins Act funding allowed the department to strive for excellence in all areas. Yet the fullest blossoming of the program would not occur until the opening of the Applied Technology Center in 1991.

Buildings Multiply—College Park Plaza

In 1977, ground was broken for the College Park Plaza Building, designed by GRJC alumnus Adrian Swets as a banking and administrative center, not for the college, but the Grand Rapids

1975-84

1979

The Technology Division introduced the "Technology for Industry" program, with the purpose of creating course offerings tailored to meet the needs of local industries. It started with an Amway Corporation class held after hours at Amway's plant. This program later became known as Business & Technical Training and is now known as Workforce Training.

1980

The Music Center opened on the corner of Lyon Street and Ransom Avenue, in what formerly was the East Building gymnasium, to provide improved practice, rehearsal, and performance areas.

Culinary Arts program established.

Resident tuition was $494.00 per year.

Culinary Arts demonstration at Career Day, 1980. (GRCC Archives)

(above, Figure 88) Music Center, 1980. (GRCC Archives)
(right, Figure 89) Student Community Center, 1981. (GRCC Archives)

Teachers Credit Union. In time the building, standing just to the west of the North Building, would become GRJC's central administration building (1992). At present it houses the faculty offices of several college departments and the Grand Rapids Community College Foundation.

The Music Center

When the Ford Health and Physical Education Center opened in 1976, the 53-year-old East Building gymnasium fell into disuse while the Calkins' Building and Renovation Team and local architects worked to decide its fate. Once an acoustics consultant determined that the concrete floors and heavy masonry walls were "excellent sound isolators," the board of education approved a renovation plan, with the state agreeing to provide half of the $1.8 million cost. In August of 1980, the Music Department moved from the West Building to its newly-transformed facility. **(Figure 88)** The improvement was dramatic and long-awaited. The first floor had been enlarged

to provide space for nine offices, two teaching studios, 19 practice rooms, a listening center, and student and faculty lounges. The second floor, the former girls' gymnasium, became a two-story rehearsal, recital, and performance area, with 160 theater seats. The former boys' gymnasium evolved into four classrooms, with one designed for teaching piano. A third floor resulted from the construction of a floor midway between floor and roof of the boys' gym, accommodating a large classroom, a chamber music room, and a large choral rehearsal hall with seating for up to 250.[8]

Original plans for the Music Center included a 750-seat performance hall to the immediate east. Though Calkins had a major donor in place, the plans did not materialize.[9] The arts simply lacked funding available to occupational programs.

The Student Community Center

The new Student Community Center, at the midpoint of campus, opened at the start of the 1981 school year, along with a central parking ramp addition of 250 spaces. (**Figure 89**) The new SCC was literally the center of student life. At a time when state and local funding for construction were drying up, the college devised a unique self-financing plan for the nearly $7 million project: two thirds of the cost would come from tuition, rental fees, bookstore profits, parking fees, and the cafeteria, with the remainder coming from the district's Building and Sites Fund.

Shaped to the contour of Lyon Street hill and linked by walkways to the parking ramp and fieldhouse, the building effectively consolidated all student services into one location: the College Bookstore, the Student Activities Office, a student recreation room, *The Collegiate* newspaper, student government offices, The Heritage Restaurant, a cafeteria, a multi-purpose kitchen, a Community Multi-purpose Room, the Admissions and Counseling offices, a student study lounge, and the Academic Support Center (directed by Richard Bezile) containing the Tutoring Program, the Reading/Writing Lab, and Handicapped Services.[10]

The McCabe-Marlowe House

This elegant, Victorian style house had been, since 1945, the residence of Grand Rapids Junior College science instructors Marie McCabe and her niece, Wilma McCabe

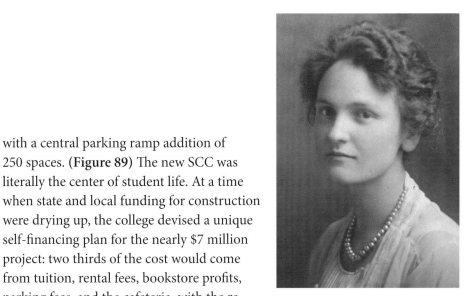

(**top, Figure 90**) Marie McCabe, undated. (GRCC Archives)
(**above, Figure 91**) Wilma Marlowe, 1938 *Olympian*. (GRCC Archives)

Marlowe. (**Figures 90 & 91**) Marie, who had begun teaching in 1922, had long been advisor of the Pre-Medic Club at the college, and with Wilma had hosted informal gatherings in their home, introducing many promising students to influential figures from the University of Michigan, GRJC's main transfer institution. Often, the meetings would provide significant nudges to students' careers in the medical field.

In 1979, the two ladies, long-retired, made the decision to move to Florida to be closer to family. When their home went up for sale, President Calkins began considering its purchase as a college hospitality house, envisioning an elegant, home-like venue for hosting college guests, small conferences, and fund-raising events, with a kitchen run by the Culinary Arts Department. The GRJC Foundation did not have the money to cover the $150,000 purchase price, so Calkins and Bob Chase approached the Steelcase Foundation and were provided a two-year, interest-free loan, which the college repaid as promised.

In 1981, Dr. Ray Boozer was appointed acting executive secretary of the GRJC Foundation and was charged with heading up a fund drive for restoration of the house. The Foundation office, upon completion of renovations, would occupy a portion of the second floor. The GRJC Alumni Association, reactivated by Calkins in 1976 and increasingly vital to the life of the college, supported the

1981

The Heritage Restaurant opened in G Building. It was relocated to the Student Center the following year and then to its current location in the Wisner-Bottrall Applied Technology Center in 1991. (The Heritage Restaurant in Student Community Center, 1981. GRCC Archives)

McCabe-Marlow House opened to serve as the college's hospitality house for hosting college guests, small conferences, and fund-raising events, with a kitchen run by the Culinary Arts Department. The house was named in honor of the previous owners, Grand Rapids Junior College science instructors Marie McCabe and her niece Wilma McCabe Marlowe for their life-long dedication to the college.

Academic Foundations Program (AFP) established. In addition to an emphasis on basic academic skills, AFP also offered students the opportunity for personal growth and development, teaching such life skills as problem solving, decision-making, and effective studying. AFP courses were offered in English, reading, math, chemistry, biology, and psychology.

(**Figure 92**) McCabe-Marlowe House, 1981. (GRCC Archives)

project by conducting a successful public fund drive led by alumnus Jack Klap that guaranteed completion by 1982.

Students and instructors of the Junior College Occupational Training Program accomplished restoration of the home over the process of 15 months. This "labor of love," supervised by instructors Chet Moore, Tom Boozer, and Ken Homrich with the administrative support of C. J. Shroll, Director of Occupational Training, proved deeply gratifying to all involved. Named the McCabe-Marlowe House in honor of Marie and Wilma for their life-long dedication to the college, the facility was declared a Michigan Historic Site in 1986.[11] (**Figure 92**)

Technical Education Center—Leonard and Ball

In 1979, the Technology Division introduced the "Technology for Industry" Program, with the purpose of creating course offerings tailored to meet the needs of local industries, extending a tradition of citizen's advisory committees at GRJC. A series of occupational deans, including Robert Duffy, Don Maine, Till Peters, and Don Boyer, helped fashion Occupational Education into the fastest growing, most community-conscious and adaptable area of the college.

In the late 1970s, newly-renovated buildings on Leonard and Ball Streets, three miles from central campus, became the Technology Center, led by Occupational Training Director C. J. Shroll and OT Coordinator, Julie Johnson. (**Figure 93**) The new center greatly improved the facilities for automotive repair and body work, welding, furniture making, and home repair, as well as enabling the creation of a number of new job training programs. A talented faculty of George Cottrell, Chet Moore, John Pifer, Harold Schurman, Ken Smith, and others ensured the Center's success. With the advent of computers and robotics, manufacturing was changing at a lightning pace. Shroll

(Figure 93) Occupational Training Center, undated. (GRCC Archives)

ran a program that was flexible and light on its feet, responding swiftly to employer needs. The program demonstrated its success by turning out skilled workers who moved quickly and effectively into the work force.[12]

A rapidly-growing non-credit Apprenticeship Program, directed by John Eister and taught part-time by people working as master electricians, plumbers, pipefitters, and a myriad of other skilled jobs, occupied the basement of the Main Building.

GVSC Presence in Downtown Grand Rapids
Competition from Grand Valley State College had, in the early 1980s, become a very real threat to GRJC. GVSC President Arend Lubbers wanted a downtown Grand Rapids presence for his college, but he was very aware that such a presence represented competition with GRJC for students. Presidents Calkins and Lubbers met and in time carved out an agreement of mutual support and coordination of resources, which benefitted both institutions. GVSC would build a downtown classroom center but restrict classes to junior and senior levels. According to Calkins, "the agreement was the salvation of both schools."

Growing Diversity
As a result of the dramatic social readjustments of the '60s and early '70s, GRJC had become an increasingly diverse student body with a diversity of wants and needs. In 1977, foreign stu-

dent population on-campus increased from 45 to 125 in a single year, and the need for English as a Second Language doubled. Nancy Johnson was named foreign student advisor. Language Arts instructor Judy Kienitz became counselor-coordinator of the newly-instituted Handicapped Student Programs, as the college sought to comply with recent federal regulations prohibiting discrimination against persons with handicaps. The Women's Resource Center, created in 1973 to serve women wishing to advance or change careers, continued to grow in relevancy. Within a couple of years, a Council for Minority Concerns would develop a strong presence.

Organized in 1981 to serve as an advisory group to President Calkins and chaired by Pat Pulliam, the Council for Minority Concerns quickly assumed a primary place in the life of the college. The group's objectives were to monitor policies affecting the recruitment of minority staff and students, to work toward retention of minority students, and to serve as crisis intervention for minority students and staff. The Council initiated a conflict resolution workshop, an annual banquet for minority high school seniors and their parents, a Student Life Board to provide a forum for students of various ethnic and cultural backgrounds, and a loan fund to assist Black, Hispanic, and Native American Students. In 1984, the college opened an Office of Minority Affairs/Affirmative Action, headed by Richard Reid.

Academic Foundations Program
The 1981 creation of the Academic Foundations Program (AFP) represented a major step beyond several decades of developmental courses offered by the college. "In addition to former emphasis on basic academic skills," reads the college's *1984 Self-Study*, "AFP would also offer students the opportunity for personal

1975-84

1981

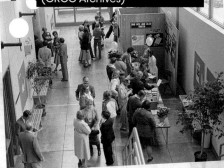

GRJC Open House, 1981. (GRCC Archives)

Telecourses were offered for the first time in the fall semester—with an enrollment of 113 students. By the fall of 1984 GRJC had more students enrolled in telecourses than any other college in Michigan. GRJC held this position through the 1980s with interest in telecourses continuing to grow. By the Winter Semester of 1990 there were 1,048 students enrolled in 25 courses. Once the college developed online classes, use of telecourses declined, and they were discontinued in 2009.

1982

The Student Life Board was formed to provide a forum for students of various ethnic and cultural backgrounds.

GRJC hosted Men's and Women's Swimming and Diving Nationals where GRJC men placed third and women second.

Beginning in Fall of 1981, students who enrolled in developmental courses were considered participants in the Academic Foundation Program (AFP). Planning was coordinated by the Dean of Arts and Sciences with program activities monitored by an oversight committee. The Director of the Education Development Center (now named CASS, Counseling and Academic Support Services) assumed responsibility for coordinating the program.

Courses included:
    English 001,002 (later changed to English 097 and 098)
    Reading 100, 102
    Mathematics 003, 004, 005
    Chemistry 100
    Biology 100
    Psychology 100 (later changed to Psychology 101)

In addition to former emphasis on basic academic skills, AFP would also offer students the opportunity for personal growth and development. Psychology 100 (renumbered 101) was altered to expose students to principles of problem solving, decision-making, goal setting, self-awareness, effective studying, stress management, etc. Instructors were encouraged to refer students for tutoring, peer counseling and use of services through the Reading-Writing Lab.

In the meantime, instructors began regular meetings to discuss students' progress, to evaluate the effectiveness of the program, and to make recommendations for revisions.

-147-

(Figure 94) *Grand Rapids Junior College Self-Study* 1984. (GRCC Archives)

uniform guidelines for classroom management and for evaluation of student progress. The program encouraged a team approach to teaching. Dean of Students Elias Lumpkins, psychology instructor Richard Bezile, and Council of Minority Concerns Chair Pat Pulliam provided the creativity and energy to make this program a reality. Given the college's open enrollment policy, a developmental program with an increased student success rate was a blessing for all concerned.

College News

1977 marked the demise of the Women's League, for 65 years one of the most popular and productive of student organizations. The beautifully decorated Women's League suite in the Main Building would continue being used as a student study area. In February of 1978, Business Division Chair Charles Chanter unveiled a new Associate in Business Degree.

In the fall of that year, Life Sciences Chair Harvey Meyaard announced that Dr. Jud VanderWal would teach a new genetics course dealing with human heredity and related social issues such as cloning, birth defects, and transsexualism. In 1979, Dean Till Peters introduced an Occupational Therapy

growth and development," teaching such life skills as problem solving, decision-making, and effective studying. (Figure 94) AFP courses were made available in English, reading, math, chemistry, biology, and psychology. AFP instructors developed

Program headed up by Pat McClellan and funded by federal monies provided by the Perkins Act. (**Figures 95a & b**) The same year, vocal music instructor Ted Pasma was chosen to lead the Grand Rapids Symphonic Choir, and Lynne Asper was hired to be the college's instrumental director. He would also conduct the Kent Philharmonia Orchestra.

In sports, 1977 brought more national recognition for Gordon Hunsberger—in his twenty-second season as football coach—for having the best record (123-60-7) of any junior college football coach in the country. All-American Charlie Wells joined the PE faculty and was named assistant wrestling coach. In March of 1978 and '79, GRJC hosted the National Junior College Athletic Association Swimming and Diving Championship. Visiting coaches had high praise for the new facilities and aquatic director Dave Clark's masterful organization that allowed a championship contested simultaneously with men and women. GRJC Coach Pinky McPherson, with

the top women's swim team in Michigan, captured second place in the nation. Coach Jim Hall's men's team, second in the state, took third place nationally. In October of 1981, Coach Skip Nelson's women's tennis team won a state championship, while in 1983, Tom Hofmann, GRJC baseball coach, was named assistant coach of the U.S. Olympic baseball team.

In the early '80s, the Art Department sponsored an annual art-craft show called RampArts, with its exhibit area at the top

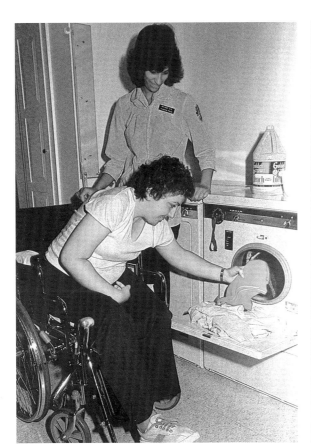
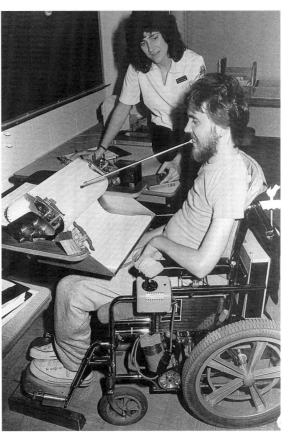

(**Figures 95a & b**) Occupational Therapy Assisting students, 1982. (GRCC Archives)

1982

Computer Applications Division was established with 24 Apple computers purchased with the assistance of federal vocational education dollars.

January 23 marked the first broadcasts from Channel G, the higher education cable channel located at the college. The channel initially aired 25 hours of telecourses weekly, affording students enrolled in those courses an opportunity to view them at a convenient time.

1983

Shuttle bus to campus offered by the Grand Rapids Area Transit Authority serving the two main GUS lots on Front Avenue and the parking lot at the John Ball Park.

Women's tennis team finished third in the National Junior College Tennis Tournament. The team would go on to participate in the national tournament in 1987, 1989, 1991-93, 2001, 2005, and 2012. (1983 women's tennis team. GRCC Archives)

(**Figure 96**) RampArts, 1982. (GRCC Archives)

of the parking ramp. (**Figure 96**) Former student editor Carolyn Medendorp assumed, in 1980, the position of *Collegiate* advisor and guided the newspaper staff through a time of transition. In the fall of '82, Language Arts instructor Philip Jung took over journalism responsibilities, leading the student newspaper more fully into the arenas of national and international issues, environmental concerns, and college financial struggles.

Funding Problems—Cooperative Solutions

Governor Milliken, in 1981, cut nearly $1 million in state aid to the college. In response, GRJC faculty, aware that the well-being of the institution was at stake, agreed to a 5 percent pay cut in exchange for 10 fewer teaching days per school year. The agreement recovered half the loss in state aid, the remainder coming from a 26 percent increase in student tuition rates ($25 per credit hour for residents, $40 for non-residents). President Reagan's first round of budget cuts hit colleges in 1982, with Michigan losing $132,000,000 in higher education funding. By 1984, given Michigan's high unemployment rate, the state cut its share of support for the GRJC budget from 52 to 34 percent. Happily, the second half of the decade would see a modest upturn in the state's financial fortunes, though the college would never again see state funding at a 50 percent level. Calkins, in response, began a series of aggressive fund-raising campaigns.

Superintendent Turnover

Dr. John Dow left Grand Rapids in the 1984 school year to become superintendent of schools in New Haven, Connecticut. Long-time GRPS administrator, Dr. Elmer Vruggink, took the job of interim superintendent with hopes of being named Dow's replacement. Instead, the board of education, in a close vote, decided on an outsider from California, Dr. Robert Ferrera. By spring of '84, with GRPS $1.5 million in the red, Ferrera had eliminated 51 administrative positions from K-12 and seemed intent on shaking up the entire system. Early on, he pledged support to the college, but over time kept his distance from it. Calkins' relationship with him was, at best, uneasy. The Runkel/Dow/Calkins rapport was a thing of the past. Over the next several years, the presence of Ferrera would, according to Bob Partridge, speaking as a former college executive vice president of finance, provide "the spur for Calkins to move the college toward separating from the Grand Rapids Public Schools."[13]

Ferrera did manage to provide Language Arts a memorable service by agreeing (in 1984) to move the division out of the West Building and into the fifth floor of the North Building (GRPS administrative offices)—rather than into the G Building as planned. Language Arts reveled in its new quarters, pleased to be back in the center of campus life. Grand Rapids City High School would for several years occupy the G Building. GRPS administration would begin vacating the college, a signal of a more dramatic separation to come.

The 1984 Self-Study

Beginning in the early 80s, knowing that a North Central re-accreditation visit was scheduled for 1984, Calkins ordered a massive evaluation involving all areas of the college. He and his staff created groups dedicated to communication among administration, faculty, support staff, and students; they orchestrated task forces for planning, community advisory committees, and the gathering and composing of what would become the *Grand Rapids Junior College 1984 Self-Study*, the most thorough and eloquently written of any the college has done before or since. Language Arts and Foreign Language instructor Richard Reid, commissioned to do the bulk of the writing, presented a detailed view of the college's successes, its building programs, its faculty accomplishments, its divisional progress, its student achievements, along with a frank assessment of college shortcomings in providing for a student body of well over 9,000.

The North Central Committee had much praise for the integrity of the document, yet, as always, the group came up with a laundry list of concerns, the most important of which was the lack of a strong, unified long-range strategic plan for the institution, which they attributed to board control of the college. "Because of...attachment to the school district," the Committee report stated, "the college leaders don't find much incentive for serious planning and fiscal control since the District manages revenue and allocation." If the college separated from K-12, the report went on, "it could reduce tuition, obtain local tax revenue from a greatly expanded area and because of its independence make better use of fiscal management to enhance planning and fiscal controls." Acutely aware of the truth of these observations, Calkins and staff, within two years, produced a detailed five-year strategic plan and set in motion another plan of even greater consequence: independence from the K-12 system.

1984

Office of Minority Affairs/Affirmative Action opened to provide personal, cultural, social, and academic growth and development for minority students. The Office acted as an advocate for minority students in order to enhance their opportunities for a successful educational experience.

The Music Department sponsored jazz saxophonist great Stan Getz and held its first triennial Magnum Opus Harpsichord Competition featuring the Magnum Opus harpsichord, donated by the Harry Samrick family of Grand Rapids. (GRCC Archives)

Enrollment was 8,913.

First annual Martin Luther King Jr. Community Peace March, January 16, 1986. (GRCC Archives)

The Builders: The Calkins Years—Part Two
1985-98

Million Dollar Faculty

President Calkins took great pride in the *1984 Self-Study*, but even more in a program that took shape a year later known as "Million Dollar Faculty." (**Figure 97**) The brainchild of Language Arts instructor Keith Longberg, who had pursued Calkins for some time before finally gaining his attention, the plan was a faculty initiative for fund-raising intended to enrich the endowment-poor GRJC Foundation and its scholarship fund. (**Figure 98**) In July of 1985, Longberg, in the caressive setting of the McCabe-Marlowe House, gathered a group of faculty identified as important supporters of the Foundation. He described a fund-raising

Grand Rapids Junior College

"Million Dollar Faculty"

and

"Matching Million"

Companion Programs To Promote Scholarship Giving

(**right, Figure 97**) Million Dollar Faculty campaign program, undated. (GRCC Archives)
(**above, Figure 98**) Keith Longberg, English faculty member and originator of the Million Dollar Faculty campaign (center) with GRJC Foundation Director Dr. Ray Boozer (left) and President Calkins. (GRCC Archives)

1985

Shades of Blue, the college's vocal jazz group, performed at the National Association of Jazz Educators conference in Dallas. During the mid-1980s they also traveled to Vancouver, British Columbia to perform in the Canadian National Finals.

GRJC launched Million Dollar Faculty campaign, developed by English Faculty member Keith Longberg.

The Language Arts Division held the first annual Communication Arts Festival sponsored to encourage writing in high schools and recognize students' original compositions by awarding scholarships to the college. (1990 Communication Arts Festival program. GRCC Archives)

GRAND RAPIDS JUNIOR COLLEGE
6th ANNUAL
COMMUNICATION
ARTS
FESTIVAL
SPONSORED BY THE
LANGUAGE ARTS DIVISION
OCTOBER 31, 1990

• ENTERTAINMENT BY
  "SHADES OF BLUE"
• WORKSHOPS
• WRITING CONTEST

(above, Figure 99) Governor James Blanchard announcing joint funding for the construction of the Applied Technology Center, 1986. (GRCC Archives)

(right, Figure 100) Governor James Blanchard, GRJC President Calkins and Ferris State President J. William Wenrich on the site of the future Applied Technology Center, 1986. (GRCC Archives)

plan driven by pledges from faculty and managed by payroll deduction, pledges with the purpose of endowing scholarships that faculty donors would both name and control. An accompanying plan called "Matching Millions" would solicit the business community to match all faculty contributions.

The response of the faculty group was stunning. Within two weeks, the Foundation had received pledges of more than $100,000 from 15 faculty members. Within a year and a half, faculty pledges amounted to $800,000. In an unprecedented move, the Grand Rapids Board of Education made available $150,000 over a five-year period to match faculty contributions alongside those from business, tripling the value of a faculty pledge. By the fall of 1986, the assets of the Foundation (a total of $24,000 in 1985) had grown to over $1,750,000. Today the Foundation has assets in excess of $23 million and awards $750,000 a year in scholarships to over 800 students.

Center for Environmental Studies

The Center for Environmental Studies, revitalized by Dr. Kay Dodge in 1983, brought to the college a local, regional, and global sense of the need for environmental education and activism. Funded by the Wege Foundation and other local sources, the Center began sponsoring major environmental gatherings. In 1985, the forum "Great Lakes Issues with Global Implications," featured marine biologist Jean-Michel Cousteau, former Secretary of the Interior Stuart Udall, and the governors and officials from states and Canadian provinces bordering the Great Lakes. In 1990, the Center opened a Costa Rican office with the mission of illuminating the global nature of environmental concerns and the need for shared solutions to ecological problems.[1] In time, Dodge would retire to Costa Rica, funding would become problematic, and the Center would separate from the college and move off-campus.

Long-term *Collegiate* Advisor

In 1986, Language Arts instructor Dr. Scott McNabb took over as head of the journalism program and as *Collegiate* advisor. He would remain in that role for 316 issues of the newspaper over 24 years, a tenure longer than any previous advisor. He (in 1987) replaced electric typewriters with computers, transforming the paper's production process. He helped students produce the first online version of *The Collegiate* in '96 and would continue teaching and advising the newspaper staff two years beyond his retirement in 2010. Under McNabb, *The Collegiate* would flourish. On 14 occasions the Michigan Community College Press and the Michigan Press Associations named it Best Overall Community College Newspaper in Michigan. It was a Pacemaker Finalist (the Pulitzer of national college newspaper awards) five times; it won consecutive Best of Show awards at the National College Media Convention in New York City in 2008 and 2009.[2] McNabb's student journalists accomplished a record unmatched by any other Michigan community college, a record placing *The Collegiate* among a handful of top community college newspapers in the country.

Things Happening

In the latter half of the 1980s, change was in the air: not only a growing momentum for separation from the Grand Rapids Public Schools, but also the escalating excitement about a new technology and training center, for which Governor Blanchard had already recommended state funding. **(Figure 99 & 100)**

(Figure 101) 1987-88 Shades of Blue with Director Duane Davis (left) leaning against the Music Center. (GRCC Archives)

Every day seemed busier than the last. A Seventy-fifth Anniversary Celebration was coming up in 1989, and a college self-study for North Central accreditation was due by 1990.

Exciting things were happening in the daily life of the college. Shades of Blue, a GRJC vocal jazz group directed by Duane Davis, had won the Best Vocal Group Award at the Aquinas Intercollegiate Jazz Festival in 1984, and was honored in 1985 with an invitation to perform at the National Association of Jazz Educators in Dallas. **(Figure 101)** In spring of the same year, the group attended MusicFest Canada in Vancouver, British Columbia, the only American group

1986

Culinary Arts Department was awarded fifth-place ranking nationwide among food service schools.

Sex therapist, media personality, and author Dr. Ruth Westheimer spoke at the Ford Fieldhouse. Her appearance resulted in protesters marching outside the facility. (Dr. Ruth Westheimer poster, 1986. GRCC Archives)

In Person
DR RUTH
Monday, September 15, 1986
8:00 PM – Ford Fieldhouse

The first annual Dr. Martin Luther King, Jr. Community Peace March was held and included participants from other area colleges. (First annual Martin Luther King, Jr. Peace March, 1986. GRCC Archives)

Grand Rapids Junior College
Communication Arts Festival

Thursday, November 7, 1985

(Figure 102) 1985 Communications Arts Festival program. (GRCC Archives)

extended an invitation. There, Shades was awarded the first-place gold medal.[3] The GRJC College Choir, directed by Davis, whose national reputation was catalyst for the invitation, would perform in 1990 at Carnegie Hall in New York City.

The Language Arts Division in the mid-1980s began hosting an annual Communication Arts Festival for high school seniors as a tool for promoting both the college and higher education. (Figure 102) In 1985, the college named Bobbi Schrader the first chairperson of a unified Health Division. In 1986, the Task Force for Gay and Lesbian Awareness established an active presence on campus.

Spectrum Theater opened its fall 1987 season with an original student production called *The Dog Ate My Homework*, a comic musical examining life at GRJC. The play was the collaborative venture of Fred Sebulske's theater students, Walter Lockwood's creative writing students, Charles Buffham's music students (original music and lyrics), and Duane Davis's vocal direction. In spring of 1987, Fred Garbowitz was hired to teach speech and resurrect the college debate team. By 1990, the JC debaters would rank second among two-year colleges nationwide. In the fall of 1987 a Culinary Arts team traveled to West Germany for the Culinary Olympics, taking home two gold, five silver, and four bronze medals. In 1988, the Assessing Student Skills for Entry and Transfer (ASSET) test was administered for the first time, ensuring more accurate placement of entering students. 1989 marked the opening of Noorthoek Academy, a first-of-its-kind program in the arts and sciences

for special needs students wishing to pursue their education in a college setting. In 1990, math students began using a new graphing calculator.

Led by Patti Trepkowski, the GRJC Laboratory Preschool for hands-on training of preschool teachers, continued to grow in reputation and importance. Social Science instructor Roger Schlosser began leading summer study tours to Europe. He would continue worldwide tours for many years, and other colleagues—Paul Chardoul, Nick Antonakis, Dick Stien, Aleta Anderson, Hillery Haney, Dr. Mike DeVivo, Dr. Robert Hendershot, Dr. Greg Forbes, and Dr. Matt Douglas among them—would follow suit, leading study travel to exotic places around the world.

In February of 1985 Fred Julian replaced Gordon Hunsberger (NJCAA Football Hall of Fame) as head football coach. Julian, the following year, would lead the GRJC football team to victory against Tyler Junior College in the Texas Junior College Bowl. In 1987, Doug Wabeke, a talented college and minor league shortstop, replaced Tom Hofmann (NJCAA Baseball Hall of Fame) as head baseball coach. In 1990, Gene Paxton (1971 Region 12 Coach of the Year) would retire after 25 years as basketball coach with a record of 517-280 and five MJCAA championships. Granville Brown replaced him, yet within two years would hand the reins to his assistant, former GRJC star Dave Selmon. Selmon would compile a 417-138 record, seven MCCAA championships and a runner-up in the 1995 Division II National Championship. (Figure 103)

Bursting at the Seams

Faculty began the 1987 school year working without a contract, and students worried about a strike. To everyone's relief, an agreement was ratified by November, though Language Arts

(Figure 103) 1994-95 basketball team. (GRCC Archives)

Chair Chuck Chamberlain feared that a failure to set limits on class size was going to create heavy burdens for composition instructors. His fears were well-founded. In spite of staff projections to the contrary, enrollment increased so rapidly that existing facilities could barely accommodate the numbers. In the fall of 1989, with 11,350 already admitted, the college's open door was forced to close early for lack of available classrooms. The Applied Technology Center, with its desperately needed teaching space, was not scheduled to open until 1991, at which time enrollment would top 12,000.

The Seventy-fifth Anniversary Celebration

In the fall of 1989, GRJC, an elder statesman among junior colleges in the country, celebrated its Diamond Jubilee. Bearing a new logo designed by Media Services graphic artist Jeremy Long, the college shared its seventy-fifth birthday party with the entire

1987

GRJC became the first public school in the area to participate in the recycling of office paper.

1988

The Culinary Arts program was awarded its initial accreditation by the Accrediting Commission of the American Culinary Federation Educational Institute (ACFEI).

After a 15-year hiatus, the GRJC Debate Team placed third in the Regional Debate Tournament held in Athens, Ohio, and finished ranked twenty-sixth in the American Debate Association Poll, one of only three from community colleges. (1987 Debate Team. GRCC Archives)

The Collegiate was again named the best community college newspaper in Michigan and received the highest ranking awarded by the Associated Collegiate Press, a national organization, and the Best College Newspaper in Michigan by the University of Michigan Press Club.

(**top, Figure 104**) Seventy-fifth Anniversary banner on the Music Center, 1989. (GRCC Archives)

(**right, Figure 105**) Seventy-fifth Anniversary world record cherry torte, October 5, 1989. (GRCC Archives)

community. (**Figure 104**) A formal ceremony honoring the college's founding fathers came first, followed by a college-wide convocation of staff recognition, the awarding of the first annual Excellence in Education award (to Dee Palmer, Secretary to Dean Marinus Swets), and a salute to the future of the college.

The main celebration continued for a week, with birthday cake and ice cream sundaes prepared for a thousand evening college students during their class breaks. A Community Birthday Party came next—imaginative and spectacular—with 75 Culinary Arts students making (at the top of the parking ramp) the world's largest cherry torte (75 feet long, on a 75-foot baking pan built by tech students), in 75 minutes. (**Figure 105**) This feast was followed by a college tour led by staff members in vintage clothing, displays of college history, musical and theatrical performances, and drawings for prizes ranging from scholarships to Health Club memberships. The

celebration ended with a formal diamond jubilee dinner dance attended by 300 of the college's most faithful supporters. All received crystal goblets etched with the anniversary logo.[4]

Committee of 53

In June of 1988, when Superintendent Ferrera resigned to take a position in Minneapolis, Patrick Sandro, a GRPS insider and a welcome, steadying presence to both the public schools and the college, was named interim superintendent. Soon after, the Grand Rapids Board of Education began serving a second role—as the College's board of trustees until a separation of GRPS and the college could take place. In the fall of 1989, at Sandro's urging, the board of education appointed a committee of 53 Kent County citizens to study a plan for separation. (**Figure 106**) In May of 1990, the committee made a recommendation for redistricting of the college to include all of the 20 school districts in the Kent

ABSTRACT

The Committee of 53 recommends that Grand Rapids Junior College be redistricted to meet the needs of the population it serves. This recommendation is based on several factors:

The College's students range in age from 18 years to over 70 from a wide range of racial, ethnic, and socio-economic backgrounds.

The College has been experiencing rapid growth in enrollment. From 1960 to 1989, JC has grown from 2,351 students to 17,400 in credit and non-credit courses and is expected to grow to 30,000 by the year 2010.

The College trains and must continue to meet demands for training the present workforce. Workforce training and retraining has grown from 600 to 6,000 individuals. The number is expected to increase to 18,000 in the year 2000.

Enrollment must not be limited. The state's two-year public colleges are under mandate by law to admit all persons over the age of 18 who live in the district and seek to enter.

The College's downtown location is landlocked and cannot accommodate present and future growth.

The Grand Rapids Public Schools District (the City of Grand Rapids) is the supporting tax base for Grand Rapids Junior College. Seventy percent (70%) of the College's students live outside the Grand Rapids Public Schools District.

JC's tax base must be expanded to meet the needs of the population it serves. It would cost the citizens of Grand Rapids 6.2 mills to support the College's projected growth. That would exceed the maximum levy of 5 mills permitted by Laws of the State of Michigan for a community college.

The Committee of 53 recommends that the College's district be expanded to include the Kent Intermediate Schools District, that not more than 1.9 mills be levied to cover costs of operations and capital outlay, and that the issue be placed before the voters in January, 1991.

Report from the Committee Studying the Redistricting of GRAND RAPIDS JUNIOR COLLEGE

Presented to Grand Rapids Junior College Board of Trustees
May 14, 1990

(Figure 106) *Report from the Committee Studying the Redistricting of Junior College*, May 14, 1990. (GRCC Archives)

Intermediate School District. The board of education unanimously approved the recommendation and set in motion plans for a redistricting vote.

A Community College at Last

Calkins, a veteran of many successful millage elections, orchestrated a campaign blitz designed to reach every eligible voter in the district. The massive effort resulted in an impressive

(February 5, 1991) victory that established Grand Rapids Community College as an independent institution with a newly-elected seven-member board of trustees and operating revenue of 1.9 mills. Though some staff felt there was wisdom in changing the college name to Kent County Community College, the board opted for tradition and name recognition. Some years later, former chief financial officer Bob Partridge would state that, in winning this critical election, "Dick Calkins proved himself the most impactful president of all."

The 1990 Self-Study

In an odd bit of timing, the college's *1990 Self-Study* was written while GRJC was a junior college, yet the North Central Evaluation Team report was completed a week after the victorious redistricting proposal that made GRJC a community college. Though the team had long recommended such a change, their report was careful to point out that many new employees and hefty expenditures would be needed to run the operations formerly provided by the Grand Rapids School District. "There will be a great deal of pressure to meet unmet needs in a short time," the report stated. It proved an understatement.

1985-98

1989

The Noorthoek Academy was established, offering a continuing education program in the arts and sciences for students with mild cognitive impairments. (Noorthoek Academy brochure, undated. GRCC Archives)

The college celebrated its seventy-fifth anniversary throughout the 1989-90 school year.

GRJC began offering classes at the Holland Careerline Tech Center in a collaborative effort with Muskegon Community College.

Wrestling team finished sixth in the National Junior College Athletic Association Tournament.

1991

Applied Technology Center opened. This technical training center was conceived as a joint venture by GRJC and Ferris State College to provide innovative, cutting-edge technical training for business and industry.

THE COLLEGIATE

GRAND RAPIDS JUNIOR COLLEGE

Vol. 35. January 23, 1991

Vote on Feb. 5

Committee plans college future

By Michael Wilson
Associate Editor

Hob-nobbing with the candidate

JC's future riding on upcoming seperation vote

By Joey Sutherlin and Chris Kuhn
Collegiate Staff Members

---

page 4 — **viewpoints** — January 24, 1991

Exercise your right: Vote on February 5

— Joey Sutherlin

Two sides to redistricting

Separating college from public schools presents some issues to contemplate

Produced by *The Collegiate* staff. Printed by Graphica & Printers

Sample Ballot of the Feb. 5th election

PROPOSITION TO ESTABLISH A COMMUNITY COLLEGE DISTRICT	PROPOSITION II TO ESTABLISH THE MAXIMUM ANNUAL TAX RATE
Yes ___ No ___	Yes ___ No ___

Vote on Feb. 5

THE COLLEGIATE

GRAND RAPIDS JUNIOR COLLEGE

Vol.35, No.X August 22, 1990

Redistricting proposal approved by JC Board

By Joe Koenig
Editor-in-chief

Projected Enrollment for JC, 1990-2010

- 11,401 in Fall, 1989 (actual)
- 11,864 in 1990
- 14,475 in 1995
- 17,660 in 2000
- 21,547 in 2005
- 26,289 in 2010

Collegiate Graphic

Photo by Jason Woods
Gov. James Blanchard meets with JC officials in a May visit to view progress on the Tech Center. See Tech Center story on pages 6 & 7.

The Guv

THE COLLEGIATE

GRAND RAPIDS JUNIOR COLLEGE

Vol. 35, No. 8 February 20, 1991

JC prepares for the Discontinuance Agreement

By Michael Wilson
Associate Editor

Free at last

JC separates from K-12

By Joey Sutherlin
Editor-in-Chief

Child support

Young supporters of American troops join the Downtown Grand Rapids rally.

photo by Steven Wright

see Free, page 2

GRJC Becomes GRCC

For 77 years, Grand Rapids Junior College had been a part of the Grand Rapids Public Schools, subject to and limited by the Grand Rapids superintendent and board of education. Talk of separation of the college from the public schools had been in the air for years. Yet when the issue at last came to the polls in 1974, voters said no to separation (and a countywide tax base for the college) by a two-to-one margin, effectively ending discussion for a long period of time.

At last, in 1991, as a result of a successful, hard-fought redistricting election guided by President Richard Calkins, the college became an independent, county-based college with its own elected board of trustees. Though many thought there was wisdom in changing the college name to Kent County Community College, the new board opted to go with tradition and name recognition, calling it Grand Rapids Community College. Funded by its own county-generated operating revenue of 1.9 mills, GRCC could now offer resident tuition to the entire Kent Intermediate School District.

The 1991 separation of all college operations, buildings, and staff from the K-12 system was a daunting task. A Separation Agreement between GRCC and GRPS helped guide the complicated process of transition. The college bought its buildings from GRPS for $9.3 million and hired away many skilled GRPS employees to do for the college what they had done for the public schools. Superintendent Patrick Sandro was forced to make a plea to President Calkins to end the poaching of his employees. The separation, now 23 years old, has never prevented a good working relationship between GRCC and GRPS.

To date, Grand Rapids Community College has not gained the full support of residents outside of the city. Though GRCC generates huge sums each year for the area's economy, every college millage election since 1991 has failed, due largely to the out-of-city vote.

(clockwise from top left) *The Collegiate*. January 23, 1991. *The Collegiate*. January 23, 1991. *The Collegiate*, page 4. August 22, 1990. *The Collegiate*. January 23, 1991. *The Collegiate*. February 20, 1991 (GRCC Archives)

The Separation Agreement

At the recommendation of the President, the board of trustees appointed new (since the retirement of John Cuthbertson) Chief Financial Officer Bob Partridge to the position of vice president of financial services. Partridge faced the daunting task of building an entire Department of Business and Finance from the ground up. A later administrator would liken it to "giving birth to a full grown child."[5] In a short period of time, the college managed to hire away a fair number of skilled GRPS employees to do for the college what they had done for the public schools. Superintendent Sandro was forced to make a plea to Calkins to end the poaching of his employees.

A Separation Agreement helped guide the complicated process of transition. One large hurdle was the fact that all college buildings belonged to the Grand Rapids Public Schools—and the board wanted $15 million from the college for these facilities. Partridge, who looked upon the campus buildings as a community investment, felt the college should pay nothing. The board disagreed. In the end the two sides compromised on a $9.3 million buyout, which the college paid off over the next 10 years.

New Board—New Applied Technology Center

The founding GRCC Board of Trustees was, according to Calkins, "a positive, supportive group that cared deeply for the college." Lyle Morrison was elected the first board chairperson. Other members included Ellen James, Teresa (Terri) Handlin, former Chief Executive Frank McCarthy, William (Mac) McPherson, Janice Maggini, and David Rodriquez. This group hit the ground running. First on the agenda was approval of another Five-Year Plan 1991-96 called *Vision '96*, the work of the

(right, Figure 107)
Vision '96 planning document. (GRCC Archives) (above, Figure 108) President Calkins' address at the opening of the Applied Technology Center, 1991. (GRCC Archives)

Long-Range Planning Task Force. (**Figure 107**) On the heels of that came the June 17, 1991, dedication and grand opening of the Applied Technology Center, a $27 million technical training center conceived as a joint venture by President Calkins and President J. William Wenrich of Ferris State University. (**Figure 108**) In one facility, the combined resources of GRCC (70 percent) and FSU (30 percent) would provide innovative, cutting-edge technical training for business and industry. The two-year/four-year college partnership was the first of its kind—and, thanks to the efforts of State Representative Tom Mathieu and others, resulted in state funding of $13 million. A capital campaign chaired by Fred Keller raised close to $5 million in cash and in-kind contributions of equipment and furnishings from 173 individuals and companies.

The planning of the ATC was the work of those who would benefit most from it—area business and industry, and faculty and staff of the Technology, Computer Applications, and Hospitality Education Division. The Technology Division, Computer Applications Division, and area business leaders oversaw the design of

1985-98

1991

Redistricting measure passed which enabled the college to separate from K-12 district.

1992

The board of trustees approved the purchase of the College Park Plaza Building which would become home to the college's administration.

GRCC began operating a mobile uplink truck for all 29 community colleges in the Michigan Community College Association. The truck uplinked debates and rallies in two presidential elections, (1992 and 1996) many professional sporting events, many syndicated talk shows and a variety of K12 and collegiate educational events.

1993

Poet Allen Ginsberg spoke at GRCC in 1993. (GRCC Archives)

Diversity Task Force formed.

(**Figure 109**) Lyon Street Parking Ramp dedication and ribbing cutting, 1994. President Calkins (left) with student representative, Board of Trustees Chair Lyle Morrison, and Mayor John Logie. (GRCC Archives)

labs for computer-aided design and drafting, plastics technology, computer applications, electronics, robotics, energy management, machine tooling, air conditioning/heating/refrigeration, materials testing, and hydraulics/pneumatics. The Hospitality Division created its own designs for a new Heritage Restaurant, Art & Bev's Café, instructional kitchens, banquet rooms, and receiving and storage areas—in the process expanding enrollment to 300 students. The Hospitality Education Division had been named the top food service program in the country in 1989. New first-class quarters in the ATC and travel to Germany for the Culinary Olympics inspired in the staff bold academic innovations—in particular, yearly international study tours for both students and faculty to broaden exposure to international cuisine experiences.

A South Campus

By the fall of 1992, enrollment stood at 14,250 students, and the college felt the pinch of trying to accommodate them. Though GRCC was committed to downtown Grand Rapids, talk of a satellite campus began to fill the air. Steelcase Corporation stepped forward with an offer to donate a large parcel of land near 60th Street, south of town, to create a second GRCC campus. Dean of Institutional Research Dr. Juan R. Olivarez was put in charge of the project. President Calkins and others envisioned a facility deeply invested in advanced technology and innovative learning. Planning went on for three years; Calkins with the help of Representative Tom Mathieu, both powerful lobbyists for the college, managed to secure millions in support from the state.

Yet in the end, Olivarez reluctantly recommended the development be abandoned. The cost was too great, technology was already the focus of the new ATC, and there was no certainty of county support for such a large undertaking. Olivarez felt the college would be better served by a new science building on the Main campus. The future was in the sciences, he told Calkins, and a first-class science facility (already in the planning stages), would prove a more significant investment for the college.

Calkins was disappointed, but took time to consider the recommendation. In the end he trusted the judgment of the man he had put in charge. Acting swiftly, he persuaded state legislators to transfer the South campus development appropriation to Main campus science building construction.[6]

Retirement Packages, Lyon Street Parking Ramp, and Other News

The redistricting of the college was followed by a wave of significant retirements. Dr. Marinus Swets was replaced as dean of Arts and Sciences by newcomer Dr. Wesley Teo and then (when Teo was promoted) Language Arts Chair Chuck Chamberlain. College veteran Dr. Pat Pulliam replaced retiring Executive Vice President Corky Eringaard, and Technology Chair Dr. Don Boyer replaced Dr. Till Peters as dean of Occupational Education. C. Richard Smith, who had done much of the planning for the Ford Fieldhouse, made the decision to retire. Buy-out packages encouraged senior staff and faculty retirements as a cost-saving measure. Times and faces were changing.

After much uncertainty about location, the board approved in 1992 a new 750-space parking ramp to be built on the northwest corner of Lyon and Bostwick. It would open in 1994, providing relief for a perennial college problem. (**Figure 109**)

In the early 1990s, voices in liberal arts divisions could be heard complaining, with some justification, that Occupational Education was receiving the lion's share of the college budget. In 1991, Language Arts instructors Dr. Veta Tucker and David Cope introduced courses in African-American literature and multicultural literature, respectively. In 1993, the college established

USA STADIUM
MILLINGTON, TENNESSEE

NJCAA II '96

(**Figure 110**) 1996 baseball team.(GRCC Archives)

1993

Lyon Street Parking Ramp opened providing 750 additional parking spaces on the corner of Lyon and Bostwick. (GRCC Archives)

1994

College connected to the Internet.

Service Learning Center opened to serve as a clearinghouse for providing students volunteer and service learning opportunities.

Enrollment was 13,726.

1995

First Diversity Conference was held. (GRCC Archives)

Winchester Alley opened.

Men's basketball team lost in the NJCAA Division II title game to North Iowa College.

First annual Math Challenge for ninth and tenth graders held.

a Diversity Task Force and in 1995 hosted its first Diversity Conference. In 1994, Dr. Robert Long created the Science Education Center to improve science education and motivate young students to pursue science careers. Master guitarist Brian Morris joined the Music Department and soon established the GRCC International Guitar Series.

Richard Steele, contracted from GRPS, became director of campus security. In 1995, Captain Cindy Kennell replaced him, and by 1999 campus police carried side arms; in 2001 her seven-officer force became a college department with full police power. The football team won the '92 Dixie Rotary Bowl in St. George, Utah. On campus, a new non-smoking policy began

limiting disgruntled smokers to designated areas. In 1993, iconic poet Allen Ginsberg ran a workshop and read from his works, guest of the college and his poet-friend David Cope. In 1994, Coach Spyke Johnson was inducted into the NJCAA Swimming and Diving Hall of Fame. The same year, internet access became available to the college, and to students the following year. Email access arrived in 1996. Biology instructor Laurie Faber was named '96 Michigan Science Teacher of the Year. Rick Vander Veen was voted top Michigan Arena Manager and Recreational Director for 1996. The baseball team, coached by Doug Wabeke, won the NJCAA Division II World Series in '96 and '97. (**Figure 110**) Wabeke was named '97 "Coach of the Year" and then

(Figure 111) President Calkins awards Delta Phi Alpha honors to students, 1997. (GRCC Archives)

college co-athletic director with Steve Kemperman, replacing the retiring Emil Caprara. 1997 also marked the induction of Coach Sigurd (Skip) Nelson into the Women's Tennis Hall of Fame.

Organizational Changes

In the 1994-95 school year, day and evening (continuing education) colleges consolidated operations and ceased to be separate entities. Dean of Continuing Education Julie Johnson thereafter took the position of dean of enrollment management in charge of financial aid, admissions, as well as registrar.[7] In 1996, Calkins and staff reconfigured administrative structure, replacing nine divisional chairs with three deans (Chuck Chamberlain, Dean of the School of Social Science and Humanities, Dr. Don Boyer, Dean of the School of Workforce Development, and David Steinfort, Dean of the School of Mathematics, Natural Science, Health and Wellness) and their three assistant deans (Dr. Joseph Becherer, Bobbi Schrader, and Dr. Velvie Green). A number of former divisions were subdivided into departments, each with its own chair. The Language Arts Division, for example, was divided into English, and Language and Thought Departments, led by Janet Paasche and Bernard Manker. The Social Science Division became Social Science and Behavioral

Science Departments, led by Steve Abid and Dr. Gary Burbridge. Faculty response to reorganization was mixed.

The Three-Year War

Independence from the Grand Rapids Public Schools did not guarantee college solvency. Within two years of the redistricting victory, the college began experiencing hard financial times. A sudden dip in enrollment, the loss of non-resident tuition as a result of countywide residency, ever-decreasing state aid, and a freeze on property taxes by Governor Engler conspired to put the college well over a million dollars in the red. Tuition hikes and budget cuts inevitably followed. Wrestling, cross-country, and swimming teams were eliminated.

The 1991 Five-Year Plan (*Vision '96*) made it a college objective to "institutionalize problem solving as opposed to labor adversarial approaches in collective bargaining." This approach to negotiations no doubt appealed to Association President Tom Hofmann and Chief Negotiator Dick Godfrey, yet during the financial difficulties of 1993, at a point when faculty was asked to give back half of a six percent raise as a gesture of good faith, the problem-solving approach gave way to the deeply adversarial. At the outset of new contract negotiations, the disagreements appeared formidable and steadily got worse. It took fact finding, arbitration, declarations of impasse, a faculty vote of "no confidence" in the President, and three years of extreme stress to reach an agreement. The *Grand Rapids Press* threw fuel on the fire with an extended story about "excessive" faculty overtime and wages—true in a handful of egregious cases—prejudicing the public view of both the faculty and the college. The unhappy period came to be known as "the three-year war." In the end, both sides compromised and a five-year contract was reached, followed by a deep, collective sigh of relief.[8]

Total Quality Management

One of the few Calkins' enterprises that did not gain traction was a leadership model from the business world known as "Total Quality Management" (TQM) or "Continuous Quality Improvement" (CQI). It was intended to be a form of shared leadership that focused on how well the organization functioned. It encouraged employees to be engaged in decision-making and to direct their work performance toward clearly stated and measurable outcomes. Though the idea fell flat in the educational environment of GRCC (a number of faculty perceived Calkins as unwilling to share leadership), later presidents would adopt CQI principles as a means of institutional self-evaluation for the re-accreditation process.

Library Automation

Dorothy Terhune and Phil Pikaart, the longest-serving GRCC librarians, participated in the 1997 modernization of the library from traditional print resources to the introduction of library automation and digital resources. In 1998, Mike Klawitter became the college's first archivist.

Since the later Calkins years, Betsy Teo, Susan Bergin, and Patricia Ingersoll have served as library directors. Library staff support of off-campus and online curriculums with ebooks, databases, and ejournals has occurred far ahead of most Michigan community colleges.

Older Learner Center

In the early 1970s, Dr. Robert Riekse of GRCC and Dr. Henry Holstege of Calvin College had formed a Consortium on Aging which developed programs to educate older adults and service providers on aging issues. In 1998, Calkins organized these efforts into the Older Learner Center of GRCC, with the mission (in Calkins' words) "of providing older people, their families and service providers with knowledge that would promote successful, independent living." Riekse, Holstege, and Michael Faber launched the center, which to date has served the needs of thousands of older people in Kent County.[9]

The Calkins Era Ends After 23 Years

The Older Learner Center would be one of the final pieces of business for President Calkins. After 23 years of doing the visionary work of reinventing the college, Calkins made the decision in the fall of 1998 to retire. The rancor and stress of the final few years had taken a toll. Having given 38 years of service to GRPS and the college, 30 years as a spokesman for the Michigan Community College Association, and 40 years as minister of music to five different churches, it was time to give himself more fully to family, friends and his wide-ranging cultural interests. Calkins would leave behind a lasting legacy of strong and creative leadership, unparalleled facilities and program development, and ongoing academic excellence. (**Figure 111**)

1985-98

1996

Baseball team won its first NJCAA Division II World Series.

Email offered on-campus.

Spectrum Theater opened on Fountain Street. This facility included a space for the Culinary Arts Baking and Pastry Arts program on the lower level.

1997

Automated registration by touchtone phone was made available. In addition, students could register via computer workstations throughout the college.

Softball team won the regional championships and advanced to the national tournament. They repeated this feat in 1998.

Baseball team won its second NJCAA Division II World Series. (1997 Baseball team. GRCC Archives)

1998

Older Learner Center established.

Students in Winchester Alley, ca. 1990s. (GRCC Archives)

The Olivarez Years
1999-2008

The First Interim President

On September 30, 1998, Executive Vice President Dr. Patricia Pulliam was named interim president of GRCC, the first woman and the first African-American to lead the college. (**Figure 112**) She would serve well for four months (throwing her own hat into the presidential ring) while the search process proceeded. She suspected, however, that she would be seen as a reflection of the Calkins administration, which had just emerged from a period of prolonged struggle with faculty. On February 10, 1999, when the board named Dr. Juan R. Olivarez (GRCC Dean of Institutional Research) the college's eighth president, Pulliam was disappointed but not surprised.[1] She retired shortly thereafter, having served the college faithfully and well—as instructor and administrator—for 30 years.

The Eighth Chief Executive

Dr. Juan Olivarez thereupon became the first Hispanic president of a Michigan college or university. (**Figure 113**) He was born in Benavides, Texas, where his family worked as migrant laborers. His parents valued education and instilled in him a strong work ethic; education to them was the surest way out of poverty. When his father and uncle managed to find work in the Gary steel mills, the family moved to East Chicago. In time Olivarez became interested in Aquinas College in Grand

(**Figure 112**) Dr. Patricia Pulliam, first Interim President, 1993. (GRCC Archives)

(**Figure 113**) Dr. Juan R. Olivarez, eighth leader of GRCC. (GRCC Archives)

Rapids, Michigan, and applied for admission. There he would earn a teaching degree and meet his future wife, Mary, who was also an education major. He began his career teaching first grade in the Grand Rapids Public Schools, one of the first bilingual teachers in the district. After two years, he entered Wayne State University, earning a master's degree in Educational Psychology and later a doctorate in Family and Child Ecology from Michigan State University. He would work for 20 years for GRPS as a school psychologist, a supervisor of special education, and finally as a director of curriculum research and development. Mary and he would have two sons.

When GRJC became a community college in 1991, President Calkins gave Vice President Bill Foster the job of persuading Olivarez to become the college's dean of institutional research. Happy with GRPS yet attracted by the challenge of a college remaking itself, Olivarez eventually accepted, never imagining that within the space of eight years, he would replace Calkins as GRCC president. By 1996, Olivarez would become CEO of the Community Learning Enterprise alongside his duties as dean.

Of 47 applicants, Olivarez was the choice of the board of trustees to become the eighth chief executive of Grand Rapids Community College. His style was different from the forceful, decisive, builder/visionary Calkins.

1999

Juan Olivarez was named the eighth leader of the college and the first Hispanic president of a Michigan college or university. Olivarez developed community partnerships through the financing and construction of the Leslie E. Tassell M-TEC Center and establishing Learning Corners. He also worked to encourage diversity at the college by pushing diversity to the forefront of hiring practices, program development, and student recruitment. Within his ten years as president, Olivarez saw the college double the number of minority students.

First annual International Harvest Festival was held. This event features food, dance, and arts from around the world. (1992 International Harvest Festival. GRCC Archives)

College hosted a teach-in on Kosovo.

Bostwick Commons opened, transforming one block of Bostwick Avenue between Lyon and Fountain from an open street with heavy traffic into a green space for students to gather, study, eat, read or to just relax.

(**Figure 114**) President Olivarez's Inauguration, October 1999. (GRCC Archives)

and local leaders, musical interludes, and all the pomp and ceremony appropriate to a presidential inauguration. (**Figure 114**)

Community Partnerships

Olivarez from the start envisioned a college stronger in comunity partnerships—wanting to broaden the sense of what it meant to be a community college. He had earlier created the Community Learning Enterprise, in which the college served as learning consultant for the community. The CLE would help move GRCC toward Olivarez's partnership goals, providing a base from which his vision could expand. The college would work with K-12, with the intermediate school districts (particularly Ottawa County, not served by a community college), with the health industry (connecting it with a new college science facility), with downtown Grand Rapids, with area colleges—with any part of the greater community facing a learning need. Donna Kragt, Frank Conner, John Cleveland, and Mark Champion worked with Olivarez as part of this initiative.[2]

Teacher Education

In 1998, GRCC chemistry instructor Dr. Joe Hesse and math instructor James Chesla received awards from the National Science Foundation for designing math and science courses that met all state and national benchmarks for future teachers. Hesse, with the support of Dr. Ruth Kurlandsky, Coordinator of Curriculum Development, and Art Armijo, Director of Upward Bound, established a Teacher Education Center in the GRCC Library. Over 30 instructors agreed to be mentors for students pursuing careers in teaching. The Center would in time become part of the Child Development and Education Program headed by Dr. Becky Brinks. A Teachers of Tomorrow Scholarship (TOTS) program, overseen by Hesse and Carole

Olivarez arrived after a time of protracted contract battles. He was a healer, a consensus-builder, a collaborator with natural people skills and a desire to strengthen GRCC as a community of care. He seemed the right choice at the right time.

The College's First Inauguration Ceremony

The board of trustees envisioned a gala inauguration ceremony for the eighth president, and Richard Austin, Director of Professional Development, was the choice to orchestrate it. On Sunday, October 17, 1999, GRCC invited the community to a Campus Open House to experience the facilities and operations of a dramatically expanded college. On Friday, October 22, Fountain Street Church filled with faculty, staff, students, and community members to share in a formal processional with fanfares and marches, congratulatory remarks from state

(Figure 115) Wealthy Learning Corner, 2004. (GRCC Archives)

Redwine, presently awards up to $20,000 in scholarships each year.[3]

The Learning Corners

From the start of his presidency, Olivarez had his staff going door-to-door interviewing community members about how GRCC could better serve them, in the process discovering that many desired the college's presence in their own neighborhoods. In collaboration with the Wege Foundation and the GRPS, Olivarez in 2003 created the first Learning Corner on Wealthy

Street, which became a hub for students who wanted to be in school but had problems with a regular high school environment. (Figure 115) The storefront operation with the GRCC name on it quickly attracted area residents who wanted to build their English language skills, computer literacy, and other abilities in preparation for the GED, for citizenship tests, or for college enrollment.[4] The experiment was an immediate success. A similar Learning Corner would later be established on Grand Rapids' West Side.

The Century Turns with Good and Bad News

1999 saw the creation of a Y2K Team to assess college readiness for the new millennium. In March, the first annual Salute to Women Awards went to Nancy Clouse, Terri Handlin, Jill Paasch, and Dr. Pat Pulliam. In April, Social Science Chair Dr. Richard Kurzhals, along with Paul Chardoul, Roger Schlosser, and Carolyn Grin presented a teach-in on the war in Kosovo. That year, Coach Sue Katerburg was inducted into the NJCAA Tennis Hall of Fame.

In November, biology instructors Dr. Greg Forbes and Dr. Robert Long wrote a grant proposal for the Michigan Department of Education called the Michigan Science Evolution Education Initiative with the goals of training educators in teaching evolution and providing them a support system. Every science teaching association in Michigan signed the proposal. Forbes would go on to champion the teaching of evolution in science classes. In 2006, the ACLU would select him for its Civil Libertarian of the Year Award for his work in favor of exclusively evolution-based curricula. He maintained that "intelligent design" was not science, that the evolution/design controversy deserved to be examined, but not in the context of a science classroom.[5]

1999 was also the year Bostwick Avenue became Bostwick Commons (rededicated as Dr. Juan R. Olivarez Student Plaza in

1999-2008

1999

First annual Salute to Women awards ceremony honoring four women within the college's community for personal and professional excellence and for serving as role models and mentors to other women. This is awarded annually during March, Women's History Month.

Joseph Kinnebrew sculpture *Aspiration of Inspiration* dedicated on the Bostwick Commons, 1999. (GRCC Archives)

2000

Richard W. Calkins Science Center opened, providing modern classrooms and laboratories for the Biological Sciences and Physical Sciences departments.

GRCC signed Concurrent Enrollment Pact with GVSU, enabling students to take courses at both institutions simultaneously, or alternate enrollment between them.

*e*GRCC implemented for online registration and access to student records.

(Figure 116)
Bostwick Commons,
undated. (GRCC Archives)

enabling degree-seeking students from one institution to take courses from the other, with all credits counting toward graduation. (**Figure 117**) The next year a similar pact would be created with Ferris State University; others would follow. The year 2000 saw the establishment of a Science Lecture Series, dramatic growth of the Early College Program, and the continued celebration of the annual Renaissance Musicall Feaste created by vocal music instructor Kevin Dobreff and hosted by the college's Madrigal Singers and Culinary Arts students. In 2001, art instructor Ron Stein's sculpture was featured in the Frederick Meijer Gardens exhibit "Master Teachers: West Michigan Sculpture Faculty." Biology instructor Dr. Matthew Douglas became regional director of the Monarch Watch, involving capture, tagging, and release of the butterflies in order to track their journeys to Mexico. Online registration (eGRCC) began. The college introduced a new professionally-created sports mascot, the Raider raccoon.

The Academic Senate (later the Academic Governing Council) held its first meeting—a group made up of administration and faculty members from each department, sharing governance by crafting adademic policies and recommending them to the provost (Dr. Velvie Green; later Dr. Gilda Gely). Eric Kunnen was appointed director of a new Distance Learning and Instructional Technologies Department. Distance Learning had begun in 1979 with the first telecourses. By 2001, online courses were already displacing them, and within seven years telecourses would be history. By 2008, GRCC would be recognized as a national leader in application of instructional technologies, including the course management system known as Blackboard.

2013), an inviting area that extended the GRCC campus the entire length of the Main and North Buildings (**Figure 116**) A Joseph Kinnebrew sculpture, *Aspiration of Inspiration* was installed and dedicated on the Commons.

In 2000, English instructor Sharon Wynkoop organized "Hemingway 101," in celebration of the writer's 101st birthday. The four-week event featured lectures, a banquet, films, a one-man play, and a traveling art exhibit. That year Provost (a title replacing executive vice president) Dr. Don Boyer announced a Concurrent Enrollment Pact with Grand Valley State University,

(Figure 117) President Arend Lubbers (center) and Juan Olvarez signing of the Concurrent Enrollment Agreement with Grand Valley State University, 2000. (GRCC Archives)

(Figure 118) President George W. Bush speaking at the Ford Fieldhouse, 2004. (GRCC Archives)

On September 11, 2001, the fall semester was just getting underway when Al-Qaeda terrorists attacked the twin towers of the World Trade Center in New York City and the Pentagon in Washington, D.C. The college and the nation were shocked, fearful, overwhelmed with angry disbelief. The October 3, 2001, Collegiate reported that Muslim students, afraid of that anger, had disappeared from classes. Staff members were trying to calm their fears. The new Bush administration would respond to the terrorist aggression with force. Prolonged wars in Afghanistan and Iraq would follow, and yet another generation of young people would find themselves doing battle for their country.

In 2002, the football team honored Coach Fred Julian in his final game with a win over Iowa Central Community College in the Graphic Edge Bowl. Jim Schulte would replace Julian. In 2003-04, the baseball team, coached by Doug Wabeke, won consecutive NJCAA Division II World Series. In 2005, coached by Mike Cupples, the team won a third consecutive Series for an overall total of five national championships.

2003 saw President Oivarez appointed by President Bush to the 10-member advisory board of the National Institute for Literacy. (Figure 118) In 2004, the GRCC Choir performed again at Carnegie Hall as part of a 225-voice chorus made up of seven community colleges from across the nation. That year, leader of the Grand Rapids Jazz Orchestra, Tim Froncek, was named a jazz instructor at GRCC. The following year, Roger Schlosser introduced a course in Irish history and Kim Wyngarden a course in Russian literature. President Olivarez hired the consulting firm Campus Works to reorganize and improve the Information Technology Department, now so vital to the functioning of the college. In 2007, wireless internet access was made available on-campus, and in November of 2008, the college became a tobacco-free facility.

Corpus Christi

As part of the 2003 season of Actors' Theater, Fred Sebulske directed *Corpus Christi*, a Terrance McNally play. The story of the life and death of a young gay man caused controversy with some

2000

GRCC organized the first annual Latino Youth Conference to motivate all youth to strive for educational excellence and higher education.

Patrick A. Thompson M-TEC opened in Olive Township, Ottawa County and was named after Pat Thompson, the owner and president of Trans-Matic Manufacturing in Holland. A joint project of the Ottawa Area Intermediate School District and GRCC, the M-TEC provided training in skilled trades.

2001

GRCC signed Concurrent Enrollment Agreement with Ferris State University.

Board of trustees swore in the seven-officer force as an independent department to afford campus police full power to ticket and arrest citizens off-campus. (GRCC police force, undated. GRCC Archives)

2002

Accuplacer first used for assessing incoming students.

(**Figure 119**) Calkins Science Center, 2000.
(GRCC Archives)

The Richard W. Calkins Science Center

In the period after GRJC became a regional community college in 1991, enrollment in the sciences began to increase dramatically. That fact and the changing landscape of science education created a sense of urgency about the need to expand GRCC science offerings and redo outmoded laboratory facilities. The same year chemistry instructors attended a conference called "Trends in Freshman Chemistry" at California Institute of Technology in Pasadena. The ideas they encountered filled them with enthusiasm about new ways of teaching—and with dreams of a facility designed to serve them in the 21st century. Two of them, Roger DeVries and Dr. Joe Hesse, began sketching out plans on airline napkins. Back home, excitement did not dissipate. Physical and biological science instructors, working together, made a strong case for a new science facility.[6] President Calkins listened, responded positively, and began marshaling legislative support. When the state agreed to transfer South campus funding to a new downtown science center, the project blossomed. Both the G Building and Violet Chapel were razed to make room for the center. Ground was broken in late spring 1997; at the building's opening in January of 2000, President Olivarez would christen the new facility— a masterwork of planning by the science faculties—the Richard W. Calkins Science Center in honor of the man who helped make it happen. (**Figure 119**)

The five-story facility was equipped with 23 classrooms, two distance learning classrooms, a science display room, 28 labs, a 150-seat auditorium, a greenhouse, a Jurassic Learning Garden, and multiple study spaces and lounge areas. Biology instructor Paul Krieger would develop a cadaver laboratory and workshops, using cadavers rented from Michigan State University. Life sciences would occupy the second and third

who felt it overstepped the bounds of community standards. Since Actors' Theater was supported by GRCC and performed at Spectrum Theater, Sebulske made the decision to move the final three performances to Fountain Street Church rather than create problems for the college. President Olivarez approved the move but held firm to maintaining the fruitful 22-year relationship with Actors' Theater. Continuing controversy (one community member repeatedly threatened to sue the college for its support of the theater group) spurred the board of trustees to adopt an academic freedom policy to provide criteria for settling such disputes. Chair Gary P. Schenk summed up the policy as follows: "The president shall not fail to protect academic freedom while recognizing community standards and allowing for community input." Though the policy placed heavy responsibility on the president, it resulted in GRCC remaining, as a college should, an open forum for ideas—with the "community standards" voices still militating to set limits on that freedom.

(Figure 120) Patrick A. Thompson M-TEC, undated. (GRCC Archives)

floors, physical sciences the fourth and fifth.[7] For GRCC science faculty, the dream had become reality.

New M-TEC Centers

Dick Calkins, in 1998, had state funding in place for a Holland M-TEC (Michigan Technical Education Center), a facility Olivarez dedicated near the start of his presidency. (**Figure 120**) In 1999, GRCC received a $3.3 million state grant as start-up funding for a new downtown M-TEC Center on the corner of Rumsey and Godfrey SW. The lot was donated to the college by Michigan Consolidated Gas Company. It was land that had lain vacant for 40 years because of contamination—the result of the burning of coal from 1880 through the 1940s. Removal of contaminated soil proved a time-consuming and expensive process. Still, President Olivarez was able to break ground for the facility in November of 2000 and dedicate it in 2002. It would be named in honor of local businessman and major donor Leslie E. Tassell and would provide workforce training—vital to the area—in automotive technology, construc-

tion trades, and manufacturing and production.[8] It would also house the Apprenticeship Program. The Leslie E. Tassell M-TEC Center, directed by George Waite, at a total cost of $13.3 million, replaced the Leonard and Ball facility which the college would put up for sale. (**Figure 121 & 122**)

Though the new M-TEC center was cause for celebration, Math Department Chair John Dersch spoke for liberal arts faculty when he voiced concern that the college had shifted its emphasis from liberal arts transfer students (now 29 percent of the student body) to occupational training students (now 71 percent of the student body).[9] Twenty-five years earlier, the balance of liberal arts transfer to occupational students had been very nearly the reverse ratio.

(**left, Figure 121**) Leslie E. Tassell M-TEC, 2002. (GRCC Archives)
(**right, Figure 122**) Grand Rapids' Mayor John H. Logie speaking at Leslie E. Tassell M-TEC dedication, 2002. (GRCC Archives)

1999-2008

2002

Football team won the Graphic Edge Bowl by the score of 12-6 over Iowa Central Community College on November 17, 2002. This was Coach Fred Julian's last game. (2002 Graphic Edge Bowl trophy. GRCC Archives)

Leslie E. Tassell M-TEC was dedicated on August 28, 2002. Named in honor of local businessman and GRCC donor Leslie E. Tassell, this center provides hands-on education in automotive technology, construction trades, and metal forming and welding.

2003

College established Center for Diversity Learning to embrace and promote respect of human differences through programs and activities supporting increased social justice and equity among all people.

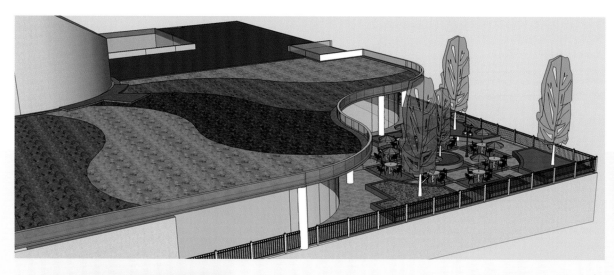

The Wisner-Bottrall Applied Technology Center Green Roof

During the tenure of President Olivarez and later under President Ender, sustainability became a top priority of Grand Rapids Community College. In 2006, Olivarez directed the college's Environmental Council to develop energy conservation plans, one of the most dramatic being the 2007 installation of a green roof on the Applied Technology Center. Designed by GMB Architecture and funded by a grant from the Steelcase Foundation, the Liveroof pre-vegetated roof was installed by Ter Horst & Rinzema Construction Co. and Summit Landscape Management, Inc. The top-floor roof of the ATC was chosen because of its broad expanse; a lower green deck was added to enhance The Heritage Restaurant viewing area and provide natural herb gardens for the Culinary Arts program.

What are the benefits of a green roof? Large concrete buildings with asphalt roofs generate enough heat to affect area weather patterns. When living plants replace vast stretches of asphalt (in this case, 25,000 square feet), the vegetation cools and cleans the air. The ATC roof garden also provides insulation that saves energy, increases the longevity of the roof, and enhances the acoustics of the entire building. Perhaps most beneficial of all, the ATC green roof absorbs rain, preventing heavy run-off into the city's storm water systems. The colorful, drought-tolerant sedum plants offer another benefit no ordinary roof can: a restorative effect on mind and spirit.

(**clockwise from top left**) Wisner-Bottrall Applied Technology Center green roof design. (GRCC Archives); Green roof construction outside of The Heritage Restaurant. (GRCC Archives); Completed green roof outside second floor of the Wisner-Bottrall Applied Technology Center. (GRCC Archives); Green roof Information panel, second floor of the Wisner-Bottrall Applied Technology Center. (GRCC Archives)

Hard Financial Times

Almost from the start, the Olivarez administration faced the hardest financial times since the recession of the early 1980s. In 2001, the United States lost 26.1 million jobs, the state of Michigan among the hardest hit. In 2000, Vice President of Finance Bob Partridge predicted a $1.2 million deficit for 2001, based on a 30 percent increase in health care, increasing retirement fund costs, and a decreasing property tax. By the time Partridge retired in 2010, he had seen (over his 19-year career as chief financial officer) state aid to the college decrease from 50 to 16 percent.[10] In 2003, when Governor Jennifer Granholm slashed state aid 1.5 percent, Olivarez announced that the college had no choice but to raise tuition, increase class sizes, and prepare for future cuts in programs. The hiring of adjunct faculty would increase as a cost-savings measure. By 2004, Partridge was projecting a $3.5 million deficit.

The worst was yet to come. The Great Recession, which officially began in late 2007, contributed to the historic election of President Barack Obama in 2008, and ended in the summer of 2009, saw a collapse of the stock market and housing prices, the near-bankruptcy of the auto industry, and an 11 percent drop of median income in Michigan. During these harsh times, GRCC enrollment increased sharply (a predictable phenomenon). To accommodate the rush of students seeking new skills, Olivarez made the decision to ask taxpayers for a millage increase—in spite of the bleak financial outlook. As part of the 1991 redistricting victory, the college had promised not to ask taxpayers for more money for the next 10 years. That promise had been kept—with six years to spare. The board of trustees supported the Olivarez decision. A 2007 millage election was hard-fought but resulted in a narrow loss. A follow-up election had similar results. Olivarez marked

those defeats as the greatest disappointments of his presidency.[11]

Collective bargaining during such thin times was difficult, especially with the Faculty Association. Yet Olivarez managed to work at positive problem-solving with Association Presidents Tom Hofmann, Fred van Hartesveldt, and Chief Negotiator Dick Godfrey to resolve important issues, including the granting of titles to faculty (largely the work of the Academic Senate) based on longevity.

Commitment to Diversity

Dick Calkins and his staff had done a good deal to encourage diversity at the college: a Women's Resource Center, a Title IX coordinator, a Gay and Lesbian Task Force, facilities and an advisor for foreign students, a Council for Minority Concerns, an Office of Handicapped Services, courses in African-American and multicultural literature, a Diversity Task Force, the first annual Diversity Conference, and a 1994 Diversity Learning Center which hosted a yearly lecture series.

President Olivarez was intent on building beyond what Calkins had begun. Diversity was deeply important to the board of trustees, and Olivarez pushed it to the forefront of hiring practices, program development, and student recruitment. Within the nine years of the Olivarez presidency, the college doubled the number of minority students enrolled. The Diversity Learning Center team offered diversity training for staff and faculty. It also sponsored the annual Giants Awards ceremony (established in 1983 by Cedric Ward and Dr. Pat Pulliam) honoring exceptional contributions to the African-American community; the annual Salute to Women; the Diversity Conference; the Martin Luther King, Jr. Celebration; and the Diversity Lecture Series featuring advocates of social

2004

RaiderCard implemented, enabling students to pay for parking, books, printing, vending and other expenses with a swipe of their identification cards. (RaiderCard, undated. GRCC Archives)

The GRCC baseball team won three consecutive NJCAA Division II World Series titles from 2003-05. (2004 NJCAA Division II World Series champions. GRCC Archives)

The GRCC Choir performed in Carnegie Hall in New York as part of a 225-voice chorus made up of singers from seven community colleges from across the nation. The GRCC Choir had also performed in Carnegie Hall in 1990 and 1999.

2005

Enrollment Center opened to create a front door at the college for new students and streamline the enrollment process.

(**Figure 123**) 2013 Diversity Lecture Series speaker LZ Granderson. (GRCC Archives)

(Figure 124) Hispanic Excellence Scholarship, presented by Presdent Olivarez, 2006. (GRCC Archives)

(Figure 125) Dedication of Woodrick Diversity Learning Center, honoring Aleicia and Bob Woodrick (center), December 2006. (GRCC Archives)

2005

The football team, ranked No. 2, played No. 1 Glendale (Arizona), Community College at the National Junior College Athletic Association Championship in the Valley of the Sun Bowl I, coming up on the short end 50-48.

GRCC Hospitality Education Department hosted the Nation's Cup, an International Culinary Competition, with culinary arts students representing Scotland, Argentina, Canada, Chile, the United States and Mexico. The college hosted this event again in 2007 and 2009. (2005 Nations Cup. GRCC Archives)

Mariachi Band created, performing traditional and modern Hispanic music. (GRCC Archives)

justice and spokespersons of often controversial minority views. **(Figure 123)**

In 2006, the college hosted a "Women in the Arts" celebration for Women's History Month, featuring poets Mursalata Muhammad and Linda Nemec. Katie Kalisz introduced a Women's Literature course that year. In April, the International Students Organization put on its seventh annual festival featuring international culinary and cultural events. In October 2006, Olivarez joined a protest march against a Michigan initiative intending to put an end to Affirmative Action, a national policy he strongly embraced. In November, the college held the first Hispanic Excellence Scholarship gala to honor the values of César E. Chávez. Awards were presented to five West Michigan people for their dedication to the teaching and legacy of

Chávez and a $1,000 scholarship in Chávez's name to a worthy student. **(Figure 124)** Michael Gillan of the Music Department founded the college's own mariachi band, featuring Hispanic folk music.

In December of 2006, for their active role in promoting diversity and challenging racism in West Michigan, as well as for their generous donation to the improvement of the Diversity Learning Center, Bob and Aleicia Woodrick became the namesakes of the new Bob and Aleicia Woodrick Diversity Learning Center. **(Figure 125)**

The Open Door Campaign

To fill the gaps left by decreased state funding, the GRCC Foundation, in 2006, undertook a $10 million, three-year

(above, Figure 126) Open Door fund-raising campaign, 2006. (GRCC Archives)
(right, Figure 127) President Olivarez and Trustee Gary P. Schenk toasting Peter and Pat Cook at the renaming of the North Building, 2006. (GRCC Archives)

fund-raising campaign known as Open Door and headed by co-chairs David Custer and Win Irwin with the support of many other community leaders. (**Figure 126**) The college had been forced to make more than $5.3 million in cuts since 2000. A number of college buildings were deteriorating; the cost of maintenance and upgrade projects would be in the tens of millions.

Continuing "deferred maintenance" decisions would only multiply future costs. Enrollment was increasing steadily; the college needed more classrooms and new technologies to accommodate students. Replacing outdated electronic equipment alone was costing the college over $500,000 per year. Student Support Services lacked sufficient space. Mandatory expenses such as utility costs, health insurance, and retirement contributions were all on the increase. Professional development of faculty and expanded student scholarships also made the list of high priorities. Thanks to the diligence of the co-chairs and the efforts of many others, the Open Door Campaign met its goals and more.

Legacy donors became an important part of the Open Door strategy. In 2006, the North Building was renamed the Peter and Pat Cook Academic Hall to commemorate their major donation to the campaign. In 2007, Peter and Joan Secchia's interest in and support for the hospitality program resulted in the program being renamed The Secchia Institute for Culinary Education. In 2008, the Applied Technology Center would be renamed the Wisner-Bottrall Applied Technology Center to honor the generous financial support of Tom and Joyce Wisner and David and Michelle Bottrall. (**Figures 127-129**)

Visual Arts Accreditation

In 1996, when the nine college divisions were eliminated, Art and Photography combined to form a new Visual Arts

Department, headed by Nick Antonakis. Photography was moved from the Learning Center to more spacious studio, lab, and classroom facilities in the Main Building beside the Art Department. The move was a positive one, resulting in a closer working relationship between art and photography students and faculty, as well as a shared gallery. In 1998, the Visual Arts Department started on a path toward National Association of Schools of Art and Design (NASAD) accreditation, which would acknowledge the department as having achieved the na-

tion's highest standards for programs, instruction, and facilities. The Visual Arts Department's first self-study was submitted to NASAD in 2003. A visitation and evaluation took place the same year. Accreditation was delayed, however, because programs in interior decorating and graphics communication had to be added to the accreditation application. The photography curriculum needed to be improved with the addition of digital courses. Ultimately, though, NASAD accreditation was conferred on GRCC and the Visual Arts Department in 2008.[12]

(left, Figure 128) Culinary Arts Department renamed the Secchia Institute for Culinary Education. Peter Secchia (left) and President Olivarez (right), 2007. (GRCC Archives)
(above, Figure 129) Ice sculpture created by Secchia Institute students for the renaming of the Applied Technology Center, which became the Wisner-Bottrall Applied Technology Center, 2008. (GRCC Archives)

2005

First study abroad program to Northern Ireland featured classes in history of Ulster and politics of Northern Ireland and a trip to Ireland. (GRCC Archives)

2006

A study prepared for the college by CCbenefits Inc. showed GRCC's economic impact in West Michigan was an estimated $977.5 million annually.

First annual Hispanic Excellence Scholarship Gala held.

The Diversity Learning Center was relocated to a newly remodeled space in the Learning Resource Center and renamed the Bob and Aleicia Woodrick Diversity Learning Center in recognition of their work in and financial support of diversity education at GRCC.

Campus offered wireless network access to students and staff.

Sustainabiility

When the Center for Environmental Studies moved from the college, Dean of Arts and Sciences Dr. Gary Burbridge assumed responsibility for the Environmental Council, which under his leadership would soon become the Sustainability Council. In 2006, Provost Dr. Velvie Green put him in charge of writing a Sustainability Plan, which reflected the college's commitment to recycling, reducing energy use, managing storm water, installing a green roof on the ATC (funded by a Steelcase Foundation grant), and moving toward energy neutrality.[13] In 2007, the college committed to an energy conservation program in partnership with Energy Education, Inc.

The Michigan Quality Leadership Award and Accreditation

In fall of 1997, the long-standing North Central re-accreditation process was resuscitated for yet another seven-year cycle, starting with a college self-study. Provost Dr. Don Boyer appointed Dr. Ruth Kurlandsky and a team of 35 to begin work on it, but the faculty was hesitant to participate, based on what they perceived as the college's failure to act on the recommendations of the previous North Central Review. About the same time, staff attending a Chicago conference discovered a new accreditation model called the Academic Quality Improvement Project (AQIP) based on principles of Continuous Quality Improvement (CQI), the leadership model President Calkins had unsuccessfully attempted to adopt several years previous.

The new approach, a yearly, ongoing institutional self-evaluation, gained the interest of both faculty and staff, many of whom had been trained in CQI principles. Participation in the new system had the benefit of exempting the college from the '97 self-study. So in 1999, GRCC was admitted into

(above, Figure 130)
Collins Art Gallery, undated. (GRCC Archives)
(right, Figure 131)
Paul Collins appearing at opening of the Collins Art Gallery, 2004. (GRCC Archives)

The college's Paul Collins Art Gallery opened for its first season in fall of 2003. **(Figures 130-31)** Named for Grand Rapids artist Paul Collins whose collectors donated a number of his works to the college to be sold to raise funds for the gallery's construction and operation, the facility now provides space for diverse and high-quality exhibitions.

the AQIP pilot program for re-accreditation. A requirement for participation was commitment to a state-level quality award process (the Michigan Quality Leadership Award) modeled after the national Malcolm Baldrige Education Award. Dr. Don Boyer put Dean of Institutional Research Donna Kragt and Dr. Gary Burbridge in charge of the award application, which would serve as the pathway to re-accreditation. In the next several years, the college diligently prepared the award application, and though the driving purpose of the application was re-accreditation, Olivarez was delighted to find that GRCC, in 2007, had become the first college to receive the Michigan Quality Leadership Award.

(**Figure 132**) Michigan Quality Leadership Award, 2007. (GRCC Archives)

(**Figure 132**) A Higher Learning Council site visit followed in 2007, resulting in re-accreditation until 2014.[14]

Early in his presidency, Olivarez had led a collaborative effort to revitalize college mission, vision, and values statements and use them as guides to strategic planning. He created a Strategic Planning Team of 65 members (close to half of them faculty), to put planning into the hands of a large cross-section of college employees. The work of that team has since been a vital element in the AQIP re-accreditation process.

President Olivarez Resigns

In March 2008, Juan Olivarez announced his resignation after nine years as chief executive of GRCC. He was 58 years old, and leading collaboratively over a long haul had required great patience and energy. The millage losses of the previous year, the endless financial scrambling of his tenure had exacted a price as well. Yet he had grown skillful at the increasingly necessary business of fund-raising, and when an offer to lead the Kalamazoo Community Foundation as president and CEO arrived, he found it difficult to resist.

Lamenting the loss of Olivarez, Board of Trustees' Chair Gary Schenk told a *Collegiate* reporter, "We didn't know at the time [nine years before] how good a choice we had made." Olivarez' legacy of compassionate caring and commitment to diversity had opened the GRCC doors wider than ever before.

2007

GRCC's Hospitality Program renamed The Secchia Institute for Culinary Education to recognize a sizable donation from Peter and Joan Secchia to the GRCC Hospitality Education Department.

GRCC received the Michigan Quality Leadership Award from the Michigan Quality Council for improving overall performance.

GRCC began offering night classes at West Ottawa North High School. This agreement was extended to day classes in 2009 and marked the first expansion of the Lakeshore campus.

2008

Two GRCC departments received initial accreditation, the Visual Arts Department from the National Association of Schools of Art and Design, and Child Development from the National Association for the Education of Young Children Commission.

Applied Technology Center renamed Wisner-Bottrall Applied Technology Center.

Academic Standing policy adopted by the Academic Governing Council.

GRCC became a tobacco-free campus.

Commencement, May 2, 2014. (GRCC Archives)

The Ender Years
2009 to the Present

The Second Interim President

Dr. Anne Mulder had worn many hats in her years at the college, but interim president was a new one. She had retired after seven years as president of Lake Michigan Community College and had settled into a condo in Florida. When she received and accepted a call to become interim dean of education at GVSU, it was clear retirement had been premature. Not long after, the GRCC Board of Trustees, looking for an interim president who was qualified yet uninterested in candidacy, decided Anne would be a first-rate choice to maintain college business while a presidential search was conducted. She accepted the challenge. (**Figure 133**) When an initial search failed to uncover the right presidential candidate, a second was launched, resulting in Mulder leading the college for the better part of a year.

As many in the college already knew, maintaining was not Anne Mulder's style. She had strong ideas about GRCC's importance to the central city. "The college has provided a barricade to urban decay," she stated in an interview. "It has helped keep the fabric of this community together."[1] Always a strong supporter of downtown and the arts, she secured financing and a lease agreement for St. Cecilia's Royce Auditorium to become home of the Music Department's larger performances.[2] St. Cecilia and GRCC seemed a

(**Figure 133**) Dr. Anne Mulder, GRCC Interim President 2008-09. (GRCC Archives)

(**Figure 134**) Dr. Steven Ender, ninth leader of GRCC. (GRCC Archives)

natural partnership and would further energize the downtown area.

GRCC in 2008 needed room to accommodate its rapidly increasing enrollment, capped more than once for lack of space. Vice President of Finance Bob Partridge favored accomplishing expansion by means of an Olivarez strategic plan calling for more learning corners and other off-campus offerings. Mulder saw the answer in the Davenport University downtown campus on Fulton Street, soon to be vacated as a result of the university's move to Caledonia. Nearly contiguous with the GRCC campus, the eight-acre Davenport property included six buildings, one of them a large classroom facility, and a parking area for 540 cars. The Heritage Hill Association applauded Mulder's idea. Upgrading and occupying the property for college use would go far toward preserving the historic neighborhood and strengthening the core city. Mulder would lay the groundwork for a deal; Partridge, carrying out the wishes of the next president, Dr. Steven C. Ender (**Figure 134**) (who saw the wisdom of acquiring the property, as Partridge did in time), would negotiate the $9.5 million purchase. (**Figure 135**)

The Ninth Chief Executive

Steven (Steve) Ender was born in Richmond, Virginia, an identical twin whose brother

2009

On January 29 the GRCC Board of Trustees unanimously approved hiring Dr. Steven Ender as the college's ninth leader. Ender was instrumental in the purchase and development of the Davenport University's downtown campus. He headed up the GRCC Works...Ask Anyone capital campaign which raised over $15 million for renovation projects on both the main and Davenport campuses. Under Ender, GRCC continued its significant progress in sustainability practices. The college extended its outreach with satellite facilities and programs, including the Holland Midtown Center.

Bookstore began renting books.

College purchased Davenport University's downtown campus, which included six buildings and 540 parking spaces. (GRCC Archives)

First annual Peace Studies Conference, later renamed the Race, Ethnicity and Identity Conference was held. (GRCC Archives)

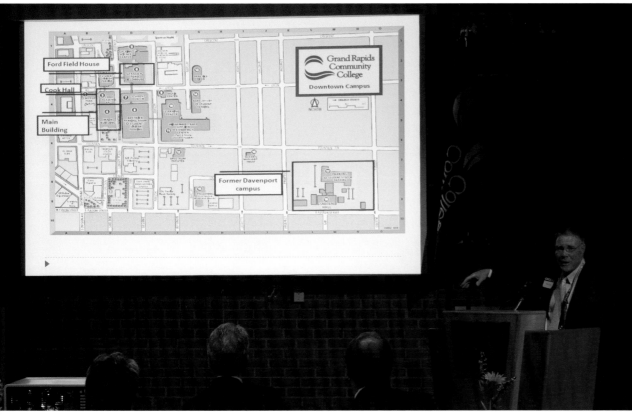

(top, Figure 135) GRCC purchased Davenport University's downtown campus, 2009. (GRCC Archives)

Ken, like Steve himself, would earn a doctorate and become a community college president. Early on, their father taught them (and two younger siblings) lessons in the value of money. He gave no allowances, expected them to work for the money they needed, and took half of everything they made. If they found this practice odd, they never questioned it. In high school, when the boys decided to save for a car, their father told them it was not necessary. They already had the money saved—the half wages they had handed over to him for all those years. It was a stunning lesson in delayed gratification, which neither boy forgot.

Achieving Eagle Scout status as a Boy Scout, Steve Ender was still (by his own admission) a mediocre high school student who, after graduation in 1968, managed to save enough to pay his way through Virginia Commonwealth University by working and living at home. Over time this passive, "gentleman C"

onlooker would become a fully-engaged college student with a passion for learning—and then a passionate educator who would spend a career opening the doors of higher education to students such as he had been. He would earn a master's degree from the University of Georgia. The University would hire him to start a developmental program, and he would finish his doctorate in the process.

Kansas State University hired Ender away as a counselor/psychologist; there he would again create a developmental program to prepare less-than-qualified students for college work. During that period, he co-wrote and edited books, consulted, and learned to love the academic culture. In 1984 he was recruited by Indiana University of Pennsylvania to head up developmental programs. There he would create college simulation courses for high schools, courses that had great success in Pennsylvania urban centers. He would spend 22 years at IUP in both faculty and administrative positions before accepting the presidency of Westmoreland County Community College (WCCC) in Pennsylvania in 2005.

At Westmoreland, Ender learned quickly that the president's most important role was as protector of the college. From the start at WCCC, he felt political interference from an appointed board of trustees, particularly in the hiring of staff. By the end of three years, the situation had not improved, and he was compelled to act on the college's behalf by reporting the trustees' ongoing manipulation to the state and to the Middle States accrediting agency. Aware that he had most likely burned his bridges, he began actively seeking other employment.

An ad for the GRCC presidency attracted him. His wife Karen was drawn to the area—she had a best friend living in Grand Rapids. At a conference in New York City, he happened into Anne Mulder and her Executive Deputy Kathy Mullins.

They chatted about the GRCC position, and shortly thereafter he made a decision to apply for it. He visited the college for a formal interview in November of 2008, returned for a final interview in January of 2009, and was offered the job the same evening in a phone call from GRCC Board Chair Gary Schenk. Ender accepted. In March 2009, he spent a month in Grand Rapids, "trying to keep up with Anne Mulder" as she showed him the ropes.[3] He assumed duties as GRCC president on May 1, the first president without roots or job history in the area.

On October 22, 2009, the college celebrated the investiture of Dr. Ender, an event every bit as dignified and grand as the Olivarez inauguration. (**Figure 136**) Ender's wife Karen attend-ed, as well as his son and daughter and their spouses. Ender's speech, following those of Mayor George Heartwell and other dignitaries, made reference to current GRCC realities: the college was a growth industry with a declining financial base. His purpose as president would be to make the college a sustainable institution. He promised transformation, which meant charting a new path for the GRCC of today and tomorrow. Faculty responded with a degree of uneasiness.

An Outsider's View

In hiring Ender, the trustees had felt that, given the struggling financial state of the college, they needed someone who was not an insider, someone with a fresh way of seeing. During the job interview, they had appreciated Ender's understanding of a community college's purpose, his student success-centered thinking, his boldness about private fund-raising, and his candor about fiscal threats.[4] Once he was on the job, they were pleased he found the college stronger academically than most community colleges and intrigued he thought it remiss that some of the community's most generous donors had never been approached to support

(**Figure 136**) President Ender with the GRCC Board of Trustees at his Investiture, 2009. (GRCC Archives)

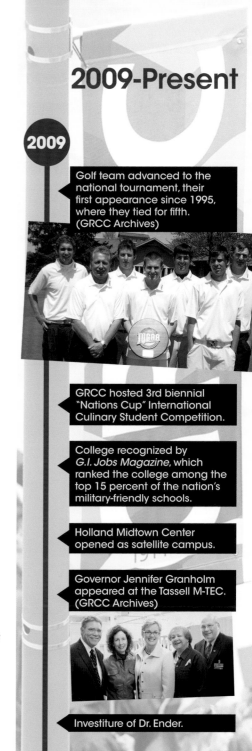

2009-Present

2009

Golf team advanced to the national tournament, their first appearance since 1995, where they tied for fifth. (GRCC Archives)

GRCC hosted 3rd biennial "Nations Cup" International Culinary Student Competition.

College recognized by *G.I. Jobs Magazine*, which ranked the college among the top 15 percent of the nation's military-friendly schools.

Holland Midtown Center opened as satellite campus.

Governor Jennifer Granholm appeared at the Tassell M-TEC. (GRCC Archives)

Investiture of Dr. Ender.

(**Figure 137**) GRCC Works Campaign. GRCC Archives)

necessary to preserve the college's existence and its tradition of excellence. They felt Ender was that man. His goals would be to create attractive, functional, up-to-date facilities, improve student success, and find a path to a balanced budget. Achieving the latter, in particular, was not likely to make him popular.

Ender was very aware of his outsider role. As a newcomer to a large institution, he found himself having to lead through difficult times without many close, personal relationships. He accepted the role, not particularly liking it, but willing to do what needed to be done.

The GRCC Works...Ask Anyone Capital Campaign

Ender barely had his feet on the ground when he found himself heading up an ambitious capital campaign called GRCC Works...Ask Anyone. (**Figure 137**) The goal of the campaign was to raise $12 million for renovation projects on both campuses to provide quality space to accommodate students. Ender, early on, had made a commitment to an open door policy—he would not turn away any first-time, full-time student (the college in recent years had been turning away a thousand a year). He had already spent time developing relationships with some of Grand Rapids' most significant donors. Dr. Andrew Bowne, Director of the GRCC Foundation and David Custer, Chair of the Foundation Board, worked beside Ender. Dr. Jim Buzzitta, a college alumnus, agreed to chair the campaign, and Doug DeVos, Hank Meijer, and Fred Keller, significant community philanthropic leaders, unhesitatingly came aboard as honorary chairs. By the time of the campaign kick-off ceremony, $6.25 million had already come in, and by 2010, the first phase of fund-raising from foundations and private donors had brought in over $10 million. Within 18 months the GRCC Works goal

the college. When he suggested that faculty and administrative contracts were, in his estimation, unsustainable (an observation Chief Financial Officer Bob Partridge had made as early as the 1990s),[5] they were deeply attentive. Full-time faculty and administrators were on a step system with yearly pay boosts and generous benefits that the college could not continue to meet. Part-time faculty wages were the highest in the area. He was distressed that faculty titles were based on longevity and not merit, and that 84 percent of total college budget went for personnel and benefits.

Exacerbating the problem was the fact that state aid was flat or decreasing. Tuition was the only source of new revenue, yet students could not bear the entire burden. There were other limits to tuition: when enrollment shrank or was capped for lack of space, the tuition dollars shrank as well. GRCC buildings needed an estimated $90 million in renovations.[6] The board of trustees wanted a president who could stand firm in support of changes

(**Figure 138**) Renaming the Davenport property DeVos campus, 2010. (left to right) Dr. Andrew Bowne and Bob Partridge. (GRCC Archives)

(**Figure 139**) The Ford Fieldhouse arena becomes the Gordon Hunsberger Arena, 2011. (left to right) Gordon and Bobby Hunsberger, Carol and David Van Andel. (GRCC Archives)

2010

Davenport property renamed DeVos campus.

GRCC hosted World Pastry Cup U.S. Team tryouts in April.

Men's basketball team advanced into the National Junior College Athletic Association Division II tournament for just the second time in school history. (GRCC Archives)

Wind Energy Technology class offered YES Safety Technology program. GRCC became first U.S. training center of this worldwide recognized safety certification program.

2011

GRCC named to President Obama's Higher Education Community Service Honor Roll, one of two state schools with the distinction.

of $12 million had been surpassed by more than $3 million. Ender and staff raised an additional $12 million in bond funding and $5 million from the state, providing the college with close to $33 million of the $90 million needed to update facilities.

The Renovations

A partial renovation of the first floor of the large Davenport classroom building, Sneden Hall, was completed in time for the fall 2009 semester, making room for 1,200 students. By 2010, major renovations to Sneden, including new décor and furniture, infrastructure, wireless connections, computer technology, and Steelcase LearnLabs, would accommodate more than 3,000 students. The renovation was made possible by gifts from the DeVos and VanderWeide families, in honor of whom the Davenport campus was renamed the DeVos campus. (**Figure 138**) For ease of passage for students, the college established shuttle bus service between the DeVos and Main campuses.

Before the Davenport purchase, there had been Main campus plans for a new classroom building with a projected cost

of $35.1 million. The entire Davenport sale and renovation, which included remodeling of Sneden Hall, the Administration Building, and Main campus renovation of Cook Hall, a portion of the Main Building, and the Ford Fieldhouse—all done in lieu of the new building—totaled $34 million. Acquiring the Davenport property turned out a wise and a frugal move, good for Grand Rapids, for The Heritage Hill area, and for both colleges.

By 2011, the Gerald R. Ford Fieldhouse had undergone a $1.1 million overhaul of the arena (as well as transformation of racquetball courts into health and wellness facilities), thanks in large part to a substantial leadership gift from the David and Carol Van Andel Foundation. The size of the gift entitled the donors to naming rights. The Van Andels chose to have the college honor someone who had made a significant impact on the athletic program. A single name rose to the top of the list: Gordon Hunsberger, NJCAA Hall of Fame football coach. "His name is synonymous with Raider athletics," Ender said at the dedication of the Gordon Hunsberger Arena, "and it's an honor for us to recognize his legacy." (**Figure 139**) In 2013, the foyer of Ford

(**Figure 142**) Dedication of the Meijer Center for Business Studies, 2013. (left to right) David Custer, Mark Meijer, Hank Meijer, and President Ender. (GRCC Archives)

(**Figure 140**) Carl Paganelli, Sr. speaks at ceremony naming the Ford Fieldhouse foyer the Paganelli Foyer, 2011. (GRCC Archives)

(**Figure 141**) Peter Secchia speaks at dedication of the Pietro and Regina Amphitheater in the Secchia Institute for Culinary Education, 2012. (GRCC Archives)

Fieldhouse would be dedicated to the Carl Paganelli family, long-time GRCC supporters and alumni, and named the Paganelli Family Foyer in appreciation of their gift of a sizable endowment to fund a yearly scholarship to a worthy student, preferably a student athlete. (**Figure 140**)

The Secchia family, in 2012, continued their support of the Culinary Education Program with the ATC building renovation dedicated as the Pietro and Regina Amphitheater, honoring the grandparents of Peter Secchia. (**Figure 141**) The 54-seat amphitheater-style lecture hall, equipped with 60-inch video monitors for close views of food preparation, a wine cooler, 25-foot granite island, and commercial, stainless steel appliances, further strengthened one of the top culinary programs in the nation.

2013 marked the dedication of the Meijer Center for Business Studies in honor of Meijer, Inc. for its interest in GRCC business students and support of the college. (**Figure 142**) Located on the second floor of the Main Building, the center featured hallway seating, three computer labs with double projection images, one LearnLab with triple projection images and powered tables for laptop use, a large collaboration suite for class projects, two small-group work spaces, a board

room for professional simulation activities, and a business center for faculty—the most dramatic departmental transformation since Business was established in 1917.

Progress in Sustainability

Ender actively supported the plans of the Sustainability Council to make GRCC a leader in sustainability practices. The college hired Dorothy Burns as its new energy manager. By 2009, 20 percent of all college electrical use was green. The college shifted to using green cleaning products and non-gasoline lawn equipment, as well as limiting use of hazardous chemicals. The same year, the college introduced SUS 101, Introduction to Sustainability, an interdisciplinary course devoted to improving environmental health. In October, GRCC students took part in a large rally for green energy in Lansing, and then marched in Grand Rapids with students from GVSU, Kendall, Calvin, and Aquinas to draw attention to global climate change and green energy advantages.

By 2010, GRCC had saved more than $1.5 million in utility expenses in the first 27 months of an energy conservation program in partnership with Energy Education, Inc. According to Ender, simple things like turning out lights and unplugging electronic devices had contributed to this dramatic savings. Recycling bins appeared on campus, school records were converted to digital form, greatly reducing paper usage, and a student group called Earth Awakening began actively promoting sustainability. In April, Maryann Lesert of the English Department organized GRCC's Spring Sustainability Series at the Grand Rapids Public Museum, featuring spoken word, visual arts, and musical presentations to promote sustainability.

In 2010, GRCC became the first training provider in the U.S. to be awarded Global Wind Organization accreditation for teaching safety training to wind farm workers. In 2012, Stuart Edward White Hall (formerly Warren Hall on DeVos campus), named for Stewart Edward White, a Grand Rapids author whose family built the house, became GRCC's first Leadership in Energy and Environmental Design (LEED) certified building. **(Figure 143)** Much of the funding for remodeling came from Meijer, Inc.

The Twin Bowl—and the End of a Storied Program

October of 2011 marked the third "Twin Bowl" football clash between GRCC and Harper College of Palatine, Illinois, where brothers Steve and Ken Ender served as college presidents. At stake was a wager between brothers involving expensive cigars, a "coveted" twin loving cup, and bragging rights. The powerful GRCC team, led by Coach Tony Annese, prevailed in the Twin Bowl as it had all season, finishing with a perfect record of 11-0, a Midwestern Football Conference championship, and a number three national ranking. In spite of the team's dominance, an NJCAA rules violation excluded GRCC from a national bowl game.

(Figure 143) Stewart Edward White Hall became GRCC's first LEED (Leadership in Energy and Environmental Design) certified building. (GRCC Archives)

By January, Tony Annese had accepted a coaching position at Ferris State University, and Ender faced the most difficult decision of his professional career. The storied GRCC football program, over 90 years in existence, was the only community college program left in the state of Michigan. Within the previous five years, four community colleges in GRCC's conference had cut football. The team now had to travel as far as North Dakota and Georgia by bus to find worthy opponents. Crowds were small, and the program lost money. Travel time and expenses had become prohibitive. The large number of players on the squad forced GRCC to violate Title IX rules governing the school's ratio of male to female athletes. According to Ender,

2011

GRCC received $2 million grant to target "academically unprepared" students.

The Gerald R. Ford Fieldhouse underwent a $1.5 million renovation including improved lighting, acoustic panels and a new natural hardwood basketball floor. The arena was renamed the Gordon Hunsberger Arena in honor of the longtime GRJC football coach and faculty member.

GRCC signed Reverse Transfer Associate Degree agreement with Davenport University, Grand Valley State University, Ferris State University and Western Michigan University. Under this agreement students could be granted an earned associate degree by combining credits earned at these transfer schools with the credits they previously earned at GRCC.

First annual Armen Awards Innovation Competition held in an effort to spark new ideas in teaching and learning. GRCC Distinguished Alumni and donor Armen Omedian partnered with the GRCC Foundation and Experiential Learning to create this competition. (2013 Armen Awards. GRCC Archives)

(**Figure 144**) Aquinas President Juan Olivarez and President Ender signing articulation agreement, 2013. (GRCC Archives)

the decision to cut the program was painful and unpopular, but "as president," he said, "it was a no-brainer."[7] Legendary coaches like Gordon Hunsberger lamented the loss but understood the realities behind it.[8] Players were inconsolable. President Ken Ender, facing the same realities, would drop the football program at Harper College three months later.

Friends of the College

Armen Oumedian attended GRJC from 1941 to 1943. His wife Pat and their three children attended the college as well. Armen and Pat began their philanthropic involvement with the college when they saw a need to support health care education. They funded a Health Care Scholarship and an Innovative Nursing Learning Fund. Other scholarship funds followed. Armen, a GRCC Distinguished Alumni, had worked for many years at Rapistan as a senior vice president. He co-chaired the Alumni Division of GRCC's Open Door Campaign. In 2011 he established the Armen Awards, a yearly team competition designed

to spark new ideas in teaching and learning. He challenged students, faculty, and community partners to form teams to create service-learning projects with community impact. His cash awards helped set the projects in motion.[9]

College News

Cindy Kennell, Chief of Campus Police, passed away in July of 2010, after a long battle with cancer. In January 2011, Rebecca Whitman, a captain in the Grand Rapids Police Department, was named the next chief.

GRCC extended its outreach with satellite facilities and programs: in 2009, the Holland Midtown Center opened as a satellite campus in Ottawa County; Early College Experience sites expanded to a larger number of area high schools: Kent City, Holland New Tech, Kelloggsville, Ottawa Hills, and Grand Rapids University Prep Academy; an educational experiment known as Middle College began at Wyoming High School, enabling a student to earn a diploma and a GRCC associate's degree simultaneously by starting college courses in the sophomore year and extending high school to five years.

Ender and staff, particularly Provost Dr. Gilda Gely, worked on cooperative agreements with four-year transfer institutions. In 2011, GRCC, Davenport, Ferris State, GVSU, and WMU signed reverse transfer associate degree agreements, aimed at students who had transferred from GRCC before completing an associate's degree. That degree could now be earned by applying transfer institution credits to the GRCC associate's degree requirements (for those wishing the additional credentials). In 2012, GRCC, GVSU, and MSU College of Human Medicine signed an articulation agreement, providing GRCC students enhanced opportunity for medical school admission. In 2013, GRCC and Aquinas College legitimized

(**Figure 145**) 2012 NJCAA Division II Volleyball champions, 2012. (GRCC Archives)

a spoken articulation agreement when President Ender and Provost Dr. Gilda Gely, Aquinas President Dr. Juan Olivarez and Provost Dr. Chad Gunnoe officially signed an agreement to create a seamless transfer for GRCC students. (**Figure 144**)

Paula Maloley, long-time GRCC head softball coach, became the 2011 recipient of the Easton Victory Club Award for 600 career wins. The sports high point of 2012 was the GRCC volleyball team, coached by Chip Will, winning its first NJCAA Division II national title. (**Figure 145**) A low point occurred the following year with the closing of men and women's tennis programs, the sole remaining Michigan community college competitive tennis teams. To replace tennis, the college restarted its cross-country team.

In 2012, Mike Light and other members of the Social Science Department orchestrated an annual weeklong Race, Ethnicity, and Identity Conference. In spring of 2012, GRCC hosted the Grand Rapids Poets' Conference, organized by Grand Rapids Poet Laureate and GRCC English professor David Cope. 2012 marked the introduction of a regular online version of *The Collegiate*. Close to 15 percent of GRCC classes were now available online. In 2013, the college was awarded $4.1 million as part of a $24.9 million grant from the U.S. Department of Labor to upgrade manufacturing programs and equipment in GRCC Workforce Training, led by Dean Fiona Hert. In July of that year, *The Chronicle of Higher Education* named Grand Rapids Community College one of its "Great Colleges to Work For."

2009-Present

2011

Football team finished the season 11-0 and a No. 3 ranking but was not invited to a major National Junior College Athletic Association bowl game.

2012

GRCC-Wyoming Middle College Program established. In the first year, 50 Wyoming High School students took advantage of the opportunity to earn both a high school diploma and an associate of arts degree in four years.

Alpha Beta Omega leadership development program organized to foster academic success by providing a positive social network and educational and cultural experiences. (2013 Alpha Beta Omega members. GRCC Archives)

White Hall received LEED silver certification for environmentally friendly design.

Musical Moods

Next to commencement, the annual Musical Moods concert is the longest-running event at GRJC/GRCC. A collage concert featuring all of the performing ensembles of the Music Department, Musical Moods was the brainchild of Albert Smith, longtime chair of the department. The first Musical Moods was held in 1948 and in its early years featured the band, orchestra and choir. Over the years, new groups have been added to the mix, including the Guitar Ensemble, the Jazz Orchestra, the Madrigal Singers, the Mariachi Band, the Percussion Ensemble, Shades of Blue, the String Quartet, and the Wind Ensemble. Today, Moods also features student soloists and duets.

The concert has bounced from venue to venue over the years due to the lack of a performing arts center at the college. Up until 1956 it was held at the East Building gymnasium. Beginning in 1957, it has utilized the following locations: St. Cecilia Auditorium, Byron Center High School Van Singel Fine Arts Center, Calvin College Fine Arts Center, Creston High School Auditorium, Forest Hills Public Schools Fine Arts Center, Grand Rapids Christian High School DeVos Center for Arts and Worship, Kenowa Hills High School Auditorium, Lowell High School Performing Arts Center, Northview High School Performing Arts Center, Ottawa Hills High School, Rockford High School, and South High School Auditorium.

In 1998, the fiftieth anniversary Musical Moods concert was held at the college's Ford Fieldhouse. In 2006, the Albert P. Smith Award began being presented at Moods in recognition of outstanding contributions to music education in Grand Rapids. Since 2011, Musical Moods has found a permanent home at the St. Cecilia Music Center's Royce Auditorium.

GRAND RAPIDS JUNIOR COLLEGE

presents

MUSICAL MOODS of '57

APRIL 26 and 27
8:00 P. M.
ST. CECILIA AUDITORIUM

(clockwise from top left) Musical Moods, undated. (GRCC Archives); 1957 Musical Mood program. (GRCC Archives); Written "Moods" with instruments and students. (GRCC Archives); 2012 Musical Moods. (GRCC Archives)

The Failed $98.6 Million Bond Proposal

The college went to district voters in 2012 for approval of a 20-year bond worth $98.6 million to pay for ongoing renovation of aging facilities, in particular the Music Building and the remainder of the Main Building, along with general renovations and tech improvement throughout campus, and future construction of a Laboratory Preschool. Those who conducted the election expected a closely contested vote. To their dismay, the proposal was soundly defeated.[10]

Many in the college were left wondering why an asset like GRCC, which generated huge sums each year for the area economy—described by local leader Dr. Jim Buzzitta as "a jewel of the community"[11]—would not enjoy the appreciative support of that community. It was the third millage loss in a row. Somehow the message was not reaching or resonating with the taxpayers. Ender would have no choice but to raise tuition, create a maintenance fee paid by students, borrow while bond rates were low, and dig in for more private fund-raising. It was a difficult and discouraging time. Armen Oumedian may have put his finger on the source of the problem when he said "GRCC is our community's best-kept secret."[12]

The 2011-16 Faculty Contract

From 2011-13, the GRCC faculty worked without a contract as negotiations trudged painfully along. Something new was in the air, something administration maintained would put the college on a more solid financial footing. The college's and the state's financial problems were no secrets. Some employees feared their wages or even jobs would be cut. A voluntary early retirement program resulted in an unusual number of experienced faculty and administrators leaving. Association President Fred van Hartesveldt, fully aware that the golden age of con-

tracts had passed, foresaw a sea change coming.[13] The college had commissioned a 2010 comparative compensation study by Municipal Consultant Services, an independent company. Their researchers found the GRCC faculty "highly compensated" compared to other Michigan community colleges.

At last, in March of 2013, negotiators reached an accord, and the GRCC Board unanimously approved a five-year faculty contract (2011-16) in which base salaries were frozen for two years, pay raises based on longevity were eliminated, and step increases were replaced by merit pay based on performance. This contract represented a profound culture shift, second only in impact to the advent of collective bargaining in 1966. Ender had managed to create an entirely new system (unique in the state) without jobs being cut or present salaries reduced, though pay increases were no longer automatic and new full-time and adjunct faculty would have lower start points for salary and fewer opportunities for salary increases. Academic rank would be tied to merit instead of longevity. Over the life of the contract, $4 million would be saved—and a great deal more over time. Ender had achieved two personal goals: he had put the college on a more sustainable financial footing, and he had motivated the revision of the evaluation system (faculty and administrators had spent months developing it) to better measure the quality of teaching performance and in the process improve chances for student success.

Though both negotiating teams deserved high praise for finding a path through the wilderness, the process did not create much good will between Ender and faculty. Some faculty members, accustomed to Juan Olivarez's gently persuasive nature, felt that Ender had muscled the contract into being. The new faculty evaluation process (according to the Higher Learning Commission's June 2014 *Quality Checkup Report*) now required, in the

Volleyball team won its first NJCAA Division II national title. The team also advanced to the national tournament in 2007, 2008, 2010.

Students observing culinary techniques at the Pietro and Regina Amphitheater, 2012. (GRCC Archives)

GRCC implemented My Degree Path, a web-based tool designed to help students stay on a clear path to graduation by reviewing coursework and evaluating degree requirements.

Secchia Institute for Culinary Education unveiled the new Pietro and Regina Amphitheater. A state-of-the-art teaching and learning culinary amphitheater named to honor the continuing support of the Secchia family.

(Figure 146) GRCC Board of Trustees and GRCC President Ender, 2012. (GRCC Archives)

view of faculty, an "onerous" amount of documentation,[14] particularly on the part of departmental chairs. Problems remained to be solved, yet the president had taken a large, albeit painful step toward ensuring the college's fiscal health.

Today, performance-based contracts govern all employee bargaining groups at the college. In spite of the jury being out on the effectiveness of "pay for performance" in the world of education, present GRCC Board of Trustees' Chair Bert Bleke, a long-time area educator, fully expects the new system (which he feels is fairer and more equitable than longevity formulas) to be successful.[15]

Board Dynamics

The present GRCC Board of Trustees has been unanimously supportive of Ender's leadership and his dramatic changes in the culture of the college. **(Figure 146)** Yet the board is oddly divided. According to former board Chair Gary Schenk, the guiding star of a trustee should always be what is best for the college. The board's mission should be the protection and advancement of the institution and its students. The position of trustee should never be a pulpit from which to wage personal battles.[16] Such battles, however, are going on regularly, at times creating an unhealthy contentiousness reflecting negatively on the college.

The 60-40 Ratio

Believing that much of the strength and leadership of a college emanates from its full-time faculty, President Ender has set a goal at GRCC of a 60-40 percent ratio of credit hours taught by full-time as compared to part-time faculty. Ongoing financial difficulties have made clear he will not reach that goal easily, particularly in departments like English. Yet he has begun the hiring of 50 full-time, tenure-track faculty members, a hopeful step.

Student Success and Retention

Today, the doors of GRCC stand open to a wider variety of students than ever before. Deeply committed to seeing those students succeed and earn degrees, the college has established Student Success and Retention Services, headed by Dean Dr. John Cowles. The programs administered by his office include the College Success Center, Achieving the Dream, and the Academic Foundations Program.

The College Success Center (headed by Domingo Hernández-Gómez), established through a Federal Title III grant, engages faculty, counselors, and academic advisors in support of at-risk students who, for any number of reasons, may be struggling to complete their college goals. A Fast Track/On Track program provides quick training for students (supported by reading and math labs, tutors, and success coaches) to build skills allowing them to bypass developmental work. An Early Alert System identifies students having difficulties in courses, refers them to the appropriate advisor, and provides support before they fall behind and abandon school. The Academic Foundations Program continues to strengthen developmental studies as a means to student success.

For several years, GRCC has been a participant in Achieving the Dream, a national program focused on discovering strategies that lead to students completing associates degrees. The Street to Completion Project, directed by Dean Tina Hoxie and Dr. Kathy Mullins, focuses on increasing success within student subgroups (such as part-time or undecided students) by planning helpful strategies for achieving a degree.

As an open door institution, GRCC is working to serve the diverse educational needs of the community—and to avoid the revolving door of early exits. The Higher Learning Commission (HLC) has made note in its latest *Quality Checkup Report* of many encouraging signs in the GRCC Success and Retention programs.

Child Development and Education

The GRJC/GRCC Laboratory Preschool has been fashioning a model Child Development program in borrowed facilities since 1974. First United Methodist Church on East Fulton Street, on the perimeter of the GRCC campus, has long provided

GRCC dedicated the Meijer Center for Business Studies in honor of Meijer, Inc. for its continued engagement with GRCC Business students and its support of the college.

Entryway of the Ford Fieldhouse renamed the Paganelli Family Foyer.

Grand Rapids Community College Board of Trustees approved the re-designation of Bostwick Commons to the Dr. Juan R. Olivarez Student Plaza in a tribute to the former GRCC president.

GRCC became first training provider in the United States to be awarded the globally-recognized Wind Organization accreditation to deliver basic safety training to wind farm workers. (Wind Safety Training at the Tassell M-TEC, 2013. GRCC Archives)

GRCC recognized as one of the "Great Colleges to Work For" by *The Chronicle of Higher Education*.

the space for this growing and vital program (directed by JaneAnn Benson), a part of Child Development and Education led by Dr. Becky Brinks. The Lab Preschool offers future preschool teachers hands-on experience with children under the guidance of college instructors, and provides parents and children the best of nurturing environments. (**Figure 147**) The 40-year program is now bursting at the seams. Thanks to a grant from the Kellogg Foundation, conceptual planning for a new leading-edge facility, to be located behind the Learning Resource Center, is presently in the works.

(**Figure 147**) Preschool student in the GRCC Laboratory Preschool, 2014. (GRCC Archives)

The June 2014 Higher Learning Commission's *Quality Checkup Report*

The Higher Learning Commission is part of the North Central Association, the familiar educational accrediting group that in 1917 conferred the first accreditation on GRJC. On April 2-4, 2014, a team from HLC paid a visit to the college. Their GRCC *Quality Checkup Report* followed on June 10, 2014, and could only be described as glowing. As the visit team expressed it, they were "so impressed with the high level of involvement and achievement that [they] raised the question of personnel burn-

(**Figure 148**) GRCC Downtown Campus, undated. (GRCC Archives)

out." Assured that excitement over the upcoming centennial celebration outweighed any issues of burnout (and that Provost Dr. Gilda Gely, who guided preparations, was a master organizer), the team went on with its praise. "The institution has strong leadership, an actively involved Board that understands its role, an effective governance structure that is organized to address issues as they occur, and personnel that are delivering quality academic and personal development coursework to meet the needs of its publics."[17] The visit provided full evidence

2013

GRCC and Aquinas College signed an articulation agreement to create a seamless transfer for GRCC students.

2014

Starting in Winter 2014, students with less than a 3.0 high school GPA will be required to enroll in CLS 100, Introduction to College, designed to assist new students with the knowledge, skills and abilities to be successful in college and life.

The Secchia Institute for Culinary Education was named one of America's Top 20 Culinary Schools by *FSR* magazine.

The college reinstated men's and women's cross-country in response to student interest, availability of competition within the state, and reasonable program costs.

Helen Claytor statue dedication held on the Dr. Juan R. Olivarez Student Plaza July 23, 2014. In 1967 Claytor became board president of the national YWCA and worked to eliminate racism in that organization (GRCC Archives)

that GRCC had met its goals in "exemplary fashion." It was an impressive showing, confirming that the college continues to be a "best practice" model for other institutions. The HLC's decision on re-accreditation will be made during the 2014-15 school year.

More To Do

The college is indeed functioning at a high level. Still, Steve Ender, into his fifth year as president, knows he has more work to do, especially when it comes to creating stronger relation-ships within the college community. Yet already he has fashioned a clearer and more sustainable future for the college, and he will leave his successor in a stronger financial position than the one he inherited in 2009. The college has reached its 100th year, and remarkable leaders, each gifted in different ways, have guided the college through every threat to its well being, through explosive growth and dizzying change—and have never lost sight of Jesse Davis's commitment to excellence in all things. **(Figure 148)**

Commencement, May 1, 2014. (GRCC Archives)

Final Thoughts

Just over a year ago—to fill a mid-semester resignation—I returned to work as a GRCC adjunct English instructor (with the arrival of titles, I may well have become a professor while I was away). I found that students had not changed much since I retired in 2001—with the exception of their cell phones. But life had indeed changed for faculty. The site of my former office was now part of a large adjunct common space from which I came and went, anonymous and unconnected (was it a feeling shared by adjuncts?). I would on occasion run into former colleagues in the department office, but the rich, daily hallway and lounge conversations seemed to have diminished. Colleagues explained it had in part to do with the size of the department. I remembered a Language Arts Division of around 25 functioning very much like a family. I heard that the former Social Science Division—that oddly collegial mix of large and conflicting personalities led for years by Chair Jim Bogdan—was now a wholly different entity.[1] Such was no doubt the case throughout the college.

Years ago, a colleague nearing retirement confided to me that the college had gotten too big and impersonal for him. Most of my career was ahead of me then, and his assessment seemed amusing. I now caught myself echoing his complaint. Things had changed. The college, incredibly enough, had moved on without me.

Fortunately, I also noticed that the hallways, the library, the campus, the fieldhouse, the multitude of buildings were all still crackling with energy. From classrooms I could hear the sounds of earnest voices, laughter, applause, the low hum of brains making synaptic connections. It struck me how very good it was to be back. Later, when my return opened the door to writing this history, I found myself growing more appreciative of the institution and its people than I'd been when I worked as a full time instructor. I'd always known the college had been good to me. I hadn't known how widespread that feeling was, how many lives the institution had touched. I hadn't understood the depth of commitment of so many staff and faculty—and I regret every important name left out of this story. To all those deserving faculty and administrators, indispensable secretaries and administrative assistants, gifted support staff, I offer my heartfelt apologies.

Some time ago, one of my sons attended this college, played baseball, and thrived on the rich experience offered him here. Now, two daughters are GRCC students in different fields. One sings in college choruses and works as an editor on *Display* magazine. The other has seen duty as photographer and writer for *The Collegiate* (may *The Collegiate* go on forever—it is an essential source of the GRCC story). Both girls love the fact that downtown Grand Rapids—its museums, galleries, coffee shops, restaurants, riverfront walkways, concerts, festivals—*is* the GRCC campus, an area that grows more vital every day. With savings earmarked for college, each girl is appreciative of how tuition expenses—thanks in part to scholarships—have not eaten deeply into those funds. Both have discovered mentors who have opened doors to new and larger worlds.

Former Director of the Theater Program Fred Sebulske tells a story of accepting a job at GRJC in 1966, intending to teach two or three years and then move on. Instead, he stayed for nearly 40 years—all the way to retirement. "Everything I wanted to do in my career I got to do here. It's a great school," he told me—and I heard the story again and again from employees who had signed on and discovered themselves in an environment with the freedom to work, to nurture students, to create, and to grow. I was one of them. I pray that the next 100 years of GRCC will be as generous of spirit.

Is the beauty of the school year the fact that it ends and then begins again? A semester comes to a close; students and teachers are able to start over fresh, determined to do better. The story of 100 years, like a long semester, ends here. But tomorrow the tale begins anew, full of hopeful anticipation.

—June 2014

Endnotes

Chapter One — Beginnings 1914-20

1. Jesse Buttrick Davis, *The Saga of a Schoolmaster* (Boston, Massachusetts, Boston University Press, 1956), 66-69.
2. Ibid., 126.
3. Ibid., 145-150.
4. Billie Wright Dziech, "Editor's Notes," *New Directions for Community Colleges*, Issue 78, Summer 1992, available online, 1.
5. Google. Joliet Junior College Website, accessed April 16, 2013. Also Davis, 161.
6. Google. http://education.stateuniversity.com/pages/1873/Community-College.html.7, accessed April 16, 2013.
7. Davis, *Saga,* 161.
8. Robert James Riekse, "Analysis of Selected Significant Historical Factors in the History of the Pioneer Junior College in Michigan: Grand Rapids Junior College, 1914-62," (unpublished Ed.D. dissertation, Michigan State University, 1964), 21.
9. Davis, *Saga,* 162-63.
10. Z. Z. Lydens, *The Story of Grand Rapids*, (Grand Rapids, Michigan: Kregel Publications, 1966), 491-93.
11. *The Grand Rapids Press*, September 19, 1914.
12. Davis, *Saga,* 164.
13. Ibid., 166.
14. Ibid., 212-13.

Chapter Two — The Andrews Era—Act One The 1920s

1. Official Proceedings of the Board of Education of Grand Rapids, meeting of January 24, 1920.
2. *The Grand Rapids Press*, January 28, 1920.
3. L. Richard Marousek, "A History of the Grand Rapids, Michigan Junior College," (unpublished M.A. thesis, Graduate College of the State University of Iowa, 1940), 52. Also "Proceedings of the Grand Rapids Board of Education," 1924.

4. Fiftieth Anniversary GRJC Athletic Directory and Record.
5. Riekse, "Analysis," 87.
6. Dr. Karin Orr, *Seventy-fifth Anniversary GRJC History*, 1989.
7. Arthur Andrews, unpublished "Autobiographical Review of 35 Years as President of Grand Rapids Junior College," 1955, 22.
8. Arthur Andrews, unpublished "Information Summary of the Accomplishments of Grand Rapids Junior College," undated, 3.
9. Clarence E. Meyers, "The Public Junior Colleges in the North Central Association." (Unpublished Ph.D. thesis, University of North Dakota, 1939), 177.
10. Anne Mulder-Edmondson, unpublished "Musical Moods and Other Memories: A History of the Music Department at Grand Rapids Junior College," 1982, 5.

Chapter Three — The Andrews Era—Act Two The 1930s

1. Lydens, *The Story*, 495.
2. Ibid., 495-96.
3. George E. Carrothers, *History of the Michigan College Association*, (University of Michigan, 1961), 8-10.
4. Ibid., 10.
5. E. Ray Baxter, unpublished "Fifty Years of Educational Leadership—Grand Rapids Junior College, 1914-64,) 1964, 7.
6. Ibid., 8.
7. Ibid., 9.
8. Mulder-Edmundson, "Musical Moods," 6.
9. Ibid., 6.
10. Lydens, *The Story*, 564.
11. Marousek, "A History," 65.
12. Ibid., 65-66.
13. Orr, *Seventy-fifth Anniversary,* and Lydens, *The Story*, 172, 207.

Endnotes

Chapter Four   The Andrews Era—Act Two
1940-55

1. Marousek, "A History," 68-70.
2. Ibid., 71.
3. Interview with Dr. Robert Riekse, June 7, 2013.
4. Lydens, *The Story*, 603.
5. Arthur Andrews, "Annual Report of the President, Grand Rapids Junior College," June, 1944.
6. Lydens, *The Story*, 604-6.
7. Orr, *Seventy-fifth Anniversary*.
8. Baxter, "Fifty Years," 9.
9. Arthur Andrews, "Annual Report of the President," June, 1945.
10. Riekse, "Analysis," 137.
11. Baxter, "Fifty Years," 10.
12. Mulder-Edmundson, "Musical Moods," 9.
13. Riekse, "Analysis," 123.
14. *The Grand Rapids Press*, April 26, 1955.
15. *The Grand Rapids Herald*, June 11, 1954.

Chapter Five   Years of Transition
1955-65

1. Riekse, "Analysis," 95-96.
2. Ibid., 99.
3. *The Junior Collegiate*, October 12, 1956, 3.
4. Riekse Interview.
5. *The Collegiate*, May 1, 1991, 3.
6. Telephone interview with Betty Robbins, former Director of Student Services, August 21, 2013.
7. Interview with John Dersch, Math Department Chair, August 15, 2013.
8. Lydens, *The Story*, 497.

Chapter Six   The Builders: The McCarthy Years
1965-75

1. *The Grand Rapids Press*, May 13, 1967.
2. Citizens and Alumni Study Committee, "Recommendations for Grand Rapids Junior College," 1968, 11.
3. Riekse interview.
4. North Building Brochure, prepared by the Grand Rapids Board of Education, 1971.
5. 1974 Grand Rapids Junior College self-study, *A Self Analysis*, 14.
6. Telephone interview with Keith Longberg, October 29, 2013.
7. Interview with Jack VanAartsen, October 28, 2013.
8. Telephone interviews with Jack VanAartsen and Dr. Robert Riekse, September 28, 2013.

Chapter Seven   The Builders: The Calkins Years—Part One
1965-84

1. Interview with Richard Calkins (all Calkins quotes that follow will be from the interview), May 7, 2013.
2. Interview with Fred Sebulske, May 8, 2013.
3. Spectrum Theater Brochure, 1997, 5-6
4. Interview with Bruce and Tina Lockwood, July 19, 2013.
5. Dersch interview.
6. Interview with Jonathon Russell, May 8, 2013.
7. Interview with Bob Garlough, September 5, 2013.
8. Grand Rapids Junior College Music Center brochure, 1980.
9. Calkins interview and Music Center brochure, 1980.
10. Student Community Center brochure, 1981.
11. Calkins interview, and McCabe-Marlowe House brochure, 1981.
12. Interview with C. J. Shroll, 2012.
13. Interview with Bob Partridge, May 10, 2013.

Endnotes

Chapter Eight   **The Builders: The Calkins Years—Part Two**
                                      1985-98

1. Orr, *Seventy-fifth Anniversary*.
2. Telephone interview with Dr. Scott McNabb, October 30, 2013.
3. Interview with Duane Davis, November 18, 2013.
4. Orr, *Seventy-fifth Anniversary*.
5. Vicki Janowiak, quoted in http:/mlive.com, December 20, 2010.
6. Calkins interview; interview with Dr. Juan Olivarez, June 28, 2013.
7. Interview with Deb DeWent, February 24, 2014. Notes from Julie Johnson.
8. Interviews with Tom Hofmann, May 21, 2013, Fred van Hartesveldt, October 7, 2013, Chuck Chamberlain, September 13, 2013; VanAartsen, Calkins, and Partridge interviews.
9. *The GRCC Alumni News*, fall 1998, 4.

Chapter Nine   **The Olivarez Years**
                                   1999-2008

1. Interview with Dr. Pat Pulliam, September 23, 2013.
2. Telephone interview with Dr. Juan Olivarez, December 13, 2013.
3. Notes from Dr. Joseph Hesse, December 4, 2013.
4. Olivarez interview.
5. *The Collegiate*, November 10, 1999.
6. Notes from Dr. Joseph Hesse.
7. Calkins Science Center brochure, April, 2000.
8. Leslie E. Tassell M-TEC brochure, August 28, 2002.
9. *The Collegiate*, April 12, 2006.
10. Partridge interview.
11. Olivarez interview.
12. Notes from Nick Antonakis, December 18, 2013.
13. Interview with Dr. Gary Burbridge, October 29, 2013.
14. Interview with Donna Kragt, December 4, 2013.

Chapter Ten   **The Ender Years**
                                 2009-Present

1. Interview with Dr. Anne Mulder, May 16, 2013.
2. Notes from Music Department Chair Kevin Dobreff, January 1, 2014.
3. Interview with Dr. Steven Ender, July 16, 2013.
4. Interview with Gary Schenk, former Board Chair, January 17, 2014.
5. Partridge interview.
6. Ender interview.
7. Ibid.
8. Interview with Gordon Hunsberger, December 19, 2013.
9. *GRCC Foundation Annual Report, 2012-13*, 9.
10. Ibid, 9.
11. GRCC Works Kick-off Ceremony, YouTube, 2009.
12. *Foundation Annual Report*, 9.
13. van Hartesveldt interview.
14. Higher Learning Commission, *Quality Checkup Report*, Grand Rapids Community College, June 10, 2014, 6 (based on the team visit of April 2-4, 2014). Also interview with English Department Chair Janice Balyeat, Sept. 10, 2013.
15. Interview with Bert Bleke, present GRCC Board Chair, January 22, 2014.
16. Schenk interview.
17. HLC *Quality Checkup Report*, 3.

Final Thoughts

1. Burbridge interview.

1963-2014 GRJC/GRCC
Distinguished Alumni Recipients

The Distinguished Alumni Award honors a GRCC/JC alumnus who has achieved substantial public recognition for his/her accomplishments or success.

1964	John T. Bangert	Engineer	Bell Telephone Laboratories
	E. Ray Baxter	Dean	Grand Rapids Junior College
	Russell Christopher	Musician	The Metropolitan Opera
	Edward N. Cole	Industrialist and Executive	General Motors Corporation
	R. Hiley Davis	Industrialist	American Seating Company
	Lawrence J. Fuller	Brigadier General	United States Army
	Richard M. Gillett	Chairman	Old Kent Bank
	Arnold Gingrich	Publisher	*Esquire* magazine
	Dr. John Hannah	President	Michigan State University
	Dr. Andrew Kosten	Minister	Ridgefield Park, NJ
	Robert Lindquist	Banker	Harris Trust and Savings
	The Honorable K. William Stinson	Congressman	U.S. House of Representatives
1965	Harry E. Chesebrough	Product Planning and Development	Chrysler Corporation
	George Huebner	Director of Research	Chrysler Corporation
	Dr. Jay L. Pylman	Superintendent	Grand Rapids Public Schools
	Dr. Clarence Straatsma	Professor	Plastic and Reconstructive Surgery, New York Medical College
1966	Dr. Gould A. Andrews	Surgeon and Administrator	Oak Ridge Institute of Nuclear Studies
	Rev. Robert J. Lignell	Minister	Faith Lutheran Church
1967	Rev. John M. Burgess	Bishop	Episcopal Diocese of Massachusetts in Boston
	Dr. Howard J. Schaubel	Orthopedic Surgeon	Grand Rapids, MI
1968	Bernadine DeValdis, M.D., F.R.C.S.	Physician	Holland, MI
	Christian Sonneveldt	Businessman, Mayor	City of Grand Rapids, MI
1969	Russell N. DeJong, M.D.	Neurology	University of Michigan
	Vernor H. Eman, D.D.S.	Dentist	Grand Rapids, MI
1970	Dr. Ray B. Loeschner	President	Olivet College
	Arthur S. Nicholas	Founder	Leon Chemicals, Inc.
1971	Harvey M. Andre, M.D.	Surgeon	Grand Rapids, MI
	Dr. Henry A. Bruinsma	Educator	Calvin College
1972	Edward Goebel	Industrialist	Holland, MI
	Ray E. Stevens, Jr., D.D.S.	Dentist, Photographer	Grand Rapids, MI
1973	James A. Ferguson, M.D.	Physician	Ferguson Hospital
	Elizabeth Wilson	Actress	Broadway stage, screen, and television
1974	Richard L. Cooper	Journalist, Pulitzer Prize	Rochester, NY
	Isla G. DePree, M.D.	Physician	Fort Meyers, FL
1975	Dr. Clarence A. Boonstra	Foreign Service Officer	U.S. Government
		Ambassador	Costa Rica
	Rev. Fr. Robert Hesse, C.S.C.	Catholic Missionary	Holy Cross Fathers, Ankole, Uganda, East Africa
	Jerome F. Mancewicz, M.D.	Physician	Grand Rapids, MI
	Theresa R. Palaszek, M.D.	Obstetrician and Gynecologist	Grand Rapids, MI
1976	John D. B. Luyendyk	Lawyer	Grand Rapids, MI
	Lumen Martin Winter	Artist, sculptor and muralist	New York, NY
1977	Elias Lumpkins	Dean of Students	Grand Rapids Junior College
	Jo Ellen Stuit	President of the Alumni Association	Grand Rapids Junior College
	Werner Veit	Editor and Publisher	*The Grand Rapids Press*

1963-2014 GRJC/GRCC
Distinguished Alumni Recipients

1978	Carl Morgenstern	Past President	Old Kent Bank
	Marjorie Shepard	Retired Principal	South High School
	Adrian Swets	Writer and Designer	College Park Plaza Building
1979	Dorothy L. Judd	Educator and Civic Leader	Grand Rapids, MI
	The Honorable John P. Steketee	Attorney, Judge	Kent County Juvenile Court
1980	Gerald A. Elliott	Writer	*The Grand Rapids Press*
	Calvin Jeter	Administrator, Businessman	Grand Rapids, MI
1981	Abe Drasin	Mayor	Grand Rapids, MI
	Bonnie Marris	Wildlife Artist	Saranac, MI
1982	Helen Morsink	Instructor	Central Michigan University
	O. Steward Myers	Instructor	Grand Rapids Junior College
	David E. Post	Architect	Post Associates, Inc.
1983	Marvin DeWinter	Architect	DeWinter Associates Inc.
	George Nelson	Superintendent	Grand Rapids, MI
	Caroll Streeter, CLU	Community Leader	Grand Rapids, MI
1984	David Cope	Poet, English Instructor	Grand Rapids Junior College
	Roy Roberts	Executive and Civic Leader	General Motors Corporation
	Vern Terpstra	Professor Emeritus	International Business, University of Michigan
1985	Harry Bloem	Executive Vice-President	Bissell Inc.
	Dr. Robert Gill	Educator, Cartoonist	Grand Rapids Public Schools
	William Lewis	Educator	University of Michigan
1986	Dr. Kenneth Fellows, Jr.	Educator	Harvard Medical School
	Hugh D. Hammerslag	Partner	Seidman & Seidman
1987	Richard M. Tooker, M.D., M.P.H.	Physician	Kent County Health Department
	Audrey Wright	Educator	East Grand Rapids High School and Louisiana State University
1988	Winfred Ferrell	Computer Consultant	New York, NY
	Rev. Russell McConnell	Founder	Grand Rapids Area Council of Churches (GRACE)
1989	Timothy D. Leuliette	President	Siemens-Bendix Automotive
	Josephine Shears	Coordinator	Veteran's Facility
		Adjunct Instructor	Grand Rapids Junior College
1990	Sara E. Glover	Nurse	Grand Rapids, MI
	William C. Woodson	Director of Graduate Studies in English	Ilinois State University
1991	Richard Reid	Foreign Language Instructor	Grand Rapids Community College
	James Robinson	Partner	Honigman Miller Schwartz and Cohn
		President	State Bar of Michigan
1992	Myrna Granderson	Health Services Manager	Grand Rapids Job Corps Center
	Gary J. Horton	Executive Vice President	Creative Services, D'Arcy Masius Benton and Bowles
1993	Billie Alexander	Director	Project Rehab
	Wallace "Pete" DeMaagd	Columnist	*The Grand Rapids Press*
1994	William LaPenna, M.D.	Cardiologist	Borgess Cardiology Group
1995	Beverly Drake	Executive Director	Area Community Services Employment and Training Council
1996	Armen Oumedian	Senior Vice President	Pinnacle Automation Inc.
1997	Howard Stovall	Attorney	Baker & McKenzie

1963-2014 GRJC/GRCC
Distinguished Alumni Recipients

1998	Gary Goode	Partner	Arthur Andersen
1999	Robert J. LaPenna, M.D.	Cardiologist	Borgess Cardiology Group
2000	Donald Maine	President	Davenport University
2001	Steven Pestka	State Representative	76th District, Michigan House of Representatives
2002	John Selmon	Senior Vice President	Davenport University
2003	The Honorable Sara J. Smolenski	Chief Judge	63rd District Court
2004	Dr. Donald R. Boyer	Retired Provost and Vice President of Academic and Student Affairs	Grand Rapids Community College
2005	The Honorable Edward "Ned" Fenlon	Retired Attorney	State Representative and Circuit Court Judge
2006	Bill Hardiman Michael Sak	State Senator State Representative, Speaker Pro Tempore	29th Senate District, State of Michigan Michigan House of Representatives
2007	Jim McKay	Chairperson	West Michigan Northern Trust Bank
2008	George Lessens	Chief Meteorologist	WZZM 13
2009	Gary Schenk	Board of Trustees (1997-2009) Lawyer	Grand Rapids Community College Schenk, Boncher, Rypma P.C.
2010	Dave Custer	President Chairperson	Custer Workplace Interiors Board of Directors, GRCC Foundation
2011	James V. Buzzitta, M.D. Janice L. Maggini	Founder Chief Executive Officer Board of Trustees (1991-2011) Retired Administrator	Michigan Medical P.C. Hughes Management Grand Rapids Community College Wyoming Public Schools
2012	Dr. Kevin O'Neill	Retired Superintendent	Coopersville Public Schools
2013	Kevin Belk Tom Rademacher	Chief of Police Columnist	Grand Rapids Police Department *The Grand Rapids Press*
2014	The Honorable John A. Hallacy	Chief Judge	10th District Court

1985-2014 GRJC/GRCC
Emeritus Faculty Recipients

The purpose of the Emeritus Faculty Award is to recognize and confer emeritus status to a retired faculty member or administrator who has been recognized by colleagues as an outstanding instructor/administrator, made a significant contribution to GRCC and its students, brought distinction to his or her field through activities inside and outside of the classroom, and served as a role model to aspiring instructors and administrators.

Year	Name	Role	Department
1985	Alecia DuRand	Faculty	Art Department
	Albert Smith	Faculty	Fine and Performing Arts
1986	E. Ray Baxter	Faculty and Administrator	President's Office
	Wendell Shroll	Administrator	Continuing Education
1987	Gordon Hunsberger	Faculty, Coach	Physical Education
	Richard Wherity	Administrator	Student Activities
1988	Elisabeth Day-Knapp	Faculty	Social Sciences
	Theodora Quick	Faculty	Mathematics
1989	Anne Miller	Faculty	Life Sciences
	Orson Stewart Myers	Faculty	Technology
1990	Ray Boozer	Administrator	Continuing Education, GRJC Foundation
	Lucille Thomas	Faculty	Language Arts
1991	Leonard Anderson	Faculty	Business
	John Regenmorter	Faculty	Speech
1992	Albertus Elve	Faculty	Chemistry
1993	Marinus Swets	Faculty and Administrator	English
1994	Anthony LaPenna	Administrator	Registrar's Office
1995	Francis J. McCarthy	Administrator and College Chief Executive	Dean's Office
1996	Allen Gerrard	Faculty	French and Spanish
1997	Harvey Meyaard	Faculty	Biology
1998	Harvey Olsen	Faculty	Sociology
1999	Anne Mulder	Administrator and Interim President	President's Office
2000	James Skidmore	Faculty	Business
2001	Bobbi Schrader	Faculty and Administrator	Nursing
2002	Nancy Clouse	Faculty	Visual Arts
2003	Phyllis Fratzke	Administrator	Child Development
	Till Peters	Dean	Occupational Education
2004	Alice Donahue	Faculty	Occupational Therapy
2005	Richard D. Kurzhals	Faculty	Social Science
2006	Granville Brown	Faculty and Administrator	Manufacturing
2007	Keith Longberg	Faculty	English
	Richard Calkins	College President	President's Office
2008	Roger DeVries	Faculty	Physical Science
2009	Charles Chamberlain	Faculty	English
		Dean	Social Science and Humanities
2010	Cornelius Eringaard	Executive Vice President	President's Office
2011	Marilyn Smidt	Faculty	Nursing
2012	Velvie Green	Dean and Provost	Business Faculty
2013	Gary Burbridge	Faculty and Dean	Social Science
2014	Paul Chardoul	Faculty	Social Science

1989-2014 GRJC/GRCC
Excellence in Education Recipients

The Excellence in Education Award was established in 1989 to honor an individual GRCC employee for his or her contributions to the College, higher education and the community. In 2000, the award was expanded to honor an outstanding faculty and staff member.

Year	Name	Department
1989	Dee Palmer	Dean's Office
1990	Robert Long	Biological Sciences
1991	Marinus Swets	Arts and Sciences
1992	Earl Mandeville	Financial Aid
1993	Duane Davis	Performing Arts
1994	Don Boyer	Occupational Education
1995	Roger DeVries	Physical Sciences
1997	Eric Flynn	Information Technology
1998	Alice Donahue	Occupational Therapy Assistant Program
1999	Jan Benhan Jerry Benham	Human Resources Food Services
2000	Fred Sebulske Sue Merizon	Performing Arts Information Technology
2001	Sandra Andrews Elias Lumpkins	Physical Sciences Student and Alumni Services
2002	Lynn Asper Donna Kragt	Performing Arts Institutional Research and Planning
2003	James Chesla Peg Burn	Mathematics Financial Services
2004	Marilyn Smidt Marianne Pierson	Nursing Student Affairs
2005	Mike Kasperlik Klaas Kwant	Radiological Technology Media Technologies
2006	Laurie Foster Chris Arnold	Biological Sciences Diversity Learning Center
2007	Linda Spoelman Becky Yoder	English Applied Technology Center
2008	Joe Hesse Bruce Morrison	Physical Science Institutional Research and Planning
2009	Bob Partridge	Business and Financial Services
2010	Steve Abid Julie Parks	Social Sciences Training Solutions
2011	John Dersch Laurie Witczak	Mathematics Academic Support Center
2012	Diane Sparks Mike Kidder	Education and Child Development Secchia Institute for Culinary Education
2013	Judy A. Jankowski Nanci Guigue	Psychology School of Workforce Development

1999-2014 GRCC
Salute to Women Recipients

Salute to Women honors four women within the college's community for personal and professional excellence and for serving as role models and mentors to other women. This is awarded annually during March, Women's History Month.

Year	Alumna	Employee	Former Employee	Student
1999	Terri Handlin	Nancy Clouse	Patricia Pulliam, Ph.D.	Jill Paasch
2000	Theresa R. Palaszek, M.D.	Kathleen M. Owens	Barbara McCarty	Annetaa Chan
2001	Virginia Moralez, RN	Velvie Green, Ph.D.	Patricia Oldt, Ph.D.	Lisa Satayut
2002	Shelly Urbane	Martha Cox	Marcia Tiesinga	Rina Modak
2003	The Honorable Sara J. Smolenski	Carole Redwine	Anne E. Mulder, Ph. D.	Belen Ledezma
2004	Jean Reed Bahle	Laurie Faber-Foster	Shirley A. West, Ph.D.	Crystal Knoll
2005	Janice Maggini	Audrey Mayfield	Geneva Hosler	Rocia Garcia
2006	Olivia Margo Anderson	Gertrude Croom	Patty Gunn	Yamaka Bracey
2007	Glenes Hamersma	Mursalata Muhammad	Phyllis Fratzke	Tami Allen
2008	Diann Gilliam	Liz Timmer	Malinda Prince Sapp, Ph. D.	Mary Adams-Powers
2009	LaTarro Traylor	Tina Hoxie	Lea Tobar	Fonda Kingsley
2010	Bonnie K. Miller	Fatima Nieves	Rosalyn M. Ghysels	Jillian Woodruff
2011	Anika Smith	Patti Mumaw	Not Awarded	Shannon Woodall
2012	Jane Doyle	Nancy Forrest	Julie Johnson	Tonja Lofton
2013	Myrna P. Granderson, ADN	Misty McClure-Anderson	Joan C. Berends, RN, Ph. D.	Carly Misech
2014	Teresa Weatherall Neal	Kathryn K. Mullins, Ph.D.	Elizabeth (Beth) Foster	Nicole Bowl

2011-13 GRCC Excellence in Teaching by Adjunct Faculty Recipients

The Excellence in Teaching by Adjunct Faculty Award was established to honor a Grand Rapids Community College adjunct faculty member for his or her contributions to the institutional goal of constantly improving the learning environments and success for our students.

2011	Melanie Forbes	Math
2012	Dawn Cheikh	Language and Thought
2013	Cheryl Kautz	Computer Information Systems

GRCC Program Level Accreditation

In addition to institutional accreditation through the Higher Learning Commission of the North Central Association of Colleges and Schools, the following GRCC programs hold separate accreditations.

Program	Accrediting Agency
Associate Degree Nursing and Licensed Practical Nursing Programs	Accreditation Commission for Education in Nursing, Inc.
Automotive Technology	National Automotive Technicians Education Foundation
Child Development	National Association for the Education of Young Children
Child Development Laboratory Preschool	National Association for the Education of Young Children
Criminal Justice - Corrections	Michigan Correctional Officers' Training Council
Dental Assisting and Dental Hygiene Programs	Commission on Dental Accreditation, American Dental Association
Heating, Ventilation, Air Conditioning and Refrigeration Technology (HVACR)	Partnership for Air-Conditioning, Heating, Refrigeration Accreditation
Law Enforcement (Police Academy)	Michigan Commission on Law Enforcement Standards
Medical Assistant Program	Commission on Accreditation of Allied Health Education Programs
Music Department	National Association of Schools of Music
Occupational Therapy Assistant	Accreditation Council of Occupational Therapy Education of the American Occupational Therapy Association
Radiologic Technology	Joint Review Committee on Education in Radiologic Technology
Secchia Institute for Culinary Education	American Culinary Federation
Visual Arts	National Association of Schools of Art and Design
Wind Energy	Global Wind Organization

1914-Present GRJC/GRCC
Full-time Employees

Disclaimer: an attempt was made to include every full-time employee who worked for or is currently working for the College. If a name has been inadvertently omitted or misspelled notify mklawitt@grcc.edu with the correction.

Amr Abdel-Wajab
Steve Abid
Ivette Acevedo
Wanda Acevedo-Ferrer
Ardreen Adair
Donna Adams
Sesime Adanu
Joseph Aderholdt
Joshua Aderholdt
Alexander Afendoulis
Lorena Aguayo-Marquez
Antonio Aguillon-Huerta
Nedim Ahmetovic
Michael Ahrendt
Stanley Albers
Drew Albritten
Ann Alexander
Martin Alexander
Nickie Alexander Mulder
David Alger
Mary Alkevicius
Ardath Allen
Barbara Allen
Christopher Allen
Dennis Allen
Hugh Allen
Penny Allen-Cook
Allen Allington
Rebecca Allington
Tess Alliston
Robert Alquist
Laura Alsgaard
Elisa Alvarez
Raul Alvarez
Beth Amante
Zakie Ambrose
Aleta Anderson
Daniel Anderson
Darwyn Anderson
David Anderson
Glenda Anderson
Helen Anderson
Leonard Anderson
Lilly Anderson
Teresa Anderson
Emiko Ando
Richard Andre
G. Arthur Andrews
Curtis Andrews
Sandra Andrews
Jennifer Andrzejewski
Laura Angulo
Anthony Annese

Howard Antoine
Nikolaos Antonakis
Thomas Antor
Suzanne Antrim
Karren Antvelink
Mary Jane Anway
Barbara Appleton
Arturo Armijo
Cresencio Armijo
Christopher Armstrong
Donald Armstrong
Christina Arnold
John Arnold
Laurie Arnswald
Marcia Arp
Elisa Arreola
Lisa Arsenault
Pranoti Asher
Stephanie Ashford
Lynn Asper
Brett Atchison
Elizabeth Atkinson
Marjorie Atkinson
Robert Atterberry
Jennifer Attila
JoAnn Atwood
Richard Austin
Chris Avison
Terri Ayers
Margy Ayuso
Clare Baar
Daniel Babcock
Eugenia Babcock
Jo Bader
John Badgerow
Susan Baglien
Yan Bai
Lowell Bailey
Rebecca Bailey
Ronnie Bailey
Elly Bainbridge
Glenn Bainum
Jack Bajema
David Baker
Frederick Baker
John Baker
Kimberly Baker
Peggy Baker
Omar Bakri
Patrick Baldridge
Mary Baldwin
Fanny Ball
Sandy Ball

Mary Baloyan
Janice Balyeat-Hansen
Atricia Banks
Nikki Banks
Curt Baragar
Christopher Barber
Floyd Barber
Charles Barfelz
Louis Barnes
Phillip Barnes
Richard Barnhart
Susan Barnstable
Mary Barnum
Mercedes Barnum
Irvine Barr
Sally Barrett
Stephen Barton
Jennifer Batten
Jody Battle
Karen Battle
Mary Bauer
Frederick Bauman
Robert Baumbach
E. Ray Baxter
Mary Bayer
Edith Bazen
Clayton Bazuin
Charles Beall
Gayl Beals
Eugenia Beardslee
Jyson Beasley
John Beattie
Joseph Becherer
Lakisha Beck
Colleen Becker
Jessie Beckham
Maree Beckon
Alice Beckwith
Leon Beery
Deidre Begay
Anesa Behrem
Chloe Beighley
Mary Beth Beighley
Amy Beil
Iva Belden
Jane Beld-Smith
Doris Bell
Constance Bellows
Benito Benavides
Tim Benedict
Marilyn Benefiel
Lorie Bengston
Jan Benham

Jerry Benham
Denyse Bening
Amy Bennett
Charles Bennett
Clare Bennett
Joan Bennett
Joseph Bennett
Raymond Bennett
Robert Bennett
JaneAnn Benson
Merrilie Benthin
Julie Bera
Joan Berends
Jessica Berens
Bernice Berg
Michael Berg
Susan Bergin
Betsy Bergman
Virginia Bergman
Jack Bergmans
Sidney Bernstein
Beth Berry
Wendy Berry
Mary Kay Bethune
Verdale Betts
Helen Beuker
Cora Beute
Cindy Bezaury
Judith Bezile
Richard Bezile
Patricia Bidle
Donna Bielecki
Deanna Binder
Jerilyn Binder
Ann Marie Birr
Charlene Bishop
Bruce Bjornseth
Donald Black
Robert Black
Stuart Blacklaw
Nancy Blackwel
Jodi Blair
Phyllis Blake
Terri Blanch
Laura Blandford
Dorothy Blatter
Mable Blink
Maxine Blink
Clem Block
William Bloemendaal
Patricia Bloom
Patrick Bockheim
Ronald Boelema

Jolene Boelens
Betty Boerema
John Boerema
Michael Boerman
Thomas Boersma
Diane Boettner
James Bogdan
Jan Bolhuis
Eunice Bolt
Robert Bolt
Melissa Boman
Colleen Bont
Mary Bont
Bunny Bookwalter
Joel Boone
Paul Boonstra
Ray Boozer
Thomas Boozer
Denise Borges
Augusta Borneman
Jennifer Borrello
Nick Borst
Mary Boruts
Bonnie Bos
John Bos
Kenneth Bos
Walter Boston
Cheryl Botham
Tina Bouchard
Sharon Bouman
William Bouton
Debbie Boverhof
Kari Boverhof
Mark Boverhof
Michael Bowen
Rachel Bower
William Bowers
Margaret Bowles
Andrew Bowne
Donald Boyer
Jan Boynton
Avonte Braden-Love
Thomas Brailey
Tom Brailey
Linda Bramble
Amanda Brand
Garret Brand
Malcolm Brannen
Robert Breen
E. Robert Breining
Laura Bridges
Lucy Bright
Rebecca Brinks

Joseph Briseno
Russell Brock
Mary Brody
Lenora Brogdon-Wyatt
Aaron Brooks
Bayard Brooks
Inez Brooks
Sara Brooks
Amy Broome
Avery Broome
Shari Brouwer
Carol Brown
Deanna Brown
Erica Brown
Gail Brown
Granville Brown
Irene Brown
James Brown
Kay Brown
Lloyd Brown
Marilou Brown
Mary Brown
Odell Brown
Robert Brown
Tommy Brown
Stephen Brozek
Karl Bruder
Cathy Bruinsma
Clifton Bryant
Jennifer Bryant
Judith Bryant
Harold Buckham
Flora Buckhout
Joyce Buckley
Katie Budden
Charles Buffham
Jennifer Buikema
Alice Bultman
Kenneth Bultman
Barbara Bunn
Gary Burbridge
Linda Burden
Shirley Burgen
Holly Burgess
Sandy Burgess
Glenn Burgett
Patricia Burgett
Letitia Burham
William Burhenn
Donna Burkholder
Mark Burnis
Harriet Burns
Marie Burns

GRJC/GRCC Full-time Employees
1914-Present

Peg Burns
Lyttron Burris
Anne Burt
Charles Burt
Terri Burt
Stacey Bush
Erin Busscher
Tamber Bustance
Heather Bustraan
Hayden Butcher
Carl Butenas
Lisa Butler
Agnes Buttweiler
Melissa Buurstra
Jerilyn Bydalek
Kate Byerwalter
Mary Byerwalter
Marie Byl
Jeffrey Byrd
Sherry Cain
Diane Caliendo
Charlotte Calkins
Richard W. Calkins
Adrian Callaghan
Alexander Callaghan
Helen Cameron
Angus Campbell
Marion Campbell
Michael Campo
Herbert Cantor
Emile Caprara
Charles Carlson
Donald Carlson
John Carlson
Robert Carlstrom
Gary Carpenter
Dillon Carr
Chauncy Carter
Karen Carter
La'Ontae Carter
Brenda Cary
Thomas Casaletto
Wesley Casarez
Michael Casey
Maria Cassidy
Patricia Castiglione
Phyllis Castleman
Laura Caulk
Robert Cebelak
Richard Cederholm
Margaret Cerny
Nancy Chaffee
Carrie Chaffer

Dorian Chalom
Charles Chamberlain
Sandra Chamberlain
Serena Chambers
Mark Champion
Charles Chanter
Mary Chapin
Janice Chapman
Kelli Chapman
Mary Anne Chapman
Jane Chappell
Paul Chardoul
Roosevelt Charleston
Robert Chase
Willis Chase
Amanda Chatel
Heath Chelesvig
Jianchu Chen
Gretchen Cheney
James Chesla
Janet Chesla
Laurie Chesley
Richard Chesnutt
Eva Chilton Johnson
Mary Jo Chisholm
Bertha Chivis
Wendell Chivis
Helene Christ
Kate Christian
Elleena Chrzan
Erin Cisler
Anna Clark
Daniel Clark
David Clark
Jennifer Clark
Elaine Clarke
Sharon Clawson
Chiquital Clay
LaShaun Clay
John Cleveland
Diane Closs
Nancy Clouse
Megan Coakley
Lisa Cohen
Lola Coke
Michael Colby
Cheryl Cole
Crystal Coleman
Patrick Coleman
Frank Collins
Carolyn Collins-Bondon
Juan Colon
Jan Colvin

Patricia Colvin
Linda Conde
Ralph Conger
Frank Conner
Scott Conner-Wellman
Hubert Conover
Roland Constant
Anita Cook
Daniel Cook
Gary Cook
Heather Cook
Lori Cook
Michael Cooper
Rhondo Cooper
Vikki Cooper
David Cope
Joy Copin
Colleen Copus
Casey Cornelius
Joseph Cortez
Esequiel Cortez, Jr.
Matthew Coullard
Paul Coulson
John Cowin
John Cowles
Martha Cox
Lyvonne Cramer
Rachel Crapo
LaDawn Cribbs
Jennifer Cronk
Sharon Cronkright
Gertrude Croom
Margaret Crosby
Marcia Cross
Larry Crossman
Katie Croucher
Ruth Crouthamel
Connie Crumpton-Armijo
Antonia Cruz
Lydia Cruz
Anny Cuculista
Robert Cunningham
Michael Cupples
Lera Curtis
Michael Curtis
John Cuthbertson
Marilyn Cutler
Patrick Cwayna
Steevigh Cwayna
Eugene Czuhai
Imelda Dailey
Beverly Daily
Brian Daily

Bruce Dakin
Valeria Dakin
Jacoba Dalebout
Marcille Dalgleish
Kathleen Damstra
Gayle Danevicz
Kathy Danevicz
Curt Daniels
Katherine Daniels
Rosa Daniels
Jeffrey Danner
Wilma Davenport
Joan Daves
Duane David
Charles Davidson
Christine Davis
Duane Davis
George Davis
Jesse Davis
Keri Davis
LeRoy Davis
Luther Davis
Melissa Davis
Wendolyn Davis
Gerald Dawkins
Alice Dawson
Charles Dawson
Danielle Dawson
Merle Dawson
Jackson Day
Shirley Day
Elizabeth Day-Knapp
Roger De Graff
Kay de Peraza
Delores DeAllen
Ben Dean
Donna Dean
Morris Dean
Lori DeBie
Jeannette DeBoer
Rosemary DeBruler
Ann Deckard
Glenn Deckinga
Shelley Deemter
Cecile DeGroot
Pamela DeGryse
Mary DeHaan
Donna DeKoning
Cecil DeKraker
Maria del Carmen Martinez
Susan Del Raso
Barbara DeLaRosa
Lucy DeLoof

Susan Delraso
Karen Demchuk
Amy DenBraber
C. Frederick Deneke
Mary Denhof
James Denney
Bernard DePrimo
Barbara DePuydt
John Dersch
Thomas Deschaine
Noah DeSmit
Staci Dever
Richard DeVinney
Michael DeVivo
Derek DeVries
George DeVries
Herbert DeVries
Laura DeVries
Linda DeVries
Margaret DeVries
Martin DeVries
Roger DeVries
Deborah DeWent
Debora DeWitt
Betty DeYoung
Joan DeYoung
Mary DeYoung
Elaine Dickinson
Rebecca Dickstein
Marian Dighton
Teresa Dilworth
Priscilla DiPiazza
Nancy Ditmar
William Dix
Harry Doane
John Doane
Paul Doane
Christine Dobberstein
Regina Dobberstein
Kevin Dobreff
Mark Dodd
Bette Doezema
Bryson Dolly-McGlothin
Mary Doltoske
Alice Donahue
Lisa Donaldson
John Doneth
Camille Donnelly
Nick Dood
Bryan Door
Lisa Dopke
Sara Dorer
Dominic Dorsey

Tamara Dossin
Carol Doubblestein
Matthew Douglas
Samuel Douglas
William Dow
Tommy Dowds, Jr.
Marcia Downs
Georgina Doyle
Jerome Drain
Lois Draper
Matthew Dressel
Sandra Drummond
Robert Dryfoos
Heidi Dubee
Evered Dudley
Robert Duffy
Marie Dufresne
Darlene Dugan
Ruth Dunbar
Yolanda Duncan
Kevin Dunn
Terrence Dunn
Ruben Duran
Alecia DuRand
Jim Durkee
David Dye
Karen Dykehouse
Nellie Dykehouse
Beverly Dykema
Anthony Dykema-VanderArk
Candyce Dykstra
Daniel Dykstra
Donald Dykstra
Karen Dykstra
Mary Dykstra
Barbara Eardley
Kyle Eaton
Gary Ebels
Leslie Edmondson
Maurice Edwards
Ronald Edwards
Ruth Eggerding
Louis Eich
John Eister
A. Martin Eldersveld
Adriana Elferdink
W. Maynard Ellington
Caroline Elliott
Margaret Elliott
Diane Ellis
Grace Ellis
Theresa Ellis
Julie Elston

GRJC/GRCC Full-time Employees
1914-Present

Robert Eluskie
Albertus Elve
Dan Elzinga
Dan Emelander
David Emelander
Kathleen Emery
Katie Emigh
Patricia Empie
Amari Enam
Steven Ender
Kristin Enders
Cheryl Endres
Marguerite Eness
Robert Engelman
Margaretta Engle
Robert Engmark
Janice Ensing
Cornelius Eringaard
Holly Ernst
Paul Esch
Miguel Espinoza
Austin Etter
Willette Eubanks
Ruth Evans
Edith Evans Hyde
Sharon Evoy
DeWayn Faber
Michael Faber
Stephen Faber
Victoria Faber
William Faber
Susan Fales
Cynthia Fant
James Farmer
Sue Farrell
Ellen Faurot
Laura Fausett
Pauline Fauth
David Fearnow
Milton Fehling
Joshua Ferguson
Keith Ferguson
Kevin Ferguson
Michael Ferguson
Harold Feringa
Marcia Feuerstein
Andre Fields
John Fields
Patrick Fields
Donald Fink
Carol Fiorenzo
Lee Fiorenzo
Mindy Firlan

Alice Fish
Cynthia Fisher
Marilyn Fisher
Maude Fisher
Frank Fishman
Denise Flagg
Karen Flagg
JoAnne Flak
Mike Flanagan
Shavval Fleming
Timothy Fleming
Calvin Fleser
Cheryl Floyd
Eric Flynn
Elizabeth Foetisch
David Folkert
Gregory Folkert
Penny Folsom
Elizabeth Forbes
Gregory Forbes
Donna Ford
Kathleen Ford
Ryan Ford
Stephanie Forest
Franklin Forner
Heather Forrest
Michael Forrest
Nancy Forrest
David Fortuna
David Fortuna, Jr.
Lorraine Fortuna
Mark Fortuna
Beth Foster
Bill Foster
Christine Foster
Elizabeth Foster
Harold Foster
Laurie Foster
Richard Foster
Douglas Fournier
Dawn Fox
Glenn Fox
James Fox
Joanne Fox
Winifred Fox
Denise Francis
Mary Francis
Joel Frank
Victoria Frankum
Michael Franz
Alvena Franzen
Phyllis Fratzke
Betty Freas

Helen Freeman
Peter Freeman
Theresa Freiberg
Lisa Freiburger
Helen Freidrich
Ruth Frey
Susan Fricke
William Frikken
James Fritz
Barbara Fryling
Ronald Fryling
William Fuehrer
Dorothy Fuller
Le'Vota Fuller
B. F. Fuller
Jesse Fuzi
Enid Gaddis
Cathajane Galante
Carey Gale
Elnora Gale
Paula Galloway
Claudia Galvez
Merle Gamber
Lynn Ganaway
Roland Gani
Langston Gant
Raymond Gant II
Mary Garboden
Fred Garbowitz
Abneyris Garcia
Brune Garcia
Jorge Garcia
Janet Gardner
Robert Garlough
Scott Garrard
Christine Gates
Sharon Gates
Joan Gearns
John Gebhart
Jodi Gee
Brent Geers
Glenn Gelderloos
Stephanie Gelock
Gilda Gely
Daniel Gendler
Sandra George
Jennifer Gerig
Allen Gerrard
Kelly Gessler
Patricia Gessler
Mindy Geurink-Holohan
J. Henry Geurkink
Rosalyn Ghysels

Troy Giambernardi
Joseph Giddis
Ray Gill
Michael Gillan
Cassandra Gillish
Margaret Gilman
J. Luis Giron
Lakenya Gissendanner
OB Gladyness
Sandy Glennemeier
Amanda Glick
Lisa Gloege
Harley Glover
Paula Gneym
Richard Godfrey
John Godisak
Lynn Goede
Sue Goeman
Michael Goff
Shanna Goff
Creighton Goins
Marion Goldsborough
Norwood Golson
Stephen Gonzalez
Wilfred Gooch
David Goodspeed
Lynn Goodspeed
Margaret Gorno
Edwin Graf
Joseph Graf
Jody Graves
Ronald Graves
Lorie Gravitt
Aaron Gray
Patricia Gray
Malique Grear
Cathy Green
Velvie Green
Robert Green, Jr.
Robert Green, Sr.
Phillip Greene
Jonathan Greer
William Greeson
Harold Gregorich
Ben Gregory
Sandra Gregory
Merry Anne Gregory-Barrows
William Grey
Lillian Griffin
Salatha Griffin
Denise Griffith
Edward Grimes
Carolyn Grin

Suzanne Griskait
Michael Gross
Nancy Grossman
Jane Grzesiak
Daniel Guajardo
Amber Guerreiro
Corey Guigelaar
Nanci Guigue
Robert Guigue
Mary Gunderson
Patti Gunn
Dorothy Gunning
Levi Guppy
Leanne Gusky
Robert Gutek
Adeline Gyte
Carol Haadsma
Kathleen Haas
Barbara Hackley
David Hager
Barbara Haglund
Donna Hale
Karen Hale
Cheryl Haley
Amanda Hall
James Hall
Judi Hall
Sandra Hall
Jodie Hallman
Steven Hallmark
Monica Halloran
Janet Ham
John Ham
Jacqueline Hamer
Glenes Hamersma
Nathaniel Hamilton
Sandra Hamilton
Joan Hammond
Margaret Hammond
James Hanafin
Hillery Haney
Gary Hankins
Ernest Hansen
Pat Hansen
Richard Hansen
Susan Hansen
Andrew Hansson
Robert Harasim
Jeanne Hare
Bunnita Haring
Joan Harker
Helen Harman
Fenis Harmon

Katherine Harmon
Eugene Harmsen
Whitney Harper
Ernestine Harris
Herman Harris
Juanita Harris
Sheryl Harris
Harry Hart
Kathy Hart
Douglas Hartgerink
Kathrine Hartigh
Jeffrey Hartman
Laura Hartuniewicz
James Harvey
Robert Harvey
Nancy Haun
James Hausman
Kaye Haven
Wilton Hawes
Andrea Hayes
James Hayes
Pamela Hayes
Kerry Hayward
Donald Hazelswart
Jesse Heard
Carrie Heaton
Gene Hecker
Paul Hecker
Benjamin Hecksel
Audrey Heckwolf
Danyel Heft
Bharadwaj Hegde
Jeremy Heide
Joyce Heinz
Stacey Heisler
Amy Hekman
Albert Heldt
Timothy Heldt
Robert Hellem
Mary Lynn Helsel
Robert Hendershot
Nancy Henderson
Carol Hendricks
Stephen Henkelman
Patricia Hennie
Ann Henning
Paul Herdegen
John Heredia
Gloria Herlong
Domingo Hernández-Gómez
Nathan Herremans
Maria Herrera-Belmares
Stacey Herrick

GRJC/GRCC Full-time Employees
1914-Present

Hazel Herringshaw
Fiona Hert
Julie Hess
S. Paul Hess
Stephen Hess
Joseph Hesse
Marvin Hesselink
Virginia Hewitt
Patricia Hewnnie
A. Jack Heydenberg
Ruby Hickman
H. Ralph Higgins
Ronald Higgins
Ronald Hight
Janet Higley
Ella Hildebrandt
David Hill
Dorothy Hill
Susan Hill
Charles Hillary
Kristen Hilton
Mary Hiner
Mary Hinsdale
Mildred Hinsdale
Judy Hinton
James Hitchings
Ray Hoag
Holly Hoare
Sara Hochsprung
Judy Hockemeyer
Jill Hodsdon-Benner
Louis Hoeskstra
James Hoffman
Karl Hoffman
Rodolphe Hoffman
Carl Hofman
Joyce Hofman-McHugh
Tom Hofmann
Mary Hofstra
David Holkeboer
Marcia Holmberg
Arthur Holmes
Camille Holmes
Alicent Holt
Karen Holt
Janice Holton
Doris Holtrop
Betty Holyfield
James Holyfield
Mary Holzgen
Kenneth Homrich
Lois Homrich
Ronald Hoogerwerf

Michael Hopson
Donald Hopwood
Thomas Hornak
Robert Horner
June Horowitz
Gerald Horstman
Curtis Horton
Tempi Hoskins
Geneva Hosler
Edward Hotchkiss
Joan Hough
Betsey Houting
Timothy Hoving
Myrna Hovlid
Kathy Howard
Melissa Howse
Tina Hoxie
Margaret Hoyle
Betsy Huber
Bruce Hudon
Victoria Hudson
Terrance Huff
Joseph Huffman
Katherine Hughes
Elsa Huhta
John Huizinga
Cornelia Hulst
Gayle Hulswit
Gordon Hunsberger
John Hunt
Robert Hurd
Todd Hurley
Willie Hurst
James Hyatt
Arthur Hyde
Julie Hyde
Patricia Ingersoll
Moss Ingram
Evelyn Ireland
Susan Irwin
Ann Isackson
Allen Jackson
Carl Jackson
William Jacoby
Christopher Jacques
Alicia James
Camesha James
Marie Jamison
Richard Janke
Judy Jankowski
Victoria Janowiak
Elaine Jansen
Mary Jansen

Morgan Jarema
David Jarnegan
Susan Jarrell
Mark Jasonowicz
Mary Jaye
Mary Jellema
Mildred Jelsma
Edwina Jendrasiak
Hertha Jenkins
Jerry Jennings
Geri Jessup
Jeanne Jett
Mauricio Jimenez
Oskars Jirgensons
Elmer Jirtle
Areli Johnson
Arthur Johnson
Eric Johnson
Jared Johnson
Jason Johnson
Josiah Johnson
Julie Johnson
Marie Johnson
Nancy Johnson
Oscar Johnson
Russell Johnson
Shirley Johnson
Timmy Johnson
Lela Johnson-Feree
Kristi Johnston
Linnea Johnston
Thomas Johnston
Antoinette Joiner
Anna Jones
Claudia Jones
Glen Jones
Justin Jones
Russell Jones
Ivory Jorgenson
Lois Jotter
Fred Julian
Philip Jung
Rachael Jungblut
Darlene Kaczmarczyk
Thomas Kaechele
Mary Kain
Katrina Kalisz
Patrick Kamau
Elaine Kampmueller
John Kamstra
Mary Kay Kane
Lynee Karamol
Gayle Karatkiewicz

Carol Karcher
Lee Karcher
Robert Karns
Michael Kasperlik
Abbot Kastanek
Karen Katerburg
Katherine Keating
Linda Keegstra
Brian Keelean
Jennifer Keessen
Luann Keizer
Patricia Keller
Roger Kelley
Diana Kelly
Jennifer Kelly
Nelda Kemperman
Steve Kemperman
Joyce Kennedy
Lucille Kennedy
Cindy Kennell
Ruth Kenney
Joseph Kent
Theresa Kent-Williams
Amy Kerkstra
Ann Kerkstra
Debra Kermeen
Mary Lou Kersjes
Therese Kersjes
Marjorie Kerwin
Dan Keyes
Gary Kidder
Michael Kidder
Judith Kienitz
Erin Kincaid
Carol King
Cindy King
Jack King
Amy Kirkbride
Michael Kiss
Jeffrey Kissinger
Simon Kittok
Ross Kladder
Marjorie Klander
Mike Klawitter
William Klein
Leigh Kleinert
Winifred Klenk
Holly Kleyn
Joan Kleynenberg
Patricia Kline
Virginia Klinesteker
Elizabeth Knapp
Jennifer Knauf

Walter Knauss
Regina Kneeland-Harrington
Joseph Knol
Donna Knoper
Sherry Knoppers
Patricia Kobel-Poll
Dorothy Koebl
Timothy Koets
Norma Kole
Katherine Kolehouse
Janice Kolkman
Amy Koning
Dirk Koning
Marianne Kooiman
Diana Kooistra
Tina Koopmans
Randi Koperski
Marianne Korivan
Margaret Koron
Deirdre Kosak
Leonard Kosiorowski
Amanda Kossack
Everilda Koteskey
Richard Kotovich
Dan Kovats
Jennifer Kowalski
Kelly Kozloski
Donna Kragt
Sarah Krajewski
Carol Kramer
Christine Kramer
George Kremble
Lauri Kremers
Johannes Kreuyer
Paul Krieger
Mitchell Kring
Robin Kritzman
Walter Krueger
Stewart Krulikoski
Courtney Krull
Ila Krumheuer
Joseph Krussell
Randall Kuberski
Jane Kubiak
David Kubik
Agnes Kugel
Jane Kula
Jan Kulesza
Eric Kunnen
Paula Kunst
Gayle Kupris
Connie Kupris-Myers
Ruth Kurlandsky

Harry Kurtzworth
Richard Kurzhals
Sheryl Kuzniar
Klaas Kwant
Barbara LaBelle
Tyjuanna LaBennett
Julie Lackscheide
Kyle Lackscheide
Jeanne Lacy
Robert Lacy
Jaime Lagenour
Mary LaHuis
John Lally
Rita Lally
Kay Lammers
Scott Lampe
Melissa Lancaster
Sandra Lancaster
Laurine Landheer
Pat Lange
Robert Langerak
Gordon Langeris
James Langeweg
Tudor Lanius
Anthony LaPenna
Patrick LaPenna
Elizabeth Laponsie
Bessie Larion
Dolores Larsen
Judith Larsen
Lori Larsen
Jonathan Larson
Kristen Larson
Laurence Larson
Brenda Lascari
Heather Lashuay
Patricia Laufer
Pamela Laureto
Kevin Lawson
Alfred Lazo
Andrew Lee
Harold Lee
Jacquelyn Lee
Marcia Lee
Pamela Lee
Patricia Lee
Randy Lee
Sammy Lee
Sang Lee
Cecile Leech
Lillian Leeson
Jay Leiffers
Iolanda Leigh

GRJC/GRCC Full-time Employees
1914-Present

George Lemke
Karen Lemmon
Karen Leneway
Susan Lepech
Daniel Lerner
Maryann Lesert
Melissa Leslie
Robert Leunk
Estelle Leven
Angela Leverence
Carolyn Levi
Calien Lewis
Lynden Lewis
Tina Lewis
Yvonne Lewis
Nina Lewis-Sleet
Jeff Lezman
Bernard Liburd
Susan Lichtenberg
H. Martin Lier
L. Mike Light
Elizabeth Lightner
Nygil Likely
Loretta Lind
Anna Lindberg
L. June Linderholm
Nancy Lindhout
Lisa Lindsay
Agnes Lisle
Cathy List
Steven List
Ronald Little
Blakeslee Lloyd
Jeanette Lochan
Bruce Lockwood
Tina Lockwood
Walter Lockwood
Chad Lodenstein
Brianne Lodholtz
Etta Lohman
Mark London
Dorothy Long
Jeremy Long
Robert Long
Keith Longberg
Michelle Lorenz
Dee Lorion
Linda Love Stewart
Susan Lovell
Joel Lowe
William Lozano
Yoko Lozano
Roland Lubbinge

Wendell Lubbinge
Mary Lucas
H. James Ludwick
Elias Lumpkins
Renel Lund
Rose Lunsford
Sarah Lusk
Alfred Lussky
Andrew Lussky
Gabrielle Luster
Nicole Luster
Sandra Luth
F. Earle Lyman
Kevin Lyons
Hailey Mabrito
Tami MacDonald
Mark MacFadyen
Szymon Machajewski
Donald MacKenzie
Evan Macklin
Mary MacLennan
John MacNaughton
Craig MacPhee
Molly Maczka
Cindy Mader
Peggy Mahaney
Elnur Maharramov
Lawrence Mahoney
Darryl Mahoy
Donald Maine
Frank Mallo
Elaine Maloley
Alice Malzahn
Carol Manciu
Marcus Manders
Earl Mandeville
Marilyn Mandigo
Lawrence Manglitz
Bernard Manker
Ricky Mann
Erica Manning
Jeremy Manning
Dorothy Mapes
Verdell Marble
Florence Marcek
Fay March
Almazine Marine
Adrian Markus
Catherine Marlett-Dreher
Wilma Marlowe
Robert Marmo
L. Richard Marousek
Alfredo Marquez

Webb Marris
Nicole Marshall
Cynthia Martin
Helen Martin
Scott Martin
Lisa Martinez
Carol Maser
Edward Maskevich
Andrew Masters
Geraldine Masters
Mansfield Matthewson
Scott Mattson
Jean Matyczn
Harold Matzke
Vicki Maxa
Richard Maycroft
Audrey Mayfield
Kristine Maze
Denise Mazur
Meredith McAfee
Dorothy McBride
Marie McCabe
Francis McCarthy
Barbara McCarty
Jim McClain
Patricia McClellan
Delbert McCloyn
Misty McClure-Anderson
Marilyn McCobb
Elaine McCormack
Florence McCormack
Elizabeth McCormick
Barb McDonald
Carol McDonald
Katherine McDonald
Mary Ann McDonald
Priscilla McDonald
Tammy McDonald
Christina McElwee
Sheila McGarvey
Essie Mcghee
Neal McGladdery
John McGrail
Duane McIntyre
Elizabeth McKinney
Joan McLain
Randall McLenore
William McMillan
Scott McNabb
Toy McNeal
Donald McNeely
Neil McPheeters
Ruth McVeigh

Lloyd Meadows
Wanda Medina
Marguerite Meengs
Mary Meholic
Anne Meilof
Kurt Meinders
Donald Meinke
Heida Meister
Matthew Mekkes
Leonard Melefsky
Marion Melefsky
Elina Melkonyan
Kim Mellema
Sharon Merizon
Susan Merizon
Scott Merlo
Harvey Meyaard
Clarence Meyer
Mildred Meyer
Sharon Meyer
Victoria Meyers
Nora Michael
Etta Michailovits
Shona Middleton
Sue Middleton
Marc Miedema
Scott Miklaszewski
Maureen Milarch
Joseph Milito
William Millar
Amy Miller
Anna Miller
Anne Miller
Douglas Miller
Edith Miller
Janet Miller
Jerome Miller
Karen Miller
Kathleen Miller
Kimberley Miller
Nancy Miller
Beatrice Milton
Peter Minasola
Frank Minervini
Scott Minton
Ashlee Mishler
Patricia Missad
Jennifer Mitchell
Lawrence Mitchell
Patrick Mitchell
Katherine Mittner
Jane Mohr
Heather Mol

Katherine Moll
Mary Moll-Styles
Matthew Molter
Robert Monaldo
Magdalena Montes-Spruit
Jon Montgomery
Laura Moody
Alex Moore
Chester Moore
Ellen Moore
Fred Moore
James Moore
Joanne Moore
Claude Moorhead
Grace Moorman
Jose Mora
Haydn Morgan
Brian Morris
David Morris
Michael Morris
Lauretta Morrisey
Bruce Morrison
Carolyn Morrison
Barbara Morrow
Linda Mosketti
Patricia Mosketti
Tammy Mosley
Jacqueline Motari
Susan Mowers
Ralph Mowry
Judy Mroz
Emma Muehlen
Mursalata Muhammad
Anne Mulder
Mark Mulder
Nancy Mulder
Eric Mullen
Nancy Mulhall
Kathryn Mullins
Kelsee Mullins
Patricia Mumaw
Dawn Mumford
Lyvonne Munger
Maureen Munger
Louis Murillo
Karen Murphy
Patricia Murray
Vada Murray
Alice Mursch
Kimberly Musser
C. Robert Muth
James Muth
O. Stewart Myers

Tony Myers
Irene Nantz
Carol Natte
Gary Natte
Jason Natte
Paula Naujalis
Ryan Nausieda
Samuel Naves
Oscar Neal
Jane Neil
Nora Neill
Thomas Neils
Anna Nelson
Evar Nelson
Martha Nelson
Sigurd Nelson
Beth Nesseth
Patricia Nethercot
Jeffrey Neumann
Jeffery Newberry
John Newberry
Kaye Newberry
Elleena Newton
Kishen Newton
Lee Newton
Eugene Nichols
Malea Nicolet
S. Lisbeth Nielsen
Signe Nielsen
Timothy Nielsen
Lisbeth Nielson
Glenn Niemeyer
Glenn Nienhuis
Fatima Nieves
Marcia Nink
Emily Nisley
Leah Nixon
Halina Nogorka
Mark Nordblom
Candace Norder
Deborah Nordman
Henry Nordmeyer
Peter Northouse
Matthew Novakoski
Cathy Noviskey
Dorothy Nowak
Karla Nowak
Sandra Nowak
Terry Nowak
Jill Nutt
Virginia Nye
Rick Nyenhuis
Daniel Nyhof

GRJC/GRCC Full-time Employees
1914-Present

Danielle Nyland
Kathie Oakes
Margaret Oatley
Tracy Obiedzinski
Nancy O'Brien
Kevin O'Halla
Glen Okonoski
Charles Olawsky
Patricia Oldt
Juan Olivarez
Lawrence Olivia
Mary Jane Olivier
Harvey Olsen
Rick Olsen
Pat Olson
Diane Omer
Ellen Ondersma
Libor Ondras
Ruth Opdendyk
Karin Orr
Diane Orth
Louis Orth
James Orzechowski
Jeremy Osborn
Julie Otte
Chris Otterbacher
Kimberly Overdevest
Griffith Owen
Kathleen Owens
Hazel Paalman
Janet Paasche
Linda Paasche
Judy Pace
Dwight Packard
Jeffrey Painter
Ruth Palma
Alec Palmer
Delores Palmer
Marian Palmer
James Palmeri
Julie Parks
Doris Parsons
Melissa Parsons
Matthew Partridge
Robert Partridge
Theodore Pasma
Michael Passer
Diane Patrick
John Patton
Rachel Paulucci
Quynh Pavlov
Karen Pavlovic
Gene Paxton

Imelda Payne
Tracy Payne
Gerald Payton
Sella Pearson
Charlotte Pease
Barbara Peay
Cathy Peck
Alfred Pelikan
Hanlina Pelissier
Nicky Pelissier
Delores Pelton
Fran Pepper
Felix Pereiro
Billy Perez
Lille Pernell
Kevin Perrin
Wes Perrin
Donald Person
Sharon Peterman
C. Conway Peters
Robert Peters
Till Peters
Bonnie Peterson
Cindy Peterson
James Peterson
Joan Peterson
Linda Peterson
Pamela Peterson
Lubov Petrash
Michael Petrilli
Sarah Petz
Paul Phifer
Magdalena Phillips
Stella Phillips
Jean Piccard
Peggy Pierce
Laurence Pierson
Marianne Pierson
Mark Pietrusza
John Pifer
Philip Pikaart
Kimberly Pike
Nicholas Pinckney
Sharon Pinckney
Ashlee Pipoly
Glenda Pittman
Pat Plachecki
Nancy Pleume
John Plummer
Patricia Podein
Marie Pokora
Melissa Polanco-Nunez
Leo Polega

Marcia Policka
Patricia Poll
Thomas Poll
Tina Pollard
Oene Pomper
Thomas Poollard
Lisa Poortenga
Christian Poquette
Lynda Possett
Marie Possett
Thomas Post
Robert Postma
Felix Potapa
Harriet Pothoven
Ruby Potter
Denise Potvin
Malinda Powers
Mary Powers
Britt Price
Emeral Price
Peter Price
Priscilla Price
Josephine Prince
Angel Prinzi
Dia Proctor
David Pruis
Patricia Pulliam
Suzanne Pullon
Charles Purvis
Jay Pylman
Janis Qualls
Theodora Quick
Julie Quillan
David Quint
Glenn Quist
Carrie Raap
Lisa Rabey
Matuir Rahman
Jillian Rainwater
Ronald Ralya
Kay Ramer
Angie Ramirez
Francisco Ramirez
Linda Randle
Benjamin Randolph
Marcia Rango
Patricia Rasch
Andrew Raschid
Glen Raymond
Belinda Reding
Carole Redwine
Kathy Reed
Mary Reed

Tracy Reed-Motta
John Regeczi
John Regenmorter
Esther Rehm
Richard Reid
Gilles Renusson
Phyllis Reyers
Ivette Reyes
Martha Reyna
Beverly Reynolds
Sherry Rhoden
Candy Rice
Donald Rice
Karla Rice
Elizabeth Rich
Heather Richards
Helen Richardson
Ruth Richason
Jodi Richhart
Ethel Richter
Jodi Richter
Michelle Richter
Ellen Riekse
Robert Riekse
Peter Rigas
Karen Riggs
Lyvonne Riisberg
Ian Riley
Al Ritter
Rebecca Rivera
Betty Robbins
Brynne Roberts
Christine Roberts
Kristin Roberts
Lynn Roberts
Maureen Roberts
Merrie Roberts
Amy Robinson
Gretchen Robinson
June Robinson
Ruth Robinson
Virginia Robinson
Kellie Roblin
Brad Roche
Michael Roche
Nancy Rockwell
Mildred Rodgers
Wayne Rodgers
Ilda Rodriguez
Luis Rodriguez-Cruz
Colleen Roersma
Monica Rogers
Joanne Rollenhagen

Eileen Rooney
William Root
Harriette Roozenburg
David Rosander
Joan Rosario-Martinez
Juan Rosario-Martinez
Anna Rose
John Rose
Margaret Rose
Sarah Rose
Raynard Ross
Constance Rourke
Michael Rowe
Hazel Rowley
John Roy
Erin Rozek
Sophie Rubin
Mary Rudd
Martin Ruiz
Harriet Russell
Jonathon Russell
Kathleen Russell
Scott Rusticus
Judy Ryan
Michael Rydman
Sue Sacha
Dorothy Sadony
Randy Sahajdack
Christopher Sain
Alejandro Saldivar
Angela Salinas
Sylvia Salinas-Moser
Kirk Salvati
Dana Sammons
Ann Sandberg
Shirley Sandee
Helen Sander
Deborah Sanders
Javon Sanders
John Sanders
Annette Sanderson
Emily Santellan
Charles Sargent
Susan Sarniak
Clarence Sauer
John Sauer
Barbara Saunier
Mark Saur
Raymond Saxe
Mark Sayer
Mary Scanlan
Cherryl Scaturro
James Schafer

Thomas Schaner
Laurie Schaut
Michael Schavey
Margaret Scheetz
Eleanor Scheifele
Stemen Scheulle
B. Nan Schichtel
Melanie Schiele-Gady
Shari Schippers
Roger Schlosser
Janet Schmidt
Kathy Schmidt
Paula Schmidt
Virginia Schmit
Louise Schmitt
Wilamena Schnooberger
Emily Schoen
Kathy Schoen
Laura Schoenborn
Peggy Schoenborn
Rita Schoeppe
Roberta Schrader
Donald Schriemer
Geraldine Schubel
Cecilia Schuck
Jason Schueller
Steven Schueller
Michael Schuler
Teresa Schuler
James Schulte
Joseph Schulte
Bob Schultz
Debra Schultz
James Schultz
Robert Schultz
Vicki Schumacher
William Schumacher
Harold Schurman
Holly Schut
Roger Schut
Donald Schutte
Emmarie Schuyt
Pamela Scott
Tamara Scott
Ingrid Scott-Webb
Dan Scribner
Douglas Scripps
Natasha Scripter
Frederick Sebulske
Jane Secord
Danelle Sedore
Alma Seegmiller
Donald Seekel

GRJC/GRCC Full-time Employees
1914-Present

Kristen Seevers	Magdalen Skiver	Kristen Spoelman	Ellen Stuart	Gloria Thomas	Samuel Upton
Lynnae Selberg	Jennifer Sklener	Linda Spoelman	Craig Stutzky	Lucille Thomas	Michelle Urbane
Karen Self	Tore Skogseth	Brenda Spratling	Alice Styles	Maurice Thomas	Olwen Urquhart
Alfred Sellers	Sarah Slachter	Cynthia Springer	Robert Suchy	Sarah Thomas	Aina Valdmanis
Sheila Sellner	Mary Slager	Frank Springer	James Sulentich	James Thompson	Jack VanAartsen
David Selmon	Lyle Slagh	Amy Sprouse	Charles Sullivan	Miriam Thompson	Ethel Van Dam
John Selmon	John Sloan	Jean St. J. Plant	Minnie Sullivan	Joann Thrush	Vern Van de Vooren
Judy Selvius	Doris Slot	Keith St. Clair	Paula Sullivan	Gary Tidd	James Van Dokkumburg
Daniel Sempangi	Linda Slotsema	Helen Stacey	Rick Sullivan	Marcia Tiesenga	Robert Van Eyck
Chad Senna	Eugene Smary	Peggy Stadt	Bernadette Sutherlin	Rebecca Tift	John Van Krimpen
Margaret Sesselmann	Marilyn Smidt	Donald Stalker	Joseph Sutherlin	Elizabeth Timmer	Mark Van Linden
Sharana Shackelford	Elizabeth Smiley	Bessie Stalsonburg	Dennis Sutton	John Tirrell	Lorraine Van Naastricht
Rolland Shackson	Albert P. Smith	Karen Stanfield	Rosario-Montes Sutton	Fawn Tobolic	Andre van Niekerk
Howard Shanken	Benjamin Smith	Alyce Stark	Justin Swan	Mary Toland	Donald Van Ostenberg
Beverly Shannon	Burton Smith	Judy Stark	Norma Swanson	David Tolhurst	Nancy Van Strien
Agnes Sharp	C. Richard Smith	Paula Stark	Simon Swartz	Gary Tolhurst	Ronald Van Unen
Ronald Shassberger	Colleen Smith	Thomas Stasiak	Joel Swets	Karen Tolhurst	Loraine VanBroekhoven
William Shattuck	Denise Smith	Otis Staten	Marinus Swets	Kathleen Tolhurst	Myrna Vanbronkhorst
Alice Shaw	Diane Smith	Shirley Staton	Pamela Swiderski	Greta Tolliver	Thomas Vandam
Richard Shea	Gene Smith	Nicholas Stauffer	Paula Swiderski	Emery Toogood	Melvin Vande Gevel
Katherine Sheehan	Jamy Smith	Frances Stearns	Darcy Swope	Lawrence Topolski	Ethel VandeBunte
Nancy Sheldon	Jennifer Smith	Donald Steeby	David Syckle	Todd Torrey	Dale VandenBerg
Twylla Shelley	June Smith	Harold O. Steele	Mary Ellen Syswerda	David Tower	Leanna VandenBerg
Anne Sherman	Ken Smith	James Steensma	Richard Szudzik	Harold Tower	Stephanie VandenBerg
Frances Shew	Kenneth Smith	Travis Steffens	Steven Tagg	Joyce Townsend	Susan VandenBerg
James Shew	Lennon Smith	Elizabeth Stegman	Filippo Tagliati	Kevin Tran	Leah VanDenTop
Kathleen Shite	Lynden Smith	Maureen Stein	Bethann Talsma	Thomas Trasky	Marcia Vander Woude
Raymond Shoberg	Michelle Smith	Ronald Stein	Lidja Tarbunas	Bernice Treat	Nancy Vanderboom-Lausch
Larry Shoemaker	Millicent Smith	David Steinfort	Michael Taubert	Marguerite Treat	Henri VanDerEnde
Karen Shough	Thomas Smith	Michael Steinfort	Karla Taverniti	Patricia Trepkowski	Amanda Vanderhill
Nancy Shovandoane	Victoria Smith	Allen Steinhurst	Ellen Taylor	Marco Trimble	C. Warren VanderHill
C. J. Shroll	Jeffrey Smoes	Tenisha Stephens	Gene Taylor	Rebecca Troeger	Donna VanderKodde
Wendell Shroll	Wayne Sneath	David Sterken	Holly Taylor	Gail Trowbridge	Carol VanderMeer
Angela Shuart	Lisa Snider	Ronald Stevenson	Jimmie Taylor	Amelinda Trujillo	Judy VanderMeer
Brian Shultz	Rick Snook	Megan Stewart	Robert Taylor	Peter Trzybinski	Elaine VanderMeulen
Eve Sidney	Darin Snyder	Richard Stien	Robert Teele	Lurene Tubbs	Robert Vandermolen
Phillip Sidwell	Harold Snyder	Cary Stiff	Christina Teijeiro	Veta Tucker	Theodore VanderPloeg
Paul Siegel	James Snyder	Kate Stoetzner	Paulo Teles	Bethany Tuffelmire	Albert VanderStett
Tricia Siegel	Eleanor Sochanek	Katherine Stoetzner	Eleanor Temple	Lois Tuinenga	Jeffery VanderVeen
Leanna Siegrist	Mike Solon	Gregory Stoike	Karen TenBroeke	Stephanie Tuinman	Rick VanderVeen
Lou Sigler	Terry Sommerdyke	Cristina Stoll	Delbert TenDyke	JoAnne Tumbling	Alice VanderVelde
Mary Sikkema	Dorothy Sonke	Bonnie Stone	Elizabeth Teo	Robert Tupper	Judson VanderWal
Gladys Silsby	Lloyd Soper	Jeff Stone	Wesley Teo	Steven Turner	Ruth Vanderwal
Charlene Silva	Crystal Sorrells	Merle Storr	Dorothy Terhune	Wendell Turner	Janice VanderWeert
Geoffrey Simmon	A. Edward Sosa	Debra Stout	Elizabeth Termeer	Charlotte Tursky	Sue VandeVelde
Terry Simmons	Nathan Spahn	Jean Strang	Arnold Terpstra	Jeffery Tyler	Terry VandeWater
Tammy Simon	Diane Sparks	Barbara Stratton	Dunn Terrance	Marvin Tyler	Debbie VanDyke
Barbara Simons	Carolyn Spaulding	Thomas Street	Jayme Thayer	Elizabeth Tyrell	Mary VanDyke
Janet Simpson	Alice Spielmaker	Dolores Strickland	Sandy Thayer	Ralph Ubaldo	Marcia VanDyke
Eugene Sims	Jennifer Spindler Goulooze	Leola Strong	Bonnie Thomas	Sandy Ubaldo	Seymour VanDyken
Judith Sink	Brent Spitler	May Strong	Colleen Thomas	Arthur Ullrey	John VanElst
Julie Sizemore	David Spitler	Leora Stroup	Darlene Thomas	Ric Underhile	Elva VanHaitsma
James Skidmore	Jeffrey Spoelman	Rhosan Stryker	David Thomas	Esther Underwood	Barbara VanHaren

GRJC/GRCC Full-time Employees
1914-Present

Frederick vanHartesveldt
Janis VanHof
Elizabeth VanNoord
Donald VanOeveren
Heather VanOort
Cheryl VanPutten
Carol VanRandwyk
Robin VanRooyen
Terri Van'tHof
Lorna VanTil
Julie Vantine
Vivian VanVessen
Jennifer VanVoorst
Thomas VanWingen
Anita Varela
Michael Vargo
Ricardo Vasquez
James Vaughn
Ivette Vazquez
Zoraida Velez-Delgado
Debra Veltkamp
Todd VerBeek
Melissa VerDuin
Joyce Verhaar
Dwayne Verly
Thomas VerStrate
Daniel Verwolf
Douglas Victoria
B. Lewis Vilchez
Debra Vilmont
Carol Visser
Helen Visser
John Visser
Jodi Vitale
Joseph Viventi
Bryan Vliem
Michelle Vliem
Mark Vogel
Michelle Vollema
Duane Vore
Lori Vos
Thomas Vos
Harriet Vossen
Kristine Voth
Gordan Vurusic
Sally Waalkes
Douglas Wabeke
Lorene Wabeke
Edward Wagner
Jodie Wagner
John Wagner
Stephen Wagner
Christopher Waid

Luanne Wait
George Waite
Roger Walcott
Joseph Waldo
Edward Walker
Ethel Walker
Gail Walker
Karen Walker
Marjorie Walker
William Walker
Donovan Wallace
Marilyn Walsh
Bruce Walski
Judith Walters
Troy Walwood
Ann Walz
Susan Wambach
Ming Wang
Jennifer Wangler
Ryan Warblow
Cedric Ward
Jarrod Ward
Charles Warner
Emma Warner
Kate Washburn
Yumiko Watanabe
Carol Watson
Elizabeth Watson
James Watson
Tracel Watson
Elizabeth Watts
Maija Watts
Faye Weatherall Davis
Linda Weaver
Kelly Webber
Charles Weber
Kenneth Weber
Joan Webster
Karl Wecker
Luanne Wedge
Milly Weeber
Laurie Weeks
Hermine Weersing
Ronald Weidenfeller
Kristen Weis
Marjorie Weisgerber
Kellie Welch
Darrell Weller
Nancy Weller
Christine Welling
Kristine Welling
Scott Wellman
Charles Wells

Edward Wells
Penni Weninger
Robert Wepman
Kent Wesenberg
Mlen-Too Wesley
Hazel West
Kelly West
Shirley West
Margaret Westerhof
Cynthia Westra
Elizabeth Westveld
Gerard Weykamp
Richard Wherity
Denise White
Gregory White
Jonathan White
Joyce White
Kathleen White
Nancy White
Roy A. White
Sally White
Winifred White
Bernice Whitley
Lisa Whitley
Michael Whitman
Rebecca Whitman
Bryan Wible
Nancy Wieringa
Virginia Wieringa
W. B. Wiers
Douglas Wiersma
Mary Wiersma
Steven Wiersma
Robert Wikstrom
Felix Wilcox
Meegan Willi
Cedric Williams
Eric Williams
James Williams
Jonnie Williams
Joye Williams
Karl O. Williams
Mary Williams
Robert Williams
Saibo Williams
Stacy Williams
Susan Williams
Theresa Williams
Wendy Williams
Carey Williamson
Tassara Willies
Janis Willis
William Willyard

Robert Wilmes
Delicia Wilondja
Angeline Wilson
Catherine Wilson
Michael Wilson
Nannette Wiltjer
Robert Wing
Lowell Wingerd
Jerry Winkhart
Sally Winn
Harry Winsemius
Bette Winters
Emmet Winters
Laurie Witczak
Deanna Witte
Linda Witte
Joann Wojewski
Johnathan Wolff
Andrew Wolinski
Jill Woller-Sullivan
Diane Wolter
Cindy Woltjer
Janice Wood
Laurie Wood
Angela Woodard
Marcia Woods
Jill Woodward
Harold Woolworth
Frieda Wordelman
Eric Worm
Crystal Worner
Marsha Worsham
G Worthington
Tom Worthington
George Wright
Martel Wright
Michael Wyckoff
Tara Wykstra
Kimberly Wyngarden
Sharon Wynkoop
Linda Wyskochil
Sandra Wysocki
Janelle Yahne
Sara Yob
Becky Yoder
Ruth Yokom
Marie Yonkman
Seth York
Sheryl York
Dale Young
Ennis Young
Maxine Young
Melvin Young

Raul Ysasi
Maria Del Carmen Zapata
Camilla Zawacki
Chris Zeef
George Zeeff
Paul Zellar
James Zemboy
Tim Zerfas
Jacqueline Zimmer
William Zoellmer
Carolee Zoerhoff
Sally Zokoe
Sammye Zollman
Frederick Zomer
Paulette Zubel
Dawn Zuidgeest-Craft
Wendy Zuziak
Mary Zwaanstra
Marvin Zwiers

Index

Index

Index

Index

Index

Index